D0079544

Resource Management
and the Oceans

Westview Replica Editions

The concept of Westview Replica Editions is a response to the continuing crisis in academic and informational publishing. Library budgets for books have been severely curtailed. Ever larger portions of general library budgets are being diverted from the purchase of books and used for data banks, computers, micromedia, and other methods of information retrieval. Interlibrary loan structures further reduce the edition sizes required to satisfy the needs of the scholarly community. Economic pressures (particularly inflation and high interest rates) on the university presses and the few private scholarly publishing companies have severely limited the capacity of the industry to properly serve the academic and research communities. As a result, many manuscripts dealing with important subjects, often representing the highest level of scholarship, are no longer economically viable publishing projects--or, if accepted for publication, are typically subject to lead times ranging from one to three years.

Westview Replica Editions are our practical solution to the problem. We accept a manuscript in camera-ready form, typed according to our specifications, and move it immediately into the production process. As always, the selection criteria include the importance of the subject, the work's contribution to scholarship, and its insight, originality of thought, and excellence of exposition. The responsiblity for editing and proofreading lies with the author or sponsoring institution. We prepare chapter headings and display pages, file for copyright, and obtain Library of Congress Cataloging in Publication Data. A detailed manual contains simple instructions for preparing the final typescript, and our editorial staff is always available to answer questions.

The end result is a book printed on acid-free paper and bound in sturdy library-quality soft covers. We manufacture these books ourselves using equipment that does not require a lengthy make-ready process and that allows us to publish first editions of 300 to 600 copies and to reprint even smaller quantities as needed. Thus, we can produce Replica Editions quickly and can keep even very specialized books in print as long as there is a demand for them.

About the Book and Author

Resource Management and the Oceans: The Political Economy of Deep Seabed Mining
Kurt Michael Shusterich

The exploitation of valuable resources beyond the boundaries of national sovereignty has provoked international confrontations and made clear the need for some form of resource management control. In particular, the potential for mining the deep seabed for strategic minerals has raised several legal, political, and economic questions, and it is likely that the management structure of the International Seabed Authority will influence the nature of technology transfers, revenue-sharing arrangements for other resource commons, and the overall relationship between the developed and developing nations of the world for at least the next two decades.

This book addresses various questions concerning the management of the global commons by focusing on the case of deep seabed mining. The author analyzes the major issues and developments associated with U.S. and international laws on marine policy and resource management, at the same time pointing to the broader range of political implications that may influence exploitation of other resource commons. His unique compilation of material derives from government and UN documents and from consultations with key individuals in the U.S. government, representatives of the ocean mining industry, and resource policy specialists.

Dr. Kurt Shusterich is a research fellow in the Marine Policy and Ocean Management Program at the Woods Hole Oceanographic Institution. Currently, he is working on an economic, legal, and political analysis of polymetallic sulfide ore deposits.

Resource Management and the Oceans: The Political Economy of Deep Seabed Mining

Kurt Michael Shusterich

Westview Press / Boulder, Colorado

DABNEY LANCASTER LIBRARY
LONGWOOD COLLEGE
FARMVILLE, VIRGINIA 23901

HD
9506
.U62
S53
1982

A Westview Replica Edition

All rights reserved. No part of this publication may be reproduced or
transmitted in any form or by any means, electronic or mechanical, including photocopy, recording, or any information storage and retrieval system,
without permission in writing from the publisher.

Copyright © 1982 by Westview Press, Inc.

Published in 1982 in the United States of America by
    Westview Press, Inc.
    5500 Central Avenue
    Boulder, Colorado 80301
    Frederick A. Praeger, President and Publisher

Library of Congress Cataloging in Publication Data
Shusterich, Kurt Michael.
    Resource management and the oceans.
    (A Westview replica edition)
    Bibliography: p.
    Includes index.
    1. Ocean mining--Government policy--United States. I. Title.
HD9506.U62S53   338.2   82-4748
ISBN 0-86531-901-4   AACR2

Printed and bound in the United States of America

10 9 8 7 6 5 4 3

DABNEY LANCASTER LIBRARY
LONGWOOD COLLEGE
FARMVILLE VIRGINIA 23901

This book is dedicated to
the challenge, mystery, and
beauty of the oceans

82-12472

SVASTI SE

Contents

Tables, Figures, and Maps

Tables

Figures

Appendix 6

Maps

Preface

The exploitation of valuable resources beyond
national sovereignty has provoked international confrontations and stressed the need for some form of management
control at various conferences over the past ten years.
With major advancements in technology, mankind is just
beginning to fully utilize the tremendous resource potential of the oceans, outer space, and Antarctica. The
potential exploitation of the deep seabed for strategic
minerals, however, has raised several legal, political,
and economic questions. The Third United Nations
Conference on the Law of the Sea, which has attempted to
codify an international law for the resource exploitation
and use of the oceans, leaves open almost as many problems
as it sought to resolve. For example, the management
structure of the International Seabed Authority will
likely influence the nature of technology transfers,
revenue-sharing arrangements for other resource commons,
and the overall relationship between the developed and
developing nations of the world for at least the next two
decades. If, or how, such an Authority could function
remains very uncertain.

This book analyzes the various domestic and international issues that have been raised about the management
of the global commons. It provides an analysis and
history of the major issues and developments of United
States and international laws on marine policy and
resource management. The book does so by focusing on the
case of deep seabed mining, while pointing to the broader
range of political implications involved that may influence exploitation for other resource commons. Material
is drawn from government and United Nations documents, as
well as consultations with key individuals in the United
States government and ocean mining industry, and from
resource policy specialists. It provides a unique
compilation of material on the major inputs into the
domestic and international decision-making process
surrounding ocean mining, strategic minerals supply and

international resource management in general. It is of particular value to those who seek to understand the full range of issues surrounding deep seabed mining and for those interested in North-South relations, international resource management, and strategic minerals supply.

As of 1982 the legal and economic prospects for deep seabed mining do not appear very promising. The staying power and strength of that industry will be well tested over the next five to ten years. Legal uncertanties persist and market conditions remain poor.

The book was completed just as the Eleventh and Final session of the Third United Nations Conference on the Law of the Sea came to a conclusion on April 30, 1982 in New York. Lacking a hoped for consensus the Convention was adopted after nine years of negotiations. At the request of the United States a vote was taken which resulted in 130 nations voting in favor to 4 against with 17 abstentions. Voting against were Israel, Turkey, the United States, and Venezuela. Abstaining were several West and East European nations including, West Germany, Holland, the United Kingdom, and the Soviet Union and its satellites.

There were various reasons why the United States did not vote for the Treaty. Those reasons include a divided U.S. delegation (for and against the final Treaty text), the intransigence of the Group of 77 to satisfactorily negotiate President Reagan's six main objectives (derived from the Administration's "review" study), the non-negotiable goal of the Group of 77 to conclude the negotiations in New York at that session, and the misperception of the U.S. delegation to seriously negotiate only with Group of 77 leaders and not the numerous African and other Third World delegations.

Unwillingness by the Soviets to make up the financial difference for a full operating budget of a Law of the Sea bureaucracy (given that the U.S. and several other Western countries might not sign the Treaty) led to their abstention when the vote came. The final signing of the Treaty will take place in December 1982. The United States will be in a difficult political and legal position if it finds itself alone in not signing the Treaty. However, if one or more West European nations and the Soviet Union refrain also, then the Treaty will not be a viable one.

Although the text was completed before the New York session had concluded, the value and timeliness of the book are not adversely affected. In fact the non-conclusive finale to the Law of the Sea negotiations and the uncertain future of the Law of the Sea Treaty suggest the need for a careful reading of the complex issues addressed in this book.

K.M.S.

Acknowledgments

There are several people who have been particularly helpful in the preparation of this book. I would like to briefly mention them by name and offer a public "thank you" to each.

A special thanks goes to Dr. Judith Kildow of the Department of Ocean Engineering at the Massachusetts Institute of Technology. Her early and continued intellectual support have both stimulated and challenged my research and ideas. Dr. Kildow's comments on early and final drafts were invaluable. I would like to thank Judy, Alfred, and Meredith for their hospitality and friendship during my visits to Boston.

I would also like to thank Thomas Kitsos of the House Merchant Marine and Fisheries Committee; Conrad G. Welling, Senior Vice-President of Ocean Minerals Company; Edward Dangler, Special Assistant to Mr. Welling; Jeffry Amsbaugh, President, Ocean Mining Associates; J.P. Moreau, Chantiers de France-Dunkerque; Ray Meyers and Milt Drucker of the State Department; Alan Ryan of the National Oceanic and Atmospheric Administration, Department of Commerce; and all the other individuals in Washington D.C. who spoke with me at length on ocean resource policy issues.

Dr. Arvid Pardo, of the Center for Marine and Coastal Studies, University of Southern California, was also very helpful in providing information and insights that are unique to a man who has been directly involved with ocean policy and politics for so many years.

Professors Wolfram Hanrieder, Dean Mann, and Michael Gordon of the Political Science Department, University of California at Santa Barbara were very helpful in offering guidance and advice in the early version of this book. I would like to thank Phyllis Griffman for her help proofreading that material and her continued friendship.

During several research trips to Washington, D.C., Maureen and Laurence provided the opportunity to mix business with pleasure. I am most grateful. I would also like to thank Jon for introducing me to ocean kayaking. Our many days on the beautiful waters off Santa Barbara provided a much needed diversion from writing about the politics of the ocean.

The final draft of the book was completed after several months of revision at the Woods Hole Oceanographic Institution in the Marine Policy and Ocean Management Program. Several individuals there helped in many ways. Special thanks to Dr. K.O. Emery, Department of Geology and Geophysics, and Robert Knecht, Senior Research Fellow, and former director of the Office of Minerals and Energy in the Commerce Department for their advice and help. I would also like to thank Ann Martin and Maynard Silva for their suggestions for improvements in some of the chapters; and Roz, Trina and Ethel for their help in proofreading. A very special thanks goes to Ann Goodwin whose skills on a word processor are only excelled by her sense of humor, willingness to work, and ability to put up with the author's demands.

Thank you all for your help and friendship.

Although the above individuals have been instrumental in the completion of this work, the author must take full responsibility for its content.

Kurt Michael Shusterich

1
Ocean Mining:
A Complex Policy Issue

INTRODUCTION

This book is about deep seabed mining and the political problems that surround it. It explores the politics and policy inputs of private industry, of the United States government, and of the international community as they pertain to ocean mining in international waters. The terms "ocean mining" and "deep seabed mining" are used interchangeably in the text--they refer specifically to the mining of the deep seabed for manganese nodules. A central focus of the study is on the formulation and results of United States policy goals as they relate to trade-offs between economic efficiency and an equitable distribution of the ocean's wealth and resources for the world community. At the heart of the problem is a debate between the rich and poor nations over different types of economic, political, legal and juridical systems that will, in the future, have a major impact on the management of resource exploitation in areas beyond national jurisdiction.

Deep seabed mining is on the nation's policy agenda for several reasons. There has been an increasing awareness by the Congress, successive Administrations over the past ten years, and resource analysts that secure access to natural resources in the coming decades is crucial for the security of the nation. This political significance stems from finite supply of the raw materials, increased demand, and politically motivated supply disruptions. There are important differences in policies for obtaining access to national resources and those for international resources; this study, however, is concerned primarily with resources that are beyond national sovereignty, in an area often referred to as the global commons. Because international mechanisms designed to manage the exploitation of the seabed will set legal precedents for other global commons and will determine the structure and authority of international institutions dealing with a wide range of issues between the developed and developing countries, deep seabed mining has taken on increasing

1

significance in the 1980s.

Another reason ocean mining is on the nation's agenda is because the technology to economically exploit a wide variety of resources that lie beyond national sovereignty has only recently been made available. The ownership and distribution of benefits derived from those resources is thus becoming a major economic and political issue.[1] The United States and a handful of other technologically advanced nations are alone in their ability to exploit these resources. These nations are eager to pursue deep seabed mining in order to decrease their heavy dependence upon Third World land-based mineral supplies. Because the technology to exploit the deep seabed is unevenly distributed among nations, there are differing views on how the resources should be exploited and their benefits shared. The views are difficult to reconcile because ocean mining is embedded in the larger controversies of ocean management, territorial rights, and issues of economic equity between the developed and developing nations.

The political and ideological differences of the rich and poor countries are made more complex by the increasing economic interdependence that has evolved between these two groups of nations over the last ten years. Interdependence is now recognized as a two-way street between the industrially advanced nations of the North which seek access to the raw materials of the developing countries of the South, and the technological and financial dependence of the Third World on the developed nations. The forum for discussing these problems as they relate to ocean mining has been the Third United Nations Conference on the Law of the Sea (UNCLOS III), which began formal meetings in 1974. Domestically, the United States Congress worked for nine years to get unilateral deep seabed mining legislation passed that would protect long-term American ocean mining resource interests. Although UNCLOS III has not yet produced a ratified treaty, United States legislation for deep seabed mining was signed into law by President Carter on June 28, 1980.

The study evaluates the extent to which access to resource areas in the global commons is of major importance to the economic and political security of the United States. Deep seabed mining can be regarded as a major test of the resolve of the United States to secure access to such resources in an era when several other nations will acquire the technological capability to exploit them.

Deep seabed mining is closely related to the efforts of the developing nations to establish a New International Economic Order (NIEO). The negotiating group of Third World nations at international conferences, known as the Group of 77, which now consists of 120 countries, is pursuing this goal in order to bring about

what they consider a more balanced and equitable distribution of the world's wealth.[2] The resources and wealth
of the oceans are just one facet of these negotiations,
but it has come to the forefront because the proposed
regime for deep seabed mining is crucial in the debate
between the rich and poor nations over technology transfer
as well as resource access, distribution, and revenue.
There is an ideological dimension to the demands in
multilateral negotiations. Most lesser developed
countries (LDCs) lack economic and social infrastructures
for successful competition with private industry of the
technologically advanced nations; their governments have
become virtually the sole spokesmen for economic demands
in the international environment. Consequently, the
connection between the negotiating stance taken by the
Group of 77 on ocean mining and their desire to shape a
NIEO adds a political dimension that tends to exacerbate
an already complicated situation. The Law of the Sea
negotiations have been made especially difficult because
the primary objective of UNCLOS III has been a comprehensive Treaty to cover all items on the agenda. The option
of reaching a compromise agreement by temporarily leaving
out troublesome issues to be dealt with later, has therefore not been possible.

Given the increasing need of the United States and
other industrialized nations for secure supplies of
resources such as those in manganese nodules, the
precedents set in determining the use of the ocean commons
will determine not only which state or group of states
will control this new source of minerals but also other
uses of the oceans and other resource commons in the
future in Antarctica, the Moon, and outer space.

Previous studies have approached ocean mining and
international resource management in a number of different
and specific points of view: the New International
Economic Order/redistribution of wealth issue; the politics of issue-linkage in regime formation, the character
of United States bureaucratic politics and how trade-offs
are worked out; and the consistency/inconsistency of
United States national legislation and policy concerning
the Law of the Sea negotiations. Because most of these
analyses have focused on a particular aspect of deep
seabed mining, international resource management, or the
Law of the Sea negotiations, the interested reader has
had to seek out numerous studies to understand how these
policy problems fit together. This study uses those works
to help present a comprehensive analysis leading to better
understanding of the major political problems and how they
are interrelated. Readers interested in pursuing more
specific and detailed analyses of a particular problem
will find numerous references to such studies in the
footnotes and bibliography.

OCEAN MANAGEMENT: A BRIEF HISTORY

The oceans cover nearly two-thirds of the earth's surface, and for centuries people have freely used them for fishing and navigation. The oceans have been one of the few resources beyond the national territorial jurisdiction of any single state: a common resource of the entire planet to be shared by all mankind, referred to as the "global commons." Other noteworthy global commons are Antarctica, outer space, and the Moon.

Hugo Grotius, a Dutch lawyer of the seventeenth century, is usually credited with producing the first major statement regarding the legal uses of the oceans. In 1609 he published Mare Liberum, a dissertation on the concepts of the freedom of the seas.[3] In it Grotius wrote that countries were free to use the sea for whatever purpose they wanted as long as it did not interfere with another country's use of the area. Grotius also realized that a coastal state should have some control over the ocean immediately adjoining its coast. This led to the definition of a zone called the territorial sea. In this zone the coastal state had complete sovereignty. Another Dutchman, Cornelius Van Bynkershoek (1673-1743), proposed that the width of this zone should be the distance from shore a cannon could fire, which was about three miles at that time. The United States still abides by a three-mile zone although most coastal states have adopted a twelve-mile territorial zone. The Law of the Sea Treaty calls for a twelve-mile zone--which the United States will adopt when the Treaty enters into force.

In 1890 the United States Supreme Court declared that: "The minimum limit of the territorial jurisdiction of a nation over tide-waters is a marine league [three miles] from its coast...." In a note to the British Prime Minister in 1793, Secretary of State Jefferson pointed to the nebulous character of a nation's assertions of territorial rights in the marginal belt, and put forward the first official American claim for a three-mile zone.[4]

The area beyond the territorial sea, known as the high seas, was considered by Grotius as res nullius, or belonging to no one. Over the centuries this concept changed somewhat to res communis, or belonging to everyone. The original concept was not effectively challenged before World War II as most countries using the sea were able to reach a workable agreement, at least during peacetime. After World War II, and especially over the last twenty years, however, the oceans have taken on increasing significance for many nations. The new interest is due in part to actions taken by the United States and in part to an awareness that many of the resources of the sea are not inexhaustible and that some minerals on or under the seafloor, such as manganese nodules, might be extremely valuable--and exhaustible.

Consequently, just as the village commons of the Middle Ages were eventually fenced off in response to economic change, so states today are "fencing off" large parts of the oceans as technological and economic change has increased its uses. In the past thirty years there has been pressure for a change in the legal framework contained in the Grotius document. During that time the two major premises of his dissertation have proved false--plentiful, inexhaustible ocean resources and their non-expropriability.

One of the first major challenges to the three-mile territorial sea concept was made by the United States. In 1945, President Harry S. Truman established a new national policy on the natural resources of the subsoil and seabed. In what is now called the Truman Proclamations on the Continental Shelf, the President stated that: "The Government of the United States regards the natural resources of the subsoil and seabed of the continental shelf beneath the high seas as appertaining to the United States, subject to its jurisdiction and control."[5] President Truman successfully asserted United States control over the seabed from the three-mile territorial sea limit out to the 200-meter isobath. Earlier there had been challenges to the traditional free seas regime as far back as 1939 when the United States declared a 200-mile zone of security at the beginning of the Second World War. The Latin American coastal states immediately adopted a similar zone. The zone of security was lifted by all nations at the end of the war in 1945. But because of Truman's continental shelf actions in 1945, some Latin American states then felt justified in claiming a 200-mile economic zone, others claimed a 200-mile territorial zone.

In 1970 President Nixon proposed that all nations adopt a treaty under which they would renounce all national claims over the natural resources of the seabed beyond the point where the high seas reach a depth of 200 meters. He called upon all nations "to regard these resources as the common heritage of mankind." (U.S. Oceans Policy. Statement by the President, May 23, 1970.)

While technological change has brought about several new uses of the oceans and consequent challenges to customary law, many of the postwar challenges had antecedents earlier in this century. During the 1920s and '30s several ocean issues were debated, issues that continue to this day: conferences to save whales from extinction; efforts to deal with oil pollution at sea; more than two dozen claims of jurisdiction over contiguous zones; United States Congressional pressures for extension of jurisdiction over fisheries and shelf resources; and United States protests over Latin American extensions of such jurisdiction.

An international conference held in The Hague in 1930 failed to agree on exact limits for national jurisdiction at a time when the three-mile limit was being questioned. The Hague conference reaffirmed the principle of freedom of the seas, but it did not manage to reach agreement on a codification of international ocean law. Almost three decades later (in 1958 and 1960) the United Nations Law of the Sea Conferences were held in Geneva.[6] The first Conference on the Law of the Sea (UNCLOS I, 1958) produced four conventions on ocean law: on the Territorial Sea, High Seas, Continental Shelf, and Fishing. UNCLOS II (1960) failed to agree on the limits of coastal state jurisdiction (rights) over offshore waters or the seabed.

Rapid changes occurred in the 1960s and influenced ocean law. There was, for example, an increase in the number of nation states, so that there was an ever increasing number of developing countries participating in international forums. Another significant change during this period was in technological development. Advances in mineral exploration and exploitation for oil and coastal gas enabled access to these resources further and further from shore. The number of fish-processing ships also increased dramatically during this period. These technological changes did much to promote the realization (perhaps first felt on a large scale in the 1930s) that the resources of the ocean were not unlimited.

In 1967 Ambassador Arvid Pardo of Malta issued a call to action on the seabed beyond national jurisdiction before the United Nations General Assembly. He believed that the seabed beyond national jurisdiction should be considered the common heritage of mankind and the wealth obtained from it should benefit both developing and developed nations.[7] Since that time Pardo has recognized that he may have exaggerated the potential wealth from the deep sea when he declared that there were trillions of dollars worth of manganese nodules on the seabed. Pardo's speech, in which he warned against the possible appropriation of vast ocean areas by those states with the technical competence to exploit them, indirectly helped to set in motion the process which eventually led to the convening, in 1973, of UNCLOS III.

The permanent Committee on the Peaceful Uses of the Seabed and the Ocean Floor Beyond the Limits of National Jurisdiction (the Seabed Committee) was established in 1968. Its role was to explore the possibilities of establishing an international regime (laws) and machinery (organization) to govern seabed exploitation in the interests of mankind, taking into special consideration the interests and needs of the developing nations.

In 1969 the UN General Assembly approved the Moratorium Resolution, which forbids exploration and exploitation of seabed resources until such time as an international regime is established. The United States and several West European countries abstained from the vote on this resolution. In 1970 the General Assembly approved a Declaration of Principles on the seabed beyond national jurisdiction as the common heritage of mankind and called for the convening of UNCLOS III on all unsettled aspects of international law.

The Seabed Committee continued its preparatory work for UNCLOS III in 1971 and 1972. It divided its expanded agenda into subcommittee I on the seabed beyond national jurisdiction; subcommittee II on traditional uses of the sea, such as fishing, navigation, and limits on coastal state jurisdiction; and subcommittee III on the environment and marine scientific research. UNCLOS III met for the first time in New York for three weeks in December of 1973; a meeting primarily to determine rules and procedures. When it met again for ten weeks in the summer of 1974 in Caracas, Venezuela, nations attending the Conference (138) stated their positions on all the issues. The subcommittees became full committees, and committee II produced a Main Trends document listing several alternative provisions on all its agenda items. Later substantive meetings of UNCLOS III are described throughout the book, particularly in chapter four.[8]

One of the major problem areas in international ocean law over the past two decades has been creeping jurisdiction. The proposal that all nations agree to 200-mile exclusive economic zones (EEZs) in the oceans off their coasts has received wide support during the last ten years. Several Latin American states were the first to stake claims to such a wide zone. Other countries, after resistance, followed the example set for 200-mile EEZs at UNCLOS III. These economic zones have now become part of international customary law. This has occurred because all coastal states now claim and abide by the 200-mile economic zone jurisdiction. Because the Law of the Sea (LOS) has not yet entered into force, however, the customary acceptance of the concept has not been officially written into international law. The 200-mile EEZ concept has resulted in the enclosure of one-third of the oceans. (See Map 1.) Table 1 indicates the gains of individual countries given 200-mile EEZs. This area is the most resource rich of the oceans. It is generally abundant in fish and exploitable oil and natural gas. In addition, the 200-mile EEZ gives added economic jurisdiction to several European and North American nations in the Pacific and Atlantic Oceans around national or trustee status islands in those areas which can now claim 200-mile economic zones as well. Mexico, for example, will have legal access to manganese nodules in part of the rich Clarion-Clipperton fracture zones in the North Pacific Ocean because it has jurisdiction over islands in those areas off its west coast.[9]

The overriding considerations of UNCLOS III are crucial questions of peace and security, broadly defined

8

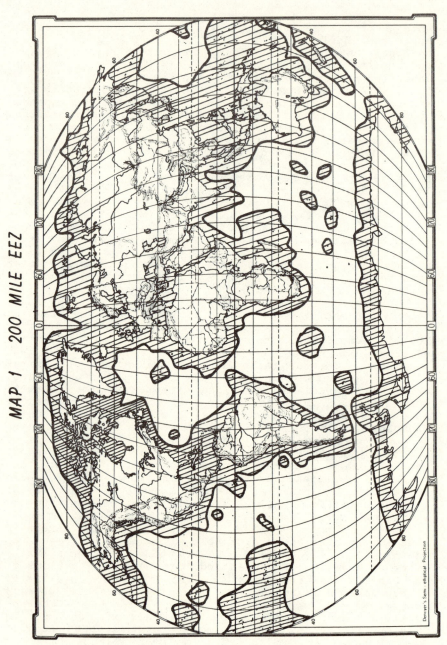

MAP 1   200 MILE EEZ

Denoyer's Semi - elliptical Projection

TABLE 1

Net Gains of Individual Countries with a 200-Mile EEZ

Country	Area Out to 200 Miles (In square nautical miles)
United States	2,222,000
Australia	2,043,300
Indonesia	1,577,300
New Zealand	1,409,500
Canada	1,307,600
Soviet Union	1,309,500
Japan	1,126,000
Brazil	924,000

in economic, strategic and ideological terms, but underlying almost all items on the agenda are struggles for power, prestige, prosperity, and ideology. On defense issues, the struggle has been between the superpowers, the major powers, and the lesser powers, over jurisdiction in the exclusive economic zone, transit through straits and freedom of action on the high seas. Economically, the issues have divided the developed and developing states over a New International Economic Order. Ideologically, they have pitted the capitalist states, the socialist states and the "nonaligned" Third World states against one another. Geographically, the struggles have been among the 122 coastal states, the 29 landlocked states, and the 26 geographically disadvantaged states. Lines have also been drawn between net producers and net consumers of raw materials, especially of strategically important metals such as those contained in manganese nodules.

The conference, which sought to establish a more equitable legal framework for ocean use, has been highly politicized. Political questions not generally associated with ocean issues, such as questions of security and disarmament, have become pervasive issues of concern to UNCLOS III, although they were not formally on the agenda.[10] The important issues of the conference can be listed as follows:

1. A definition of the width of the territorial sea and any other adjacent zones and the degree of coastal state control in these areas;

2. Ownership of the resources of the water column, seabed, and subsoil, including: (a) the resources within the area under the jurisdiction of the coastal state and the extent of this jurisdiction, and (b) the resources in the area beyond national jurisdiction or the deep or high seas;

3. Right of overflight and navigation through what are now international straits but which could be included within expanded territorial seas or are economic zones;

4. Management of living resources in the ocean, especially those species that migrate and those in areas where many countries have traditionally fished for them (such as the Georges Bank) but which now come under a single country's jurisdiction;

5. Protection and reduction of pollution in the ocean;

6. Freedom of scientific research in the ocean;

7. A regime for control or managment of the high seas.

During the past ten years, advances in the technology for exploiting the deep seabed for manganese
nodules and the continental shelf for oil and gas have
given great economic importance to these areas. Consequently, political questions have been raised between
nations about access to these resource rich regions of
the world. The minerals in manganese nodules offer the
United States an opportunity to free itself from reliance
on Third World countries for land-based supplies of
certain key minerals. New drilling technology allows ever
deeper access to oil and natural gas. Because of this,
the proportion of the world's oil that comes from under
the sea grew from almost nothing in the prewar era to
nearly 20 percent in the 1970s. In 1975 offshore oil
production was worth $40 billion, or as much as all
commercial shipping and four times the value of ocean
fisheries.[11] The value of this production has increased considerably over the last five years due to the
enormous increases in the prices of petroleum and natural
gas. Today most oil drilling occurs in waters only a few
hundred feet deep. In the near future, increasing numbers
of wells will be operating down to the 1,000 foot mark
and beyond, giving even greater importance to 200-mile
EEZs.
     Growing concern about territorial and economic
control of coastal jurisdiction is based partly on gas
and oil exploitation, and partly on tremendous increases
in coastal water fishing due to better technology such as
sonar and the use of factory ships to process huge quantities of fish at sea without returning to port. The
jurisdictional issue was one of a growing number of ocean
use problems that were created by greater technological
capabilities, increased numbers of newly independent state
actors, and a new and growing political and economic
struggle between the industrially advanced states and the
Group of 77. The area beyond coastal water jurisdiction
has become the site of increased political and economic
dispute even between close neighbors such as the United
States and Canada and the United States and Mexico. This
has put pressure on the United States government to
develop an overall oceans policy for both domestic and
international uses of the oceans. Figure 1 indicates the
major ocean areas involved in the Law of the Sea.
     Attention to ocean politics has increased consider-
ably since 1967 when Arvid Pardo dramatized the prospects
of great wealth from the deep seabed and the need for a
new regime. In 1972 the subject of the President's Report
on Foreign Policy for the 1970's included oceans under
"new dimensions of diplomacy."[12] Today the politics of
ocean uses and resources are becoming increasingly significant for a large number of nations, although in this
country it has not yet advanced in status at the Presidential level. Between 1967 and 1980 the United States

MAJOR OCEAN AREAS INVOLVED IN
LAW OF THE SEA

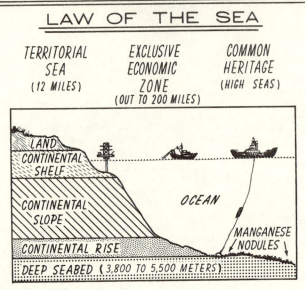

TERRITORIAL
SEA
(12 MILES)

EXCLUSIVE
ECONOMIC
ZONE
(OUT TO 200 MILES)

COMMON
HERITAGE
(HIGH SEAS)

(A)   Offshore Oil Drilling
(B)   Fishing
(C)   Seabed Mining

Territorial Zone
An area of the sea bordering coastal states over which they
claim full jurisdiction by virtue of ownership of the land.

Exclusive Economic Zone
The area just outside, but adjacent to, the territorial waters
in which the coastal states have exclusive rights to utilize
the resources, but must allow other states access for other
purposes, i.e., shipping.

Common Heritage
This term has not been given a precise legal definition, but
refers to the 1970 UN statement that resources of the seabed,
beyond the limit of national jurisdiction, are the common
heritage of mankind, not to be appropriated by one country,
but to be put under an international authority.

oceans policy agenda became increasingly complex and reflected a growing number of policy issues. Much of the agenda stemmed from the efforts of the developing and coastal states to control transnational activities, and from the dramatization of potential economic activity by the United Nations General Assembly. Efforts by other states to control transnational fishing, to benefit from private offshore drilling, to control pollution (particularly in the transport of oil), and to regulate and benefit from transnational scientific research, have politicized some issues. Others, like the debates on seabed resources and seabed arms control, arose primarily from activity in United Nations conference diplomacy. Given the comprehensive nature of the proposed LOS Treaty, it is unusual that negotiations for seabed arms control are not a part of UNCLOS III. The conference has shown that the southern nations have been, and will continue to be, divided on particular issues both related and non-related to ocean politics. In general, however, the formation of the Group of 77 has marked a new era in international conference diplomacy on many national resource management frameworks for determining the use and exploitation of the global commons.

In summary, ocean geography in the years preceding UNCLOS III was characterized by narrow coastal state jurisdictional limits, maximized freedoms of the high seas, and by decisions on ocean matters made largely by the major maritime powers of the North. The post-conference geography will feature broad belts of coastal state controls, restrictions on high seas freedoms, and a strong role in decision making on the part of the developing countries of the South.[13]

NATURE OF THE MANGANESE NODULE RESOURCE

One of the most fascinating aspects of ocean resources has been the development of the technology for mining potato-sized manganese nodules that often lie on the deep seabed at depths of 12,000 to 20,000 feet. The size and mineral content of the nodules varies a good deal, but the most common are described in Appendix 1.

The chemical composition of the nodules is unique. The nodules are oxide materials and contain no sulfur. Because of their high metallic content and the vast size of the resource, they have generated great interest in the industrialized nations as a future source of raw materials. The existence of these deposits has been known for more than a century. Nodules were first collected by the HMS Challenger during the first great oceanographic expedition from 1872-1876. While manganese nodules occur throughout the oceans, only about 3 percent of the total ocean floor has been surveyed in any detail, primarily in

the Eastern Pacific Ocean north of the Equator in the
Clarion-Clipperton fracture zones. The band or area
containing the richest deposits located thus far is about
200 kilometers wide by 1500 kilometers long and runs
roughly East-West between latitudes 6°N, and 20°N, and
longitudes 110°W and 180°W. (See Map 2.) Areas of
comparable size but different composition are believed to
exist in the South Pacific. Probably there are large
areas elsewhere, such as in the Indian Ocean.[14]
It is only since the 1960s that techniques have
been developed that promise to make available the vast
amounts of manganese, nickel, copper, and cobalt that are
contained within the nodules. Manganese nodules are
already commercially exploitable (though none have thus
far been exploited), and it is likely that within a few
decades seabed production will provide a large proportion
of the import requirements of consumer countries. The
amount of production that will be available by a given
date is difficult to estimate, and the extent of these
seabed deposits is a matter of dispute. Some marine
scientists have predicted the magnitude of the resource
to be enormous; others have concluded that the number of
commercially attractive sites, based on present technology, may be limited. The expansive view appears correct
for two reasons. First, the mining companies, which have
conducted far more prospecting than the scientific
institutions and have access to a more comprehensive data
base, assume that the extent of the resource and the
number of commercial ventures it can support over time
are very large. Second, large parts of the oceans,
particularly the Indian Ocean, are essentially unexplored,
and the probability is high that they will contain valuable deposits. Thus far, however, nodules in this area
have been found to have only a high grade of cobalt ore.
Manganese nodules have become central to many
arguments of the Group of 77 for a new international
economic order. Because ocean mining for manganese
nodules offers so much in terms of technology transfer
and precedents for other resource commons, the Group of
77 has made demands at UNCLOS III for an International
Seabed Authority that guarantees technology transfer to
mine the nodules, start-up capital ($1 billion), and has
insisted that a large portion of the wealth to be derived
from ocean mining benefit the developing nations.
Appendix 2 provides an overview of the uses of the metals
contained in ocean nodules.

UNCLOS III, NIEO, AND THE GROUP OF 77

The United States and its industrialized allies
are attracted by the possibility of reducing their
dependence on limited numbers of foreign sources for

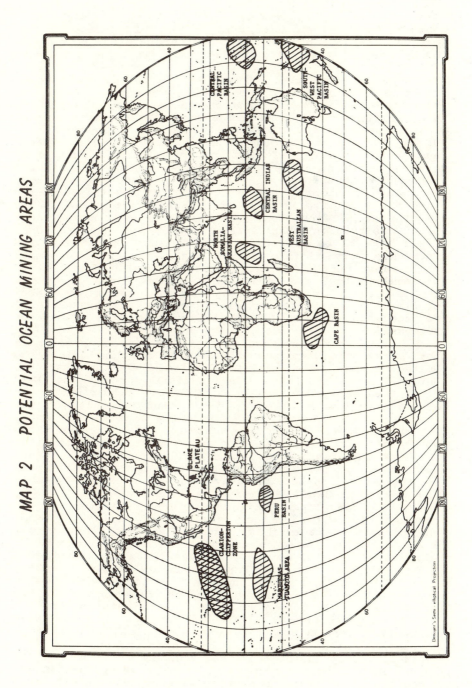

MAP 2   POTENTIAL OCEAN MINING AREAS

commodities, particularly in light of recent Soviet backed insurgent movements in Southern Africa--notably in Mozambique, Angola, and Zaire, from which regions the United States imports much of its non-oil mineral resources. The high stakes of international power politics, the uncertainty of the international arena, and the hazards of foreign policy in general, make for a potentially unstable domestic economy. This is especially true in an era of increasing economic interdependence and higher natural resource prices. But the United States and the industrialized North comprise only a few voices in the global community; of the 156 national entities in attendence at the Law of the Sea Conference as of 1980, 119 were developing nations. Because of this, multi-lateral attempts at resource management face major ideological difficulties. The United States now must deal with a situation where its domestic and international goals have to be accepted by a majority of nations with interests very different from its own. Since economic power plays such an increased role in national and inter-national policy, and because the United States lacks the economic clout it had twenty years ago, the large number of developing nations can exact demands at international negotiations such as UNCLOS III with a fair degree of success.

The common heritage concept has wide support among both developing and developed nations, including the United States. This is so despite the fact that the United States and many other nations opposed the 1970 General Assembly Declaration on General Principles on the Seabed (Resolution 2749). This Resolution called on all states to refrain from seabed resource exploitation until the establishment of an international seabed regime which would administer the area in the interest of all mankind. The United States and several other industrialized nations claim that the Resolution does not include a definition of the area itself and deny that a General Assembly declaration is legally binding.

The developed and developing countries differ considerably in their interpretations of the principle of the common heritage of mankind. The developed nations feel that free and open exploitation of the seabed, so long as territorial sovereignty is not claimed, is in the interest of all nations and allowable under both the common heritage principle and the traditional doctrine of freedom of the high seas. Most of the developing nations, however, tend to adhere to a more strict interpretation of the term "common heritage of mankind" to mean that individual states are barred from exploiting mankind's possession unless it is conducted under the auspices of a generally accepted international regime.[15]

It is not surprising that there is a North-South dimension to current ocean problems being negotiated in a

parliamentary diplomatic setting. United Nations negotiations on ocean issues were affected by North-South
considerations long before the demands of the developing
states began to be articulated coherently as a demand for
a NIEO. The two earlier UNCLOS Conferences of 1958 and
1960 took place between the two mass admissions to United
Nations membership of recently independent ex-colonies in
1955 and 1960. The impact of the presence of these new
states at both conferences was felt in terms of the style
of negotiations and their outcome. Issues were split
along developed-developing country lines, and were therefore not successfully concluded due to increasingly
different ideological approaches to a new world economic
order. In short, the industrially advanced nations wanted
to maintain the free market approach to international
economic and resource issues, while the developing states
wanted major changes in the international economic and
monetary structure.[16] These differences made agreement
impossible at all three of the Law of the Sea Conferences
as both sides felt economically threatened by the other's
goals. Many compromises made by the United States at
UNCLOS III help to explain much of the agreement reached
at that conference. The passage of unilateral deep seabed
mining legislation by the United States in 1980 also did
much to soften some of the more radical demands of the
Group of 77 at the conference. The legislation served as
a warning to the Group of 77 that the United States
government had firm goals of ensuring access to the deep
seabed for American companies. The nature of the legislation allows time for eventual agreement to be reached
at UNCLOS III, but it also sets guidelines for American
and reciprocating state ocean mining companies to proceed
with commercial exploitation in 1988 even if a Law of the
Sea Treaty is not in effect.

The obstacles encountered at UNCLOS III to final
agreement on a comprehensive Law of the Sea Treaty encountered at UNCLOS III made the formulation of a United
States deep seabed mining policy politically sensitive
vis-a-vis United States relations with developing nations.
Intense lobbying efforts by American-based ocean mining
companies have had to be balanced with international
concerns such as the demands of the Group of 77 for
changes in the world economic order. Several broad
changes on both the international and national level
indicate that American policy vis-a-vis the Group of 77
on most issues, including ocean mining, will harden
throughout the next decade.

FOOTNOTES

Chapter 1

1. The United States no longer has the same technological superiority it enjoyed from 1940 through the 1960s. The Japanese, for example, have taken over the camera, watch, radio, television and stereo component markets from the United States. Because of better technology and superior organization they have also been able to mass produce automobiles in such a way that presently threatens the very foundation of the industry in the United States. In addition, the Japanese government is helping to bring together and focus the efforts of the Japanese high technology industry in an attempt to leapfrog the American computer industry. West European nations, also, now have access to technology that was once only in the domain of American corporate interests.

2. As of 1981 there were 120 members of the Group of 77: Afghanistan, Algeria, Angola, Argentina, Bahamas, Behrain, Bangladesh, Barbados, Benin, Bhutan, Bolivia, Botswana, Brazil, Burma, Burundi, Cape Verde, Central African Republic, Chad, Chile, Colombia, Comoros, Congo, Costa Rica, Cuba, Cyrpus, Democratic Kampuchea, Democratic People's Republic of Korea, Democratic Yemen, Djibouti, Dominica, Dominican Republic, Ecuador, Egypt, El Salvador, Equatorial Guinea, Ethiopia, Fiji, Gabon, Gambia, Ghana, Grenada, Guatemala, Guinea, Guinea-Bissau, Guyana, Haiti, Honduras, India, Indonesia, Iran, Iraq, Ivory Coast, Jamaica, Jordan Kenya, Kuwait, Lao People's Democratic Republic, Lebanon, Lesotho, Liberia, Libyan Arab Jamahiriya, Madagascar, Malawi, Malaysia, Maldives, Mali, Malta, Mauritania, Mauritius, Mexico, Morocco, Mozambique, Nepal, Nicaragua, Niger, Nigeria, Oman, Pakistan, Palestine Liberation Organization, Panama, Papua New Guinea, Paraguay, Peru, Philippines, Qatar, Republic of Korea, Romania, Rwanda, Saint Lucia, Samoa, Sao Tome and Principe, Saudi Arabia, Senegal, Seychelles, Sierra Leone, Singapore, Solmon Islands, Somolia, Sri Lanka, Sudan, Suriname, Swaziland, Syrian Arab Republic, Thailand, Togo, Trinidad and Tobago, Tunisia, Uganda, United Arab Emirates, United Republic of Cameroon, United Republic of Tanzania, Upper Volta, Uruguay, Venezuela, Vietnam, Yemen, Yugoslavia, Zaire, Zambia, Zimbabwe.

3. Hugo Grotius, Mare Liberum, a dissertation by Grotius in 1618. For a translation from Latin to English see, Ralph Van Deman Magoffin, The Freedom of the Seas,

(New York: Oxford University Press, 1916). For a good historical overview of ocean policy and management see, David A. Ross, Introduction to Oceanography 2nd edition, (New Jersey: Prentice Hall, 1977). See especially Chapter 11.

4. See, Manchester v. Massachusetts, 139 U.S. 240, 257-258, (1890); Cunard Steamship Co. v. Mellon, 262 U.S. 100, 122-124, (1922); United States v. California, 332 U.S. 33, (1946).

5. Truman's Proclamation No. 2667 on the Continental Shelf, 1945. See, Donald C. Watt, "First Steps in the Enclosure of the Oceans: The Origins of Truman's Proclamation on the Resources of the Continental Shelf, 28 September 1945," Marine Policy 3 (July 1979): 211-224. For a very thorough discussion of the lawfulness of deep seabed mining and how res nullius and res communis are perceived in international law, see Ted Kronmiller, The Lawfulness of Deep Seabed Mining, Department of Commerce, 1979. Kronmiller writes that the two theories conflict on important, though not crucial, points so far as the lawfulness of appropriations of deep seabed resources is concerned. According to res nullius, the continental shelf is the property of no one and, therefore, is susceptible to ownership or sovereignty by States on the basis of occupation. Kronmiller states: "With ownership or sovereignty over the area attends the exclusive right to explore and exploit the resources thereof or to grant rights to undertake such exploration and exploitation. The requirement of occupation may be satisfied by little more than the presence of a claim by a State to a certain area and some use of, and exercise of authority over, that area."

Under the theory of res communis, the seabed, and perhaps the subsoil, beyond the limits of national juris-diction are held in common by all States. Therefore, ownership or sovereignty or soverign rights, may not lawfully be claimed or exercised by any State over that area, except in cases of acquiescence or prescription. This theory allows, however, that the resources of the deep seabed may be appropriated by any State or private enterprise on a nonexclusive basis. Kronmiller points out that while the res nullius theory is supported by some State practice predating UNCLOS III: 'by the greater weight of scholarly opinion and by dicta of the Inter-national Court of Justice, the res communis theory does have its respected adherents among the publicists." Consequently, this area of traditional law must be regard-ed as unsettled. The important point, however, is that under both theories, the resources of the deep seabed may lawfully be appropriated by State and private enterprises.

6. The four conventions of 1958 were: The 1958
Territorial Sea Convention, which did not fix the outer
limit of the territorial sea, but 12 miles was the maximum
width widely advocated and most states have now come to
accept this limit. In the high seas beyond the territorial sea, all states may exercise the freedoms recognized
in the 1958 High Sea Convention: freedom of navigation,
freedom of fishing, freedom of overflight and freedom to
lay submarine cables and pipelines. The 1958 Fisheries
Convention was an attempt to permit coastal states to
regulate the fishing of stocks around their shores, essentially from the standpoint of conservation. The 1958
Continental Shelf Convention granted coastal states
sovereign rights over the submarine areas of "continental
shelf" outside the territorial sea for the purpose of
exploring and exploiting the natural resources located
there. These four Conventions left three major problems
unresolved: the width of the territorial sea, the outer
limit of the continental shelf, and the arrangments to be
made concerning the allocation and conservation of fish
stocks. The Second U.N. Conference was held in 1960,
mainly to reach agreement on the width of the territorial
sea. The Conference failed to do so, although a proposal
for a 6-mile territorial sea and a 6-mile fishing zone
beyond was almost adopted.

7. The Common Heritage of Mankind concept was
proposed by Ambassador Arvid Pardo representing the
government of Malta in 1967 at the United Nations. It
was endorsed by the United Nations General Assembly in
1970. In 1971 the government of Malta formally proposed
that a common heritage regime replace the traditional
regime of the high seas in ocean space beyond national
jurisdiction. There are six basic elements of the
concept: (1) the area under the common heritage regime
may not be appropriated for ownership--though it can be
used; (2) all rights to resources in the area are vested
in mankind as a whole acting through an international
organization; (3) the area and its resources are managed
through an international organization in which all States
have the right to participate; (4) benefits, both
financial and deriving from participation management and
exchange and transfer of technologies, are to be shared;
(5) the common heritage area must be transmitted environ-
mentally unimpaired to future generations. See, Arvid
Pardo, "The Evolving Law of the Sea: A Critique of the
Informal Composite Negotiating Text (1977)," in Ocean
Yearbook 1, Elisabeth Mann Borgese and Norton Ginsburg,
eds., (Chicago: University of Chicago Press, 1978), pp.
9-37.

8. For an excellent historical account of the United
Nations Law of the Sea Conferences and their interaction

with United States foreign policy see, Ann L. Hollick, United States Foreign Policy and the Law of the Sea, (Princeton University Press, Princeton, New Jersey, 1981.)

9. "Scramble for the Sea," The Economist, March 3, 1976. Territorial rights to the Revillagidedo Islands will give Mexico access to a portion of the nodule rich Clarion- Clipperton fracture zone off its west coast.

10. David Larson, eds., Major Issues of the Law of the Sea, (Durham: University of New Hampshire, 1976), pp. 1-13.

11. Business Week, March 22, 1976.

12. See, U.S. Foreign Policy for the 1970's emerging structure for peace. Report to Congress by Richard Nixon, President of the United States, February 9, 1972. Also issued as House document 249, 92nd Cong. 2nd session.

13. See, Lewis M. Alexander, "The New Geography of the World's Oceans Before and After Law of the Sea," The Columbia Journal of World Business 15, (Winter 1980, no. 4): 6-16; and William T. Burke, "Critical Changes in the Law of the Sea," The Columbia Journal of World Business, op cit., pp. 17-21. Lewis M. Alexander, Geographer of the State Department, has served as Chairman of the Department of Geography and Marine Affairs, University of Rhode Island, and as Director of the Graduate Program in Marine Affairs. He was the founder of the Law of the Sea Institute. William T. Burke who teaches at the University of Washington School of Law, Seattle, Washington, has been a member of the Ocean Policy Committee of the National Research Council, of the Executive Board of the Law of the Sea Institute, and of the U.S. Advisory Committee on the Law of the Sea.

14. See, Ocean Manganese Nodules, 2nd edition, prepared by the Congressional Research Service for the United States Senate Committee on Interior and Insular Affairs, February 1977, pp. 7-12, at p. 11, and Manganese Nodule Resources and Mine Site Availability, Ocean Mining Administration, Department of the Interior, August 1976. Also see, D.S. Cronan, "Deep-Sea Nodules: Distribution and Geochemistry," in Marine Manganese Deposits, G.P. Glasby, ed., (Amsterdam: Elseiver Publishing Company, 1977), and J.Z. Frazer and M.B. Fish, Geological Factors Related to Characteristics of Seafloor Manganese Nodule Deposits, prepared for the U.S. Department of the Interior, Bureau of Mines, (University of California: Scripps Institution of Oceanography, April 30, 1980); and J.Z. Frazer and L.L. Wilson, Manganese Nodule Deposits in

22

the Indian Ocean, (University of California: Scripps
Insitution of Oceangraphy, September 1, 1979).

    15. Robert L. Friedheim, "Factor Analysis and the
Law of the Sea," The Law of the Sea: Offshore Boundaries
and Zones, Lewis M. Alexander, ed., (Columbus: Ohio
State University Press, 1967).

    16. Ibid.

2
United States Government: Political and Institutional Responses

INTRODUCTION

This chapter examines the many issues that have influenced United States policy making towards the development of national deep seabed mining policy. The issues are numerous and complex, and they have become more so, in fact, as the international political and economic context changed for the worse throughout the 1970s.

One of the major reasons it took nine years to get deep seabed mining legislation through Congress and signed into law by the President, is that State Department officials had hopes of achieving an international legal framework for the uses of the ocean's resources at the Third United Nations Conference on the Law of the Sea (UNCLOS III). By holding off on domestic action, it was hoped that an agreeable Treaty could be worked out at the conference.

A significant difficulty for American representatives to the Law of the Sea negotiations was that, at times, the ocean mining industry gave misleading information to State Department negotiators. Because their information led American negotiators to think that there were hundreds of potential mine sites, the official United States position at UNCLOS III on acceptable profit margins and grandfather rights protection clearly favored the industry. It was only from 1977 on that the government relied less on industry data. In the late 1970s, the Departments of Commerce and Interior were able to generate ocean mining data for United States negotiators. At the same time, several concessions were made to the Group of 77 by the American delegation on various provisions in the proposed Treaty on deep seabed mining issues.

Although some of the information provided by the ocean mining industry to the United States government was clearly prejudiced in its favor, similar corporate attempts to influence national policy are very common. The miners did so in an attempt to ensure a favorable operating environment that would maximize return on

23

investment. What helped make the lobbying effort so successful was that much of the State Department's data, coming chiefly from the mining industry, was especially biased toward the sole interests of that industry. But all of the interests of the industry were by no means totally satisfied. In the early sessions of UNCLOS III the Department of Defense was successful in shaping a United States Law of the Sea policy that guaranteed passage through straits--at the expense of concessions to the Group of 77 on seabed mining matters. The seabed miners were helped to some degree, though, by Leigh Ratiner--a major figure in the State Department's negotiating team up to 1976, who was very much in favor of a strong industry position.

There are some similarities between ocean mining and the oil industry that are worth noting. Both industries supply figures and data to the government, which the government then relies upon to make policies supposedly in the nation's general interest. Because ocean mining is directly tied to the North-South debate over a New International Economic Order (NIEO), the domestic and international policy framework that has grown up around it has witnessed more than the usual number of problems. The major difference between the oil and ocean mining industries is that oil is of immediate concern for the nation's leaders, while ocean mining is more of a long-term policy concern.

It would be wrong to think that what is in the best interests of industry is necessarily always harmful to the nation's best interest or that "what's good for General Motors is always good for America." At times the two mesh very nicely. As Table 1 illustrates, however, there are several basic differences in some of the objectives that industry and government have concerning natural resources.

The domestic and international policy problems that government and industry have been working with have been influenced by basic changes in the world environment over the last twenty years. Table 2 summarizes these changes. For example, two decades ago deep seabed mining would not have been an international issue on the scale it has become; the United States simply would have gone out and mined the oceans. It is important to examine exactly what has changed so drastically in the last twenty years that accounts for the many concessions at the Law of the Sea negotiations on deep seabed mining.

First, there has been a large increase in the number of nations--from approximately 100 in 1960 to over 150 in 1980. The majority of these new nations are under-developed, politically unstable, and ideologically vocal in international negotiations.

A second change that has occurred over the last two decades is the number of multilateral conferences that

TABLE 1

Resource Objectives of Industry and Government

Corporate Objectives

---

(1) Dealing with government regulations so that profits are maintained

(2) Insuring an overall healthy return on investment (usually 20-30 per cent)

(3) Deciding whether to get involved in multinational consortia

(4) Being aware of the nature of the competition (e.g., technological advances)

Government Objectives

Domestic:

(1) Determining resource needs for present and future

(2) Maintaining supply

(3) Conservation efforts

(4) Insuring a strong industry (use of aid...what type?)

International:

(1) Maintaining security of access throughout the world to resources

(2) Maintaining friendly ties through economic, political, or military means, with supply nations

(3) Evaluating the nature of foreign competition for the world's resources

(4) Negotiating at international conferences (and bilateral arrangements) for domestic interests of economic efficiency and international goals of equity and harmony

---

TABLE 2

International and Domestic Factors That Have Influenced
U. S. Ocean Mining Policy (1960-1980)

International:

---

(1) Increased number of new nations

(2) Increased number of multilateral conferences for
     dealing with basic economic and resource issues;
     and an increase in the politicization of those
     conferences

(3) A decrease in the economic power of the United
     States vis-a-vis Western Europe and Japan

(4) A decrease in the technological monopoly held by
     the United States

Domestic:

---

(1) Major role of personalities in early ocean mining
     legislation and in the official American UNCLOS III
     negotiating stance

(2) The nature of the State Department (as the key
     American negotiating apparatus at UNCLOS III):
     generally conservative

(3) Technocrats vs. bureaucrats: an increased number of
     specialists in policy-making positions

---

have been held for economic and resource issues. United States negotiators have had to contend with increasingly politicized and ideologically oriented conferences that were originally planned to deal with specific matters like technology, economics, or resources. This change has occurred because of the large number of developing nations which now take part in these negotiations.

A third change is that the United States, in relative terms, is not as economically strong as it was in the 1940s, '50s, and '60s. Western Europe and Japan have developed powerful economic bases which enable them a large degree of post-war political muscle flexing and maneuverability in the international arena that was unheard of until the 1970s.

A fourth change has been a decrease in the technological monopoly held by the United States. The United States still has many technological advantages over other nations, but not to the same degree and extent as it had between 1940 and the late 1960s. One of the reasons France, West Germany, and Japan have caught up with the United States in many high technology areas has been because of close government-industry ties in basic research and development and joint enterprises. In the French case, this has resulted in the AFERNOD ocean mining group devising a highly sophisticated second generation robot mining system that, if it proves economically viable, will out-perform most American systems for lifting the nodules from the seabed to the surface.

Technology is crucial to a nation's long-term security interests, especially in terms of resource exploitation and utilization. A monopoly in technological know-how no longer gives the United States the same competitive advantage it once did; but if the United States can secure access to critical minerals it will be in a better position to maintain its power base and influence in the world. The other industrially advanced nations also realize the necessity of securing access to key resources and have therefore been increasing government-industry ties to take full advantage of their nation's technological capabilities. For example, the Japanese and French governments have provided funds and strong encouragement for the development of manganese nodule exploitation to domestically based enterprises. The United States government ought to do the same in the case of infant high technology resource industries if American industry alone cannot compete with foreign government-industry challenges for access to the world's finite and increasingly critical resources.

Each of these four major changes is interrelated. Individually they have provided difficulties for American statesmen and conference negotiators; combined, they have altered the nature of power in international politics. For the United States, the changes have meant making several concessions to the Third World at UNCLOS III. They may also portend greater difficulties for the United States in assuring access to resources beyond national sovereignty in the next several decades.

In addition to the international changes that have occurred, it is equally important to examine the domestic factors that help account for the politics and difficulties surrounding United States ocean mining policy. One of the principal reasons a long period of time was required for completing unilateral ocean mining legislation was the role of personalities in the legislative process. For example, Senator Lee Metcalf was a major sponsor of deep seabed mining legislation. When he died, his leadership in the unilateral movement was not immediately taken up. One consequence of a lack of vigorous popular leadership behind unilateral legislation was that it took nine years for it to become law.

Personalities were also important in the UNCLOS III negotiations. While Leigh Ratiner was influential in the American negotiating team during the early meetings of the Conference there was a traditional "power politics" approach to the Group of 77. Ratiner's personal negotiating style at the Conference was much different from Elliot Richardson's who took over as head of the United States negotiating team in the mid 1970s. Ambassador Richardson was more conciliatory and somewhat of an idealist when it came to dealing with the Third World. His attempts to placate industry, United States ocean interests in general, and the Third World at UNCLOS III were good diplomacy and may have added to the short-term success of formulating a Treaty, but not to its long-term goals--an international agreement, ratified by at least sixty countries, on the uses of the oceans and its resources. Ambassador James L. Malone, who was appointed by President Reagan to head the United States delegation in 1981, worked closely with Leigh Ratiner (who maintained consultant status to the negotiating team) to present a series of changes in the Treaty text that initially shocked the Group of 77. Malone's negotiating style or "personality" was not as significant a factor as Ratiner's or Richardson's had been.

Another domestic factor that accounts for the policy problems surrounding deep seabed mining is the nature of the State Department. Because the Department of State was head of negotiations for the United States at UNCLOS III it had to be dynamic and progressive to successfully deal with the changes in the international system that occurred in the 1960s and 1970s. Unfortunately the State Department is a traditionally oriented organization that is not always noted for progressive and innovative policy formation--though there are individuals within State who most certainly are progressive. Furthermore, the data the Department was using for early negotiations was heavily influenced by industry, which tended to limit its full understanding of several ocean mining issues vis-a-vis the Group of 77--such as mine site availability. At later stages the negotiating stance was more balanced but still slightly confused and often contradictory between different bureaus within the department. In broader terms, deep seabed mining exacerbated President Carter's reorganization problems within the entire Executive branch. Because of the large bureaucracy involved with ocean mining, problems of domestic-foreign policy coordination were also made more difficult.

Finally, it is becoming increasingly apparent that technocrats (highly trained individuals with specialized knowledge and close ties with industry) run key positions in government--not traditional bureaucrats. The influx of technocrats in government is occurring at a time when corporations are making major economic decisions that affect the nation's domestic and international interests. The formation of deep seabed mining policy in the State and Commerce Departments has been typical of these changes in the bureaucracy.

These broad international and national changes have influenced both United States ocean policy in general and the Law of the Sea negotiations. In an attempt to devise an international treaty for the oceans, given these changes, negotiators at UNCLOS III have tried to cover too much in too short a time for the proposed treaty to work as hoped. Perhaps UNCLOS III should have been a series of on-going negotiations which allowed for consolidation on areas when they were reached. This process may have taken twenty to thirty years, but in the long-run, the results may have been more successful than including all the provisions currently in the Treaty into ten years of negotiating.

An estimate of the effects of the Law of the Sea on the future of international relations can be made by evaluating the changes that it has already brought about. UNCLOS III has been a major educational and learning process for the Third World--particularly for its knowledge of how multilateral negotiations function, how to join forces in order to get what they want from the developed nations, and the experience of negotiating in a legal forum for changes in the international economic order. The Group of 77 has been brought into the modern world of international politics very quickly. In the span of just ten years it has won concessions from the developed world on several economic and resource commons issues. For example, the oceans beyond national sovereignty are considered to be the common heritage of all mankind. The proposed Moon Treaty would also set aside the moon's resources as a commons area. The bargaining strength of the Group of 77 at multilateral conferences portends for possible major drawbacks for future United States resource

policy objectives--especially those for exploiting the
deep seabed and other resources beyond traditional national sovereignty. Even if the Law of the Sea Treaty as
written is not ratified, it will still serve as a
workable blueprint for future Group of 77 approaches in
international forums for resource and economic
negotiations.

The ways in which these international and domestic
influences have affected United States ocean mining policy
can be better understood by taking a closer look at the
history and politics of American deep seabed mining policy
decisions.

THE PATTERN OF UNITED STATES OCEAN MINING
POLICY FORMATION

For the past ten years the United States has been
involved in domestic negotiations for a deep seabed mining
regime. In addition, it has sought to develop world-wide
agreement on a mining regime within the context of a comprehensive United Nations Law of the Sea Treaty. Some
analysts believe that within this affirmed general
framework for the development of a mining regime, United
States policy has shown very little substantive
consistency--other than a pattern of concessions to the
policy demand of the Group of 77. Richard Darman, a
member of the United States Advisory Committee on the Law
of the Sea, believes that these concessions have been
unilateral.[1] This opinion is shared by a large number
of policy makers in Congress and the Administration--
particularly those administrators who occupy offices
concerned with the more financial and economic aspects of
UNCLOS III. Most of the concessions, however, have
served the longer-term interests of the United States in
attempting to ensure an international legal framework for
the uses of the oceans. For example, the Conference has
reached agreement on passage through straits and
territorial and economic zone limits--two goals that the
United States sought for a long time. There are, of
course, certain fundamental points on key issues that the
United States will not conceed. More than once, for
example, the former American Ambassador to the Law of the
Sea Conference, Elliot Richardson, explained that despite
the many benefits of a LOS Treaty, the United States
would not sign such a Treaty if specific aspects of the
International Seabed Authority (ISBA) did not allow
access to the deep seabed for ocean mining enterprises.

United States seabed policy at UNCLOS III has shifted
in numerous ways. It began favoring a simple decentralized, minimally conditioned licensing regime. Then it
was obliged to negotiate over a more centralized regime.

When that proved inadequate, the American position altered to consider a so-called "clean parallel system," where both the ISBA and states or states parties would have equal access to the minerals. The United States delegation then negotiated for a "balanced development system," which would ensure LDC participation in ocean mining activites. There were later negotiations for a mixed system (adding joint-ventures and more central negotiating discretion to the parallel and balanced concepts). A shift followed to a "unitary joint venture system" with clear, continuing rights of access for state sponsored parties that sought to minimize inherent competition between the internationally run Enterprise and private industry in a parallel system.[2]

In 1970, even before the formal United Nations negotiations began, the United States unilaterally proposed a draft convention with a centralized, but minimally conditioned, licensing regime. This regime included an International Seabed Resource Authority, Assembly and Council machinery, and offered provisions for revenue sharing of all mineral resources beyond the 200 meter isobath. The initial United States position skipped over a decentralized licensing alternative, implying that the United States would set a concessionary tone for later negotiations. More and more policy makers believe that the concessions have been one-sided. Also in 1970, the United States affirmed the "common heritage of mankind" principle, giving impetus to the United Nations Resolution on that subject. The notion was agreed to as a governing principle in 1970, but its operational meaning still had to be determined. The major problem has been how to resolve a common heritage concept with a capitalist free market economy that requires free access if there is to be any mining at all.

In return for these early initiatives by the Nixon Administration, the State Department hoped that a negotiating framework for a comprehensive Law of the Sea Treaty would result. Some American observers, however, believed that the United States had ceded a fundamental institutional issue of principle (the common heritage of mankind), for which the United States got a negotiating framework. In general, that was a fair deal given overall aims of attaining an international legal regime for the oceans that the United States still desires.[3]

Formal seabed negotiations began in 1974. They produced a very unsatisfactory negotiating text from the American point of view. The Informal Composite Negotiating Text (ICNT) led the United States delegation to offer further concessions in an effort to gain improvements in a revised text. In so doing, the American team entered a process of negotiation that moved away from the minimally conditioned licensing regime that it had originally proposed.

In 1975 the United States agreed to a "parallel system," that provided for both private industry and an international Enterprise that would mine the seabed for the interests of the developing countries. This was thought to be a widely acceptable compromise position (offered by Henry Kissinger), but was originally rejected by the Group of 77. It was later accepted when changes were made that more closely fit the demands of the developing countries for guarantees of technology transfer and start-up capital ($1 billion) from the developed nations. Also at this time, the United States began to introduce the principle of "balance" in the proposed parallel system. American negotiators did this by suggesting that miners should provide prospected minesites, free, to an internationally chartered competitor: the Enterprise. This was a major concession that whet the appetites of the Group of 77 for further concessions from the industrially advanced nations.

In later attempts to secure agreement on the parallel system, the United States began to negotiate a formal production control system in order to protect land-based producers. In 1976, Secretary of State Kissinger offered a specific production control formula. Production controls are needed primarily to protect a handful of land-based producers from adverse economic consequences of ocean mining. It was one of the last stumbling blocks to a final Treaty. While there is a need to protect struggling Third World land-based producers, artificial production controls are not the most efficient way to proceed. A simple tax on full-scale unrestricted ocean mining operations, to be distributed to severely affected nations, would be more effective than artificial restrictions on ocean mining. By enforcing production controls the world's economies are assured of higher prices for the minerals in manganese nodules.

Also in 1976, the United States moved further toward what was later to be termed a "balanced development system," in its continued quest for agreement. Kissinger offered to assure financing for the start-up of the proposed Enterprise and volunteered to assure the Enterprise the necessary transfer of technology. Both offers were general when made, but became quite specific in the course of negotiation. As they did so, the differences between the Group of 77 and the ocean mining nations quickly became more evident and intense.

In 1977, under the new Carter Administration, the United States attempted to regain some ground by making Kissinger's financing offer a shared debt-underwriting offer and by arguing that this would be sufficient to assure technology transfer. In fact, the United States unequivocally opposed any mandatory system of technology transfer. The negotiating text produced by the Conference, however, included both the United States' financing proposal and a mandatory system of technology transfer. This text was accepted by the American negotiators in 1978.

In 1976 the United States also proposed that the parallel system be subject to review in 20 to 25 years. In 1977 this position was reaffirmed subject to acceptance of the parallel system as a compromise, and provided that the terms of review not be prejudiced in favor of any alternative system. In 1978, however, the United States moved to accept a review system prejudiced in favor of those with biases toward a unitary system or biases against seabed development.

The United States showed more willingness to negotiate a "mixed" regime in 1977, allowing incentives for joint-ventures with the Enterprise and allowing the Authority to enjoy certain appearances of broader discretion--provided that these were to be limited by other provisions, specifications, and references in the text and its annexes.[4] The negotiating texts and annexes of 1978 failed to be satisfactorily limited. The United States thus began to reconsider whether it should really seek such extensive limitations.

In return for concessions, the United States obtained certain benefits. One was that its concessions were incorporated into the ICNT. There were, however, no substantive concessions from the Group of 77; in fact their demands remained largely unchanged. There was, though, an, expression by the Group of 77 of a continued willingness to negotiate.[5] Governments of both the Group of 77 and the industrially advanced states appreciate the benefits of an international legal regime for the oceans. One of the more obvious of these for coastal Third World states is the legality of 200-mile EEZs. The general pattern of continued United States participation in UNCLOS III and continuous United States concession can only be understood by reference to interests beyond seabed mining. As a result, there were increasing numbers of people involved with United States legislation for seabed mining who felt that no treaty would be better than the one that was being hammered out of the revised ICNT.

UNILATERAL MINING LEGISLATION

While the industrial world wants to create a climate that will stimulate private investment, the Group of 77 wants to ensure that all aspects of deep seabed mining are centrally controlled--even, it appears, at the risk of seriously constraining the investment climate. This difference in philosophy is reflected in the kind of treaty text that each group wants. The developed nations want precision, clarity, and predictability--particularly regarding security of tenure and contractual obligations.

The developing countries prefer a more generalized text--one that has broad principles but leaves the implementation of those principles to the International Authority.[6]

Former Congressman John Murphy, who had been Chairman of the House Merchant Marine and Fisheries Committee from 1977 through 1980, was one of the leading spokesmen in the Congress for unilateral action by the United States with respect to deep seabed mining legislation. His association with the ocean mining issue began in the 92nd Congress (1971-1972), and he sponsored such legislation in every succeeding Congress until it became law in 1980. Murphy served on the State Department's Law of the Sea Advisory Committee as a member of the Congressional delegation and had been a close observer of UNCLOS III since 1974.

Murphy's views, elaborated in different forums, make three or four points central to an understanding of United States unilateral mining legislation. The first concerns the Third World. The disparate perceptions and goals of the developing and developed nations are deeply ingrained and persistent. They have existed throughout the Conference, and although occasional agreement was reached on one or another issue, Murphy believed it unlikely that the nations taking part in UNCLOS III could resolve their fundamental differences on ocean mining.[7] This impasse created a dilemma for the United States--which is committed to the concept of a new and comprehensive Law of the Sea Treaty and therefore does not want the Conference to fail. Yet the United States could not permit ocean mining operations to remain stalled. The steady progress toward overall agreement in 1979 and 1980 indicates that Murphy may have overestimated the differences between the developed and developing countries or at least underestimated the efforts of both sides to reach reconciliation. The Group of 77 became less strident in some of its demands because of concessions from the United States at the Conference and the realization that American unilateral deep seabed mining legislation would become effective regardless of a Treaty.

Although concessions were made by the United States negotiating team in both the Ford and Carter administrations, it is unlikely that the Senate would have ratified the Treaty with its then current provisions on deep seabed mining. The House deep seabed mining bills of 1978 (HR 3350) and 1980 (HR 2759) were generally supported by the Carter Administration. They specifically stated that no assertions of sovereignty or sovereign rights over seabed minesites were being advanced. In recognition that the seabeds are considered the common heritage of mankind, the bills established a revenue-sharing fund to which contractors would contribute a seabed tax computed at 3.75% of the imputed value of the minerals recovered.

Upon ratification of a Treaty by the United States, funds from this trust account would then be available to make revenue-sharing contributions to the International Seabed Authority.[8]

In the Senate the Deep Seabed Mineral Resources Act (S. 2053) was "reported out" by the Committee on Foreign Relations on August 25, 1978. The Senate failed, however, to take any further action on the bill before the end of the session in October 1978. Because of procedural and parlimentary problems, the Senate failed to gain unanimous consent to consider S. 2053 and the bill died with the close of the 95th Congress. The Senate did pass S. 493, a bill very similar to its predecessor, on December 14, 1979.

In testimony before the House Committee on International Relations in 1978, Ambassador Richardson summarized the United States' position regarding domestic seabed mining by noting that the considerations underlying Administration support of unilateral legislation were independent of the Law of the Sea Conference. From 1978 until his resignation in late 1980, Richardson argued that there would be a need for some legal framework for deep seabed mining in any event between the outcome of a successful Conference and the effective date on which a comprehensive Treaty would come into force. In addition, the companies contemplating ocean mining are facing difficult decisions as to whether or not to invest money in the further development and testing of mining technology. The ocean mining industry needs to make those decisions now, before they can know definitively what the outcome of the Conference will be, and because the ratification process may take several years.

In order to get HR 2759 passed in June of 1980 before Congressional recess, all four committees involved with the bill (Foreign Affairs, Merchant Marine and Fisheries, Interior, and Ways and Means), agreed to suspend the regular rules. This enabled the various committees to work out as expeditiously as possible all remaining differences. There were also joint meetings with Senate committees which had passed their own version of the bill in 1979, so that differences could be worked out and a joint bill presented to the President for signature by early July. The legislation was signed into law by President Carter on June 28, 1980 (PL 96-283). It is commonly referred to as the Deep Seabed Hard Mineral Resources Act.

Proponents of deep seabed mining legislation asserted that the forward movement of ocean mining should be actively encouraged, and not brought to a halt while the Conference attempted to reach a seemingly elusive final agreement. One of the reasons the Conference has continued for so long is that the Carter Administration was careful not to push the Group of 77 into an intransigent position that would have killed negotiations completely. At the same time, the reality that such legislation would pass put pressure on the Group of 77 to moderate some of its demands. The general feeling on Capitol Hill was that because there was no international mechanism yet in place for the development of ocean mining, the United States should act unilaterally--through domestic legislation--to provide a proper regulatory framework. The legislation is designed to allow the commencement of ocean mining and at the same time not hinder the formation of a new international regime.[9] It has provisions which state quite clearly that an international Treaty agreement on ocean mining, if ratified by the United States Senate, would replace United States domestic ocean mining legislation. The final bills contained last minute changes that attempted to minimize Group of 77 complaints against the American action. The most important amendment provided that full-scale commercial recovery of nodules could not begin until January 1, 1988--the original date had been 1982. The legislation does allow, however, for a sufficient quantity of nodules to be mined to enable scientific and full research and development to take place for a full-scale operation.

Key Congressional movers behind domestic unilateral action claimed five major purposes for the ocean mining legislation.[10] First, it was intended to encourage the successful conclusion of UNCLOS III, creating a comprehensive Law of the Sea Treaty which will give legal definition to the principle that the hard minerals of the deep seabed are part of the common heritage of mankind. From the perspective of the United States, the successful conclusion of a Treaty requires negotiation of provisions providing nondiscriminatory and assured access to deep seabed resources for all nations.[11]

Second, the legislation provides for the establishment of an international revenue sharing fund which would receive contributions from companies that have been issued permits to engage in commercial recovery under the legislation. This revenue would be used for sharing with the international community if an eventual Treaty came into effect for the United States. In establishing this fund the United States is supposedly demonstrating good faith in working toward a legal definition of the common heritage of mankind concept.

The third purpose of the legislation is to establish an interim program to regulate the exploration for the commercial recovery of manganese nodules by American citizens, pending the ratification of a Treaty by the United States and its entering into force.[12] This purpose responds directly to the stated needs of the industry for security of tenure guarantees.

Fourth, the legislation is also designed to enhance the program of environmental assessment of the effects of exploration and exploitation of nodules from the seabed. The legislation is aimed at assuring that exploration and recovery activities are conducted in a manner which will encourage the conservation of such reserves, protect the quality of the environment, and promote the safety of life and property at sea.[13]

Finally, the legislation is designed to encourage the continued development of the technology necessary to recover the hard mineral resources of the deep seabed. One of the purposes of PL 96-283 is to help provide legal certainty to maintain industrial research and development (R&D) efforts to ensure that the required technology to mine the deep seabed--when it becomes profitable to do so--will be available. According to industry spokesmen in 1981, the domestic legislation had not provided enough legal certainty for the companies to go beyond the initial R&D phase. The next phase of development, which requires significant engineering scale-up to prototype levels, is too costly to risk investment without guaranteed access to the resources under conditions similar to domestic resource programs.[14] The low price and demand for metals throughout most of the 1970s and up to the present time (1982) indicate that market conditions are also important for understanding why R&D activities have not significantly increased. These issues will be more fully discussed in Chapter three.

With respect to the security of tenure problems for American based companies that pioneer deep seabed mining, the Act contains a statement of Congressional intent that any international agreement should provide assured and nondiscriminatory access to the resources, under reasonable terms and conditions to United States citizens. For those United States citizens who had already begun mining activities prior to an international convention, the "Grandfather Rights" statements in the Act call for the continuation of those operations under similar terms as were imposed by the domestic legislation and in such a manner as to avoid unreasonable impairment to investment.[15]

A statement of Congressional intent is not binding on UNCLOS III or on United States negotiators, yet it does represent the type of international regime favored by the Congress. Obviously the ocean mining industry benefits from this type of support as well. It is also important to all nations at UNCLOS III with respect to the type of Treaty for which the chances of Senate ratification would be enhanced and full Congressional support of additional legislation would be increased.[16]

At a session of the General Committee in New York on August 18, 1978 to hear statements regarding United States deep seabed mining legislation, the chairman of the Group of 77 voiced the concern of the developing countries:

It is incomprehensible that at a time when the conference is at an advanced state in negotiating an
internationally agreed regime for the exploration
and exploitation of the resources of the deep seabed,
states engaged in those negotiations should contemplate unilateral actions which would threaten to
jeopardize the pursuit of the negotiations and indeed
the successful conclusion of the conference itself.
Those states must be aware of the consequences of
these actions.[17]

These concerns were voiced again in 1979 and 1980 as
passage of unilateral legislation gained momentum.
Although the Soviet Union has traditionally been against
an international regime for the deep seabed, it has frequently concurred with the Group of 77 view. In 1978,
Soviet spokesmen said that the proposed legislation vio-
lated the United Nations General Assembly resolution which
called on nations not to exploit the seabed prior to
establishment of an international seabed regime.[18]

Ambassador Richardson defended the Congressional
action frequently, stating that under the freedom of the
high seas it is fully legal to exploit the seabed beyond
national jurisdiction, that the legislation was necessary
to encourage research and development preceding commercial
mining, and that it was fully compatible with a future
treaty. Instead of jeopardizing a future treaty, the
Ambassador contended that the legislation:

...should facilitate the early conclusion of a generally acceptable Law of the Sea treaty by dispelling
any impression that the governments of the countries
preparing to engage in such mining can be induced to
acquiesce in an otherwise unacceptable treaty because
that is the only way to obtain the minerals.[19]

According to proponents of deep seabed mining legislation,
the need for such action can be shown by looking at three
different scenarios for purposes of analysis: if there
is no Treaty; if there is such a Treaty; and if the United
States does not enter a Treaty agreement.

During the Congressional push for legislation, proponents argued that regardless of a Treaty there were
certain factors that support domestic action. These
include the need for a secure supply of deep seabed minerals. The United States' primary demand for nickel,
cobalt, copper, and manganese is shown in Table 3. The
figures from the executive agencies, along with the
historical demand patterns shown in this table, indicate
the average annual growth rate for the United States as
shown in Table 4.

Projections and data on worldwide consumption of
these four metals through the year 2000 are subject to

TABLE 3

U. S. Primary Demand for Cobalt, Copper, Nickel, and
Manganese (Thousands of Short Tons)

Year	Cobalt	Copper	Nickel	Manganese
1960	4.5	1107	121.6	1077
1961	5.8	1237	134.2	842
1962	6.8	1355	127.9	978
1963	6.0	1425	120.0	1096
1964	6.7	1566	132.1	1216
1965	7.1	1613	190.4	1373
1966	9.0	1898	228.8	1353
1967	7.6	1549	182.8	1207
1968	7.2	1540	162.2	1150
1969	9.6	1696	152.4	1317
1970	8.1	1572	174.7	1327
1971	6.7	1627	135.5	1170
1972	9.6	1951	167.8	1366
1973	10.9	1942	207.6	1554
1974	11.7	1953	219.1	1492
1975	6.9	1307	154.5	1133

Source: U. S. Bureau of Mines

TABLE 4

Projected U. S. Demand for Cobalt, Copper, Nickel, and Manganese (Thousands of Short Tons)

	1985	2000
Cobalt (3.7% average annual growth rate)	12.3	24.9
Copper (2.5% average annual growth rate)	2379.8	3433.6
Manganese (2% average annual growth rate)	1687.8	2224.1
Nickel (4.1% average annual growth rate)	311.1	567.9

Source: Department of Commerce. April 1979.

great variance. A report by the Department of Commerce
(Office of Ocean, Resource and Scientific Policy Coordination) in April, 1979 estimated that the average annual
rates of growth for the rest of the world (other than the
United States) in the consumption of the four metals will
be higher than the rate for the United States and most
other industrialized nations. The worldwide figures show
an upward direction because of the accelerated development
of such nations as Brazil and Mexico, and continued high
industrial growth in Japan.[20]

The need for these critical minerals thus affects
not only the United States and other industrialized
nations but also all countries in the world which consume
the products produced by such metals. One of the
"Findings" in the legislation states that the development
of seabed mineral resources is, "important to the industrial needs of the United States and other nations of the
world, both developed and developing." (See appendix 3
for a statement of "Findings and Purposes" of PL 96-283.)

Also, regardless of a Law of the Sea Treaty, there
is a great need to reduce the uncertainty of mineral
supply. Legislation is seen as a major means of helping
to minimize that uncertainty. Table 5 illustrates the
potential contribution of ocean resources to the world's
demand of these minerals between 1976 and 2000.

The need for a secure supply of critical minerals is
unquestionable. Congressional testimony from both government and industry officials presented throughout the nine
years it took to get passage of the Deep Seabed Hard
Mineral Resources Act, continually stressed that limited
producer control over supplies and prices meant that seabed mining was in the national interest of the United
States and the international interest of all mankind as
an important future alternative to potentially unreliable
sources of key minerals.[21] In testimony before
Congress, a representative of the Department of the
Interior summarized the national interest regarding a
secure supply of ocean minerals. After indicating the
Administration's strong support for enactment of deep seabed mining legislation, he stated that the best way to
provide for adequate, secure supplies of minerals is to
actively promote diversity of sources. To this end, deep
seabed nodules could be a potential alternate source of
supply in the coming decades for several minerals which
the United States imports in substantial quantities.[22]
To maintain secure supplies of the metals in manganese
nodules is important, but there are political and economic
costs to do so. Potential political costs may arise from
the alienation of the Group of 77 and land-based producer
states. Economic costs, as well as studies which indicate
that the need of the United States to secure access to
manganese nodules is not as crucial as some officials have
indicated, will be discussed in Chapter three.

TABLE 5

Potential Contribution of Ocean Resources

	Total resources (tons X 10)	Ratio of Resources to cumulative world demand, 1976-2000 (per cent)		
		Low demand	Medium demand	High demand
Nodules	2100.0			
Nickel	26.0	100%	88%	82%
Copper	22.5	8	7	6
Cobalt	5.0	439	367	328
Manganese	504.0	134	127	110

Source: "Cobalt, Copper, Nickel, and Manganese: Future Supply and Demand and Implications for Deep Seabed Mining." Office of Ocean, Resources and Scientific Coordination, Department of Commerce. April 1979.

Note: Based on nodule deposits with average metal content of 1.24% nickel, 1.03% copper, 0.24% cobalt, and 24% manganese.

Another issue for consideration, regardless of an eventual Treaty, is the need for the establishment of a legal framework. Such a framework is needed for continued investment and further technological development and resource management and environmental regulations.

The discouragement of further investments in deep seabed mining has a dimension other than the one industry claims, that may be as important, or more important, than the potential loss of the four minerals. Former Congressman John Murphy believed that obstacles in the development of the needed technology to recover manganese nodules might seriously set back other types of ocean resource exploration. He claimed that the knowledge gained from deep seabed mining may be, in the long-term, more important to mankind than the metals which are recovered:

> The nations of the world should recognize that the knowledge and technological capability necessary for recovery of seabed nodules, and not the nodules themselves, are the true resources.....The industrial and technological development that has been undertaken through major investments of capital and labor has unleashed these resources for the benefit of all--not just some--nations.....[23]

A second scenario involves the need for legislation given a subsequent Law of the Sea Treaty. If an agreed text is adopted by the Conference, there are three major reasons why domestic legislation is useful.

First, during the period between enactment of legislation and subsequent successful negotiations, it is important that the United States Congress indicate its position on the general structure of an international seabed mining regime that would be acceptable.[24]

Second, it is frequently pointed out that there will most likely be a period of several years between the conclusion of a successful LOS Conference and the date on which an international convention would enter into force with respect to states' parties. This is particularly so for the ratification process in the United States Senate, which may take a considerable period of time according to Congressional analysts and spokesmen in the State Department.[25]

Third, the continued development of United States interests in seabed mining is important under a subsequent Treaty because certain provisions in such a Treaty may place a premium on early application to the International Seabed Authority and a related premium on early investment.[26]

In the last scenario, if a Law of the Sea Treaty does not enter into force for the United States, there will be a need for unilateral legislation. It is possible that a treaty could not be binding on the United States. For example, the United States could choose not to ratify it, but would still want to retain the right to mine the seabed as an exercise of traditional law. If American citizens explored and mined the seabed within the framework of a domestic regime, then the legal position of the United States would be much stronger. There would, obviously, be major differences of opinion regarding international law in this situation. Given certain circumstances the United States could manifest its interpretation of the status of that law by exercising its proper freedom to mine under the high seas doctrine.[27] But this would be unlikely unless other ocean mining nations gave implicit support of such action.

Current ocean mining legislation[28] reflects the inputs of Congressmen,[29] legislative analysts,[30] and industry representatives.[31] Different departments and agencies of the Administration--particularly Commerce, Interior, and State--were also directly involved in the legislative process. Finally, various environmental and public interest groups such as the Environmental Policy Center, the United Methodist Law of the Sea Project, and the United States Committee for the Oceans participated in Congressional hearings and held workshops connected with the Law of the Sea.

FOREIGN AND DOMESTIC POLICY CONCERNS

Security of Supply

For two hundred years the United States has built a complex sophisticated base for its economy which draws on both the extensive resources of this nation and upon those of other nations in producing goods for domestic consumption and for trade in international commerce. The realities of our energy dependence on foreign sources over the past few years have caused many to question whether we will continue to have available sufficient supplies of other basic industrial raw materials to sustain economic growth and maintain national security.

There is increasing competition for available terrestrial sources of minerals. At the same time average ore grades are declining. This problem has been compounded by the increase in energy needed to exploit less accessible mineral deposits. Technical improvements in processing techniques, however, will lessen the pressure on known reserves of ore grade minerals by making them go further than before and by utilizing poorer grades that would otherwise be less valuable. Research and development, like other economic activities, are stimulated by the potential to earn profits. As depletion increases the costs of a mineral product, it enhances the profits to be earned from the development of any new technology that makes the mineral easier to find or process, or reduces the quantity required in its end uses, or creates a substitute material. Thus, if depletion does become severe, over the long-run one would expect greater efforts to create the technology needed to counter its adverse effects.[32]

While the United States has continued to consume an ever-expanding volume of minerals (although consumption somewhat leveled off for most of the 1970s), it has become increasingly dependent upon foreign sources for certain strategic minerals. In 1976 the $68 billion worth of domestically produced mineral raw materials had to be augmented by $31 billion worth of imported raw materials (U.S. Bureau of Mines, 1977). The United States is a major net importer of three of the metals that will be removed from ocean nodules--nickel, cobalt, and manganese. It would therefore be in the nation's best interest to have open access to manganese nodules as an additional source of those minerals.

Though there is some uncertainty about the immediate importance of ocean mining as an alternative source for copper, there is less doubt that it can become critically important for cobalt and manganese by the turn of the century. A 1979 Department of Commerce study found that available demand forecasts and past consumption patterns indicate that reserves of copper, cobalt, manganese, and nickel are adequate to the end of the century for United States needs, assuming no barriers, constraints or disruptions in the market. This report also found that seabed mining will be critical to national security as a source of manganese around the year 2000. The report concluded that although the United States economy could sustain the loss of cobalt supplies from Zaire for approximately one year, prolonged denial would make the seabed an important source of the metal for general economic growth. The report found that cobalt from other sources up to the year 2000 was adequate to meet national security requirements. In late 1980, however, it was determined by the General Accounting Office that most of the nation's cobalt reserves (collected mainly in the 1950s) were of a poor grade that would have to be sold in order to restock with higher grade ore. The better grade ore is required to meet the demands of the aerospace industry for more sophisticated metal alloys needed to build defense aircraft for the Air Force.[33]

The best way to provide for adequate, secure supplies of minerals is to actively promote diversity of sources. To this end, deep seabed nodules could be a potential alternate source of supply in the coming decades for several minerals which the United States imports in substantial quantities. With the exception of copper, the United States is very dependent on other nations for its supply of metals which could be mined from the deep seabed. United States net imports of the four major metals contained in ocean nodules as a percentage of apparent consumption is set out in Table 6.

The access to a seemingly adequate worldwide supply of minerals must be considered tenuous in view of the concentration of productive operations in only a few locations. In fact, there are one or two areas that are critical to the future supply of each metal. A brief summary of the availability and potential security of supply of each of the four minerals found in economic quantities in ocean nodules can be found in appendix 4.

Because ocean mining could supply 367% of the world demand for cobalt, there are political and economic questions which arise. For example, what will happen to the world cobalt market and what will this mean for countries such as Zaire and Zambia that rely on exports of this mineral for foreign revenue? According to one study, the effects of ocean mining on the world cobalt market would be very dramatic. In fact, the cobalt market would be the most affected of all the metals which are contained in manganese nodules. It was estimated that first generation ocean mining projects would likely lead to a cobalt price decline of 25 to 35 percent to as much as 50 percent. This would lower the normal base level price of about $10 per pound (in 1978 dollars) to $6.50 per pound.[34]

Soviet pressure on mineral rich southern Africa. The primary sources of strategic materials in southern Africa are Zaire, Zambia, Zimbabwe, and South Africa. Rebel activity and political instability in this entire region have been steadily increasing. Marxist-Leninist regimes have already taken over in nearby African nations, and further takeovers seem possible. If the Soviet Union should manage to extend its influence into these areas, it could have the power to gain political and economic concessions by "peaceful" manipulation of materials supplies to consumer countries.[35]

Table 7 shows that among the world economic powers, the Soviet Union alone is almost entirely self-sufficient in strategic materials. Even China, with large undeveloped resources at present, must import about 15 of its strategic materials. The United States is in a worse position. We must import about 30 to 40 strategic materials, and to protect against cartels or embargoes we must maintain costly stockpiles. Western Europe and Japan have even greater dependence than the United States on imported oil and other strategic materials.[36]

Zaire and Zambia appear most vulnerable to such movements, now that the Soviets are currently providing arms

TABLE 6

United States Net Imports as a Percentage of Consumption

Metal	1976	1977	1978
Cobalt	98%	97%	97%
Copper	12	13	19
Manganese	98	98	98
Nickel	70	70	77

Source: Mineral Commodity Summaries 1979, U. S. Bureau of Mines.

TABLE 7

STRATEGIC MATERIALS IMPORT DEPENDENCE

	USA (percent)	CHINA (percent)	USSR (percent)
	0 25 50 75 100	0 25 50 75 100	0 25 50 75 100
Natural Rubber			
Diamonds			
Manganese			
Cobalt			
Tantalum			
Titanium			
Platinum Group			
Chromium			
Aluminum			
Tin			
Florspar			
Nickel			
Gold			
Germanium/Indium			
Mercury			
Beryllium			
Ziconium			
Tungstan			
Zinc			
Petroleum			
Silver			
Barita			
Vanadium			
Iron Ore			
Lead			
Copper			
Uranium			
Magnesium			
Sulphur			

Sources: U.S. Bureau of Mines, Joint Chiefs of Staff; National Foreign
Assessment Center: Cong. Committee on International Relations

and military advisers, along with Cuban troops, to revolutionary movements in those countries. The repeated attempts to take over Shaba Province in Zaire, which
controls 60 percent of global cobalt resources, is perhaps
evidence of Soviet designs on mineral control of southern
Africa. After Zaire, the Soviet Union and Cuba together
are probably the largest cobalt producers in the world.
If Shaba were to fall into their control, the Soviets
would effectively control almost 80 percent of global
cobalt supplies. In addition, they would gain control
over one of the largest sources of industrial diamonds
and a significant portion of world copper production.[37]
Even if the cartels do not form, the secure supply of the
critical minerals available in ocean nodules could be
seriously threatened if the resource-rich countries of
southern Africa experience severe political and economic
instability. Both the United States and the industrialized world as a whole rely heavily on this region for
very significant quantities of manganese and cobalt. A
cut-off of supplies from one or more of these countries
due to political uprisings, transportation problems
(including sabotage), or market manipulations is likely.
The greatest national interest in seabed mining over the
long-term is in its value as a future alternative to
potentially unreliable sources of manganese. This role
can be served either by recovering manganese from the
nodules directly or by storing manganese-bearing waste
from direct processing.[38] Future supplies of various
critical minerals are never certain for numerous reasons,
including political ones. It is therefore essential to
develop, as soon as possible, alternative sources of as
many minerals as possible. Deep seabed mining for
manganese nodules offers an excellent opportunity to do
so for four critical minerals.

Defense Issues

One of the major reasons given by some United States
policy makers for making concessions on deep seabed mining
at UNCLOS III concerns national security. It is therefore
necessary to examine the specific defense issues raised
so that their linkage with ocean mining concessions can
be evaluated. Some analysts (especially those in the
Department of Defense) claim that passage through straits
is of utmost importance to the United States. Others
suggest that given the range of today's land and sea
based nuclear missiles, there are only a few straits
which are of real importance; and that too many concessions have been made to satisfy the unwarranted concerns
of the Defense Department.

In the course of the Reagan Administration's review
of the Law of the Sea Treaty text, a somewhat different
Defense Department stance became apparent. Given that
most nations had introduced a 12-mile territorial limit
and a 200-mile EEZ with assurances of innocent passage

through straits, and that only a limited number of straits were "important" because of advances in the fire and range capabilities of nuclear submarines, the Defense Department began to pull back from earlier efforts to ensure passage of the Treaty.

There are essentially five goals of the United States military in the use of ocean space. These are, maintenance of adequate capacity to project American forces overseas, maintenance of access to vital resources, maintenance of adequate surveillance capabilities, and maintenance of peacetime naval functions.[39]

Robert Osgood argues that one of the Navy's major defense concerns comes down to the problem of protecting only two straits: Gibraltar and the Indonesian straits. He suggests that from the standpoint of protecting American nuclear strategic interests in these two straits it is sufficient to carry on the kinds of operational arrangements that we already have with Malaysia, Indonesia, and Spain. Such arrangements do not require a universal law, but rather, favorable political relations with the few countries involved. Osgood believes the concessions that would have to be made in order to reach a compromise on straits for a Law of the Sea Treaty are, by comparison, not worth making. From a purely nuclear strategic position Osgood's arguments make sense. But as we learned from the Iranian crisis of 1979/80, it is very important that the United States can move conventional naval forces through various straits to any location in the world. Shows of conventional naval force are still deemed essential aspects of United States and Soviet foreign policy.

It is probable that future trouble spots in the international environment will, at times, make the movement of conventional military weapons and forces very inhospitable. For example, coastal states are, and will be, more assertive of their desire to control what goes on in waters a good way off their shores. Any ocean regime must, therefore, accommodate itself to the concerns and apprehensions of these states. Overall, the United States is doing relatively well in the present environment, which includes several bilateral working arrangements for passage through straits.

There are problems with such bilateral relationships. Even friendly nations are subject to their own domestic pressures which may not always allow the United States use of their airspace, bases, or straits. Such was the case during the Middle East crisis of 1973. In addition there are no assurances that bilateral relationships which the United States may set up with individual nations will be long lasting. Osgood points out that without a Law of the Sea Treaty guaranteeing straits passage, the United States and Iran successfully negotiated a working arrangement. This example, however, serves as an argument for a

Treaty agreement on straits passage given our present
relations with that nation. The point is that a universal
straits-passage law is not needed if the United States
can count on friendly governments in very specific areas
of the world to always permit the United States Navy use
of their straits. As the sudden and swift overthrow of
the Shah of Iran illustrates, however, the United States
does not have such guarantees.

In the final analysis any country with enough military power is going to send its navy wherever it wants.
But such actions would be very costly in terms of diplomatic and military interests. A Law of the Sea Treaty
would create a widely accepted system of international
law for the oceans, including provisions for passage
through straits. If the rules of the Treaty adequately
meet United States needs, it would be the most effective
means of insuring a legal framework which allows transit
passage through straits.

The basic conflict between the straits and the major
naval and maritime powers at UNCLOS III has come over the
efforts of the straits states to apply principles of innocent passage through territorial waters to international
straits. The problem with the requirements for innocent
passage as found in the Treaty is that the determination
is left up to the coastal state. The United States and
other major naval and maritime powers fear that such
determinations might become subjective, arbitrary and
discriminatory, placing their navies and merchant vessels
at the mercy of the coastal states, which may restrict or
prohibit passage and possibly charge exorbitant transit
fees.

Throughout the negotiations at UNCLOS III the United
States made it clear that the principle of unimpeded
passage was non-negotiable, while Indonesia and the other
straits states had the support of the Group of 77 for some
sort of straits regime similar to innocent passage in
territorial seas. (The Soviet Union had a difficult task
balancing its own desires to see as little restriction on
movement through straits as possible, and its attempts to
appear in support of the Group of 77.) The negotiations
resulted in an innovative concept of "transit passage"
for international straits, which was literally removed
from the concept of innocent passage by creating a new
chapter in the Treaty dealing with "Straits used for
international navigation," (Part III, Section 2, Articles
37 and 38). The trade-off for the apparent Group of 77
concessions on transit passage through international
straits was made because of concessions by the United
States and the developed maritime powers in regard to the
exploitation and development of the deep seabed. The
Group of 77 regards the regulation, control, exploitation,
research, and development of the deep seabed of major importance for economic, political and ideological reasons,

and from their perspective regard the control of the
International Seabed Authority as non-negotiable.[40]

Officials in different Departments in the Administration and even different bureaus within them have indicated
that at times different goals are being sought by different agencies with different interests. Those that spoke
of the need for a comprehensive Treaty, with concessions
on deep seabed mining if required, stated the need for a
clarification and definition of terms of international
law regarding the oceans. They also spoke of the need
for legal security in the high seas for deep ocean mining,
and the need for worldwide acceptance of a new legal
framework governing everything from transit through
straits to pollution control and scientific research.
The linkage between these issues is not always realized.
As a result different inputs into United States oceans
policy have frequently been uncoordinated, if not contradictory.

PROBLEMS OF AN UNCOORDINATED APPROACH TO OCEAN RESOURCE POLICY

As resource exploitation and uses of the oceans have
become more politicized over the last decade, problems of
an uncoordinated approach to United States ocean resource
policy have become increasingly apparent. The goal here
is not to solve the problem, but rather to describe its
nature and its consequences on deep seabed mining policy.

At the heart of the problem are two interrelated aspects of national policy formation which have long plagued
the policy process. The first is that ocean resource
policy combines aspects of both foreign and domestic
policy processes. And second, because of this, the
national policy making structure is not focused and is
often working at cross purposes. In the case of international ocean policy, and ocean mining in particular,
these traditional problem areas have been exacerbated by
a new set of international problems. In addition, there
is increasing pressure for better oceans policy due to
the rapid developments in the technology for ocean resource exploitation. The combination of all these factors
has resulted in an uncoordinated and inefficient international ocean resource policy framework.

One of the major objectives of a nation's foreign
policy is the maximization of political power vis-a-vis
its relations with other states in the international
system for military and economic power. The secure access
to resources from around the world is only one component
of United States foreign policy. If the securing of
resources comes into conflict with the maximizing of
political power then resource policy will be greatly

influenced by broader policy objectives.[41]

The resource component of foreign policy is often
dominated by concerns of geographic location (availability
and political security of supply), while the resource
component of domestic policy is usually dominated by more
immediate concerns of avoiding or minimizing the effects
of a crisis situation. Foreign and domestic resource
policy are two sides of the same coin--but their methods
often differ. Because the major objective of foreign
policy is the maximization of political power, and that
of domestic policy is national welfare, the two policies
often clash in the area of resources. Both spatial and
temporal consideration are essential to the efficient
management of resources. The two must therefore be
smoothly integrated into a United States resource policy
framework.[42] This is a nice goal and something that
should be aimed for. It is unlikely, however, given the
nation's present and historical tradition of domestic
political expediency surrounding the democratic process,
that many elected policy makers will venture into areas
that could possibly threaten their power bases. This is
not to say that a more integrated resource policy framework could not happen. But it will take bold men with
more foresight than we have become accustomed to, to set
the stage so that a more successfully integrated international ocean resource policy framework can be
created.[43]

Deep seabed mining highlights many of the current
and potential natural resource problems in the United
States--both at national and international levels. Conditions at the international level are changing rapidly
and have implications for United States ocean mining
policy. For example, technology transfer, the New International Economic Order, and the emergence of a new
resource diplomacy which now include Antarctica and outer
space, have created concern throughout the Federal Government. This has resulted in attempts at new policies and
new organizational structures to carry out these policies.

Deep seabed mining cuts across several categories of
policy-related issues which are currently under review by
the Federal Government. These include: United States
policy in future commons resource negotiations; nonfuel
minerals policy; United States interest in the ocean; the
United States role in relations with Third World nations
and the Group of 77 in particular; and Government reorganization to more effectively handle United States natural
resource related problems.[44] The policy stance taken
by the United States on seabed mining will in various ways
reflect the outcomes of policy decisions in all these
areas.

Only with the creation of the Office of Ocean Mining
and Energy within the National Oceanographic and
Atmospheric Administration in the second half of 1980 was

there a legally defined lead agency to overview or make policy regarding deep seabed mining. Ocean policy in general is still formulated by different actors. They can be grouped in three categories: the executive branch, Congress, and non-governmental institutions such as private corporations and interest groups, the press, and the universities. Each level has an impact on United States national ocean policy, and since the responsibility for conducting international negotiations rests with the President, the Executive branch is the crucial level for decision making concerning the Law of the Sea Treaty.

Since 1970, Law of the Sea policy in the United States has been the product of intensive negotiations among evenly matched opposing domestic and bureaucratic interests. The focus for these negotiations has been the Inter-Agency Task Force on the Law of the Sea, which was created in 1970 to coordinate the interests of the executive bureaus and agencies most concerned with Law of the Sea questions. Fourteen institutions are represented: the departments of State, Defense, Commerce, Treasury, Interior, Justice, and Transportation; the National Security Council; the National Science Foundation; the Central Intelligence Agency; the Office of Management and Budget; the United States Mission to the United Nations; the Environmental Protection Agency; and the Council on Environmental Quality.[45]

The consensus-building techniques utilized by the executive branch for determining ocean policy have left the door open for various inputs. Of these inputs, the national security interests had priority before 1971.[46] This was the result of both a reasonably small number of actively concerned bureaus and agencies and State Department support for naval positions. After 1971, however, increased participation from other sectors led to a greater proportionality between other inputs and those of the Defense Department.[47]

There have also been disputes within the Executive branch. For example, naval interests have clashed with other interests that favored extended coastal state jurisdictions. Generally, the Navy has opposed efforts to unilaterally expand United States ocean jurisdiction lest other nations follow the example and thus endanger naval mobility. Between 1967 and 1972, the Defense Department was at odds with the Interior Department which, with the United States oil industry, supported broader claims to the continental shelf.[48] The United States eventually followed the example of other countries and accepted national jurisdiction over the shelf beyond 200 meters.

A second dispute within the Executive branch began in 1973 concerning deep seabed mining. The Treasury Department supports the United States ocean mining industry and seeks United States guarantees for deep seabed

mining of manganese nodules. Money generated by the
United States companies is seen as a potential tax base
from which the Treasury would receive tax revenues. The
Treasury Department is thus very eager to see deep seabed
mining by American companies begin as soon as possible.
The Defense Department, on the other hand, has traditionally been more willing to accept an international regime
for deep seabed exploitation in negotiated exchange for
navigation rights.[49]

Difficulties in formulating a national ocean policy
are compounded by disputes between the executive branch
and Congress. Congressional criticism of United States
ocean policy extends unbroken at least into the Eisenhower
Administration. Congress has often complained that the
Executive branch has failed to manage affairs properly,
and there is a long tradition of Congressional investi-
gations into the formulation of United States ocean
policy. Most members of Congress involved with House and
Senate hearings on deep seabed mining up through 1980,
however, frequently expressed their pleasure with the way
Ambassador Elliot Richardson handled negotiations at
UNCLOS III. In fact, if there was anything in agreement
among the various agencies and branches of government
involved in ocean resources, it was the near unanimous
praise of Richardson's handling of the negotiations.
Position statements by the American Mining Congress and
testimony of Mr. Marne Dubs before the several congressional committees which examined the need for domestic
legislation during the tenure of Ambassador Richardson to
UNCLOS III were critical of the United States delegation's
handling of many of the deep seabed provisions in Part XI
and Annex III of the LOS text. The Reagan Administration
has taken an even firmer pro-industry stance.

In some respects, deepsea mining is a common resource
issue in that it represents a combination of the standard
policy problems associated with the major resource and
technology industries. It is unusual, however, because
it also brings with it new conditions of both a technical
and legal nature which are not always well understood.
These new conditions might have been more easily dealt
with if the more standard organizational and jurisdictional problems had been resolved to form a firm foundation for integrating new problems.[50]

There are some signs which indicate a move toward a
more coherent ocean mining policy framework. In 1980,
for example, the Interior Department lost to the Department of Commerce whatever jurisdiction it had over seabed
mining. There are, however, still many differences over
international ocean resource policy. Public input into
oceans policy has been minimal. How long this continues
to be the case will depend on many factors--including
possible international conflict in the oceans over
resources. While the national ocean policy process is

humming with action, debate, compromise, and conflict, it lacks a prominent spokesman.

Generally speaking, most national ocean policy is determined and kept at the sub-Cabinet level. What is needed is a more centralized Cabinet level organization and a spokesman to report directly to the President on various ocean policy problems and options. The primary impetus for such action is that ocean use and resource exploitation are becoming more and more problematic at both the domestic and international levels. The setting of priorities and policy will remain fragmented as long as jurisdiction is spread among so many different policy framers, some of which are at the Cabinet level. The ocean as a policy area is just too vast to remain in its present fragmented state if we are to achieve better policy outcomes. What is needed is a more direct and focused approach for the solving of problems and coordination of options. For the past few years former Ambassador Richardson provided some of these functions, but most of his energies were directed at UNCLOS III negotiations. With a more direct awareness and understanding of these issues, the President will, or should, become more of an executive leader in the determination and articulation of national ocean policy.

These suggestions will not, of course, stop the various interests of different departments and agencies involved in ocean issues from continuing their debates over what the nation's ocean policy should be; nor would we want that debate to cease. But a more active, aware, and articulate President would help focus the conflicting interests and help set national priorities among the many competing inputs.

The creation of the Office of Ocean Mining and Energy following enactment of deep seabed mining legislation in 1980 should help coordinate national policy efforts for ocean mining. Both the legislation and the new office are definite indications that the United States government is firm in its resolve to ensure access to the resources of the deep seabed for American security and business interests. The UNCLOS III negotiations are still considered worthwhile, but there are many signs that ocean mining companies will succeed in putting pressure on United States negotiators to demand changes in the deep seabed mining provisions of the Law of the Sea Treaty. A less conciliatory approach to the demands of the Group of 77 on deep seabed mining is already evident and is likely to increase under a Republican Senate and Administration.

FOOTNOTES

Chapter 2

1. Richard Darman, "United States Deepsea Mining
Policy: The Pattern and the Prospects," paper prepared
for presentation at M.I.T. seminar series on Deepsea
Mining and U.S. Materials/Resource Policies, January 12,
1979. Darman has been associated with Law of the Sea
policy development for a number of years: in 1976-77 he
was United States Assistant Secretary of Commerce for
Policy; in 1977, he was U.S. Representative and Vice-
Chairman of the United States Delegation to UNCLOS III;
from 1977 to the present he has been a member of the U.S.
Advisory Committee on Law of the Sea.

2. Ibid.

3. Ibid. It was hoped that an eventual agreement
would enable the United States to obtain certain economic
zone freedoms in trade. Darman suggests, however, that
the negotiating framework merely assured that the U.S.
would have to trade the operational provisions of a
centralized seabed regime in order to attempt to secure
economic zone freedoms: "that were subject to increasing
erosion and to sustained threat of further erosion."

4. Ibid.

5. Ibid.

6. John M. Murphy, "The Politics of Manganese
Nodules: International Consideration and Domestic Legislation," San Diego Law Review (April 1979): 531-554.

7. Ibid, p. 547. Thomas Kitsos, an assistant to
former Congressman John Murphy and a legislative analyst
in the House Committee on Merchant Marine and Fisheries,
has been helpful in the research for this part of the
study.

8. Report of the Comptroller General of the United
States, The Law of the Sea Conference Status of the
Issues, 1978, U.S. Government Accounting Office, March 9,
1979.

9. Ibid.

58

10. These included Congressmen John Murphy of New York, John Breaux of Louisiana and Senator Spark Matsunga of Hawaii. See John M. Murphy, Chairman of the Committee on Merchant Marine and Fisheries, "Deep Seabed Mining," Report to the Committee of the Whole House on the State of the Union, Report No. 96-411, 96th Cong., 1st sess., August 17, 1979, Report on H.R. 2759, "Deep Seabed Hard Mineral Resources Act."

11. Law of the Sea Conference Status Report, U.S. Congress, House Committee on International Relations, 95th Cong., 2nd sess., 52, 1978. Testimony of former Ambassador Elliot L. Richardson.

12. Ibid.

13. Ibid.

14. Ibid.

15. John Murphy, San Diego Law Review, p. 551.

16. Ibid.

17. Report of the Comptroller General, March 9, 1979, p. 23.

18. The Moratorium Resolution reads: "The General Assembly...declares that, pending the establishment of the aforementioned international regime: (a) States and persons, physical or juridical, are bound to refrain from all activities of exploitation of the resources of the area of the seabed and ocean floor, and the subsoil thereof, beyond the limits of national jurisdiction; (b) No claim to any part of that area or its resources shall be recognized...." This Resolution was adopted by the General Assembly by a vote of 62 to 28, with 28 abstentions, on December 15, 1969. The United States and other industrialized nations cast their votes against the resolution. See, GA. Res. 2574 (XXIV), 24 U.N. GAOT, Supp. (No. 30), 11, U.N. Doc. A/7630 (1969).

19. Report of the Comptroller General, March 9, 1979. Legislation on the subject of deep seabed hard mineral resources had been under consideration in the Committee on Merchant Marine and Fisheries since the 92nd Congress. Hearings have been held on the subject in each Congress since then. In the 93rd and 94th Congresses, bills were reported to the full Committee on Merchant Marine and Fisheries, but not to the House. In the 95th Congress, H.R. 3350 was reported to the full House by three committees, and was passed on July 26, 1978 by a 312 to 80 vote. A similar bill in the Senate was reported

by committees but was not passed prior to sine die adjournment. On December 14, 1979, however, the Senate did pass S. 493 on deep seabed mining.

20. See, Cobalt, Copper, Nickel, and Manganese: Future Supply and Demand and Implications for Deep Seabed Mining, Department of Commerce, Office of Ocean, Resource and Scientific Policy Coordination, April, 1979.

21. John Murphy, "Deep Seabed Mining," Report.

22. Charles P. Eddy, Deputy Assistant Secretary for Energy and Minerals, Department of the Interior, Statement before the U.S. Congress, House Committee on Merchant Marine and Fisheries, Hearings before the Subcommittee on Oceanography, 96th Cong., 1st sess., June 7, 1979.

23. John Murphy, San Diego Law Review, p. 553.

24. John Murphy, "Deep Seabed Mining," Report, p. 40.

25. Elliot Richardson, testimony before the U.S. Congress, House Committee on Merchant Marine and Fisheries, Hearings before the Subcommittee on Oceanography, 96th Cong., 1st sess., May 22, 1979.

26. John Murphy, "Deep Seabed Mining," Report.

27. Richard Darman, Statement before the U.S. Congress, House Committee on Merchant Marine and Fisheries, Hearings before the Subcommittee on Oceanography, "Legislative Policy for Deep Sea Mining--In the Context of International Law of the Sea Negotiations," 96th Cong. 1st sess. May 23, 1979.

28. John Murphy, "Deep Seabed Mining," Report.

29. Particularly Mr. Murphy, Mr. Breaux, Mr. Udell, Mr. Santiori, Mr. Zablocki, Mr. Bingham, Mr. Bonkers, Mr. Ullman, Mr. Pritchard, Mr. Conable, and Mr. Young.

30. Especially Tom Kitsos of the House Merchant Marine and Fisheries Committee.

31. Industry representatives such as Conrad Welling and Edward Dangler of Ocean Minerals Company (Lockheed), Marne Dubs of Kennecott Copper Corp., Ray Kaufman of Deepsea Ventures Co., and John Shaw of INCO.

32. See, John E. Tilton, The Future of Nonfuel Minerals, (Washington D.C.: The Brookings Institution, 1977). The literature on the economics of technological

60

change over the last twenty years contains a number of studies documenting the influence of expected profitability on innovation activity. See. for example, Jacob Schmoahler, Invention and Economic Growth, (Boston: Harvard University Press, 1966), and Edwin Mansfield, Industrial Research and Technological Innovation: An Econometric Analysis, 1st edition, (New York: Norton, 1968).

33. Lance Antrim, Patricia L. Spencer, and William W. Woodhead, Cobalt, Copper, Nickel and Manganese: Future Supply and Demand and Implications for Deep Seabed Mining, U.S. Department of Commerce, Office of Policy, 1979. Also see, "New for Old," The Economist, August 23-29, 1980, p. 60, regarding cobalt reserves in the United States.

34. The cobalt price figures are from John R.H. Black, The Recovery of Metals from Deepsea Manganese Nodules and the Effects on the World Cobalt and Manganese Markets, Ph.D. dissertation, Massachusetts Institute of Technology, February 1980. This was later published by Charles River Associates, Boston, Ma. 1980.

35. Bohdan Suprovicz, President, 21st Century Research, "Fear Soviet Supercartel for Critical Minerals." Purchasing, November 8, 1978, pp. 42-49.

36. See, Sub-Sahara Africa: Its Role in Critical Mineral Needs of the Western World, cited in U.S. Congress, House Committee on Interior and Insular Affairs, Hearings and Report before the Subcommittee on Mines and Mining, Oversight Hearings on Nonfuel Minerals Policy Review, 96th Cong., 1st and 2nd sessions.

37. Suprovicz, Purchasing.

38. Cobalt, Copper, Nickel, and Manganese, Department of Commerce, April, 1979, p. 49.

39. For an idea of the major defense issues raised at UNCLOS III see: David C. Larson, "Security, disarmament and the Law of the Sea," Marine Policy 3 (January 1979): 40-56; Robert Osgood, "Military Implications of the new ocean politics," Adelphi Papers, No. 122, International Institute for Strategic Studies, 1966, pl 14; Ann L. Hollick and Robert Osgood, New Era of Ocean Politics, (Baltimore: The Johns Hopkins University Press, 1974); Robert Osgood, "U.S. Security Interests and the Law of the Sea," in Ryan Amacher and Richard Sweeney, eds., The Law of the Sea; U.S. Interests and Alternatives, (Washington D.C.: American Institute for Public Policy Research, 1976); and Mark W. Janis, Sea Power and the Law of the Sea, (Boston: Lexington Books, 1976). Also

see Elliot Richardson, "Power, Mobility and the Law of the Sea," Foreign Affairs 58 (Spring 1980): 902-919.

40. David Larson, Marine Policy 3, p. 49. See also Lawrence W. Kaye, "The Innocent Passage of Warships in Foreign Territorial Seas: A Threatened Freedom," in San Diego Law Review 15 (1978): 573-602; and Michael Morris, "Have U.S. Security Interests Really Been Sacrificed?: A Reply to Admiral Hill," Ocean Development and International Law 4 (1977): 381-397.

41. Judith Kildow and V.K. Dar, "An Unusual Resource Management Problem," in Judith Kildow, ed., Deepsea Mining: Selected Papers from a Series of Seminars Held at MIT in December 1978 and January 1979, (Cambridge: MIT Press, 1980).

42. Ibid.

43. There are, obviously, differences between domestic and foreign policy objectives. The linkages between the two, though, are very real, demonstrating the need to coordinate them through an integrated policy structure. As Judith Kildow points out, however, the evolution of United States resource policy has not produced an integrated structure. She writes: "What has evolved in ad hoc fashion, is a huge and complex system of Federal agency rivalries characterized by older agencies with traditionally defined and now artificially functionally-segregated mandates vying with each other and newer ones reflecting the evolution of an integrated policy system. The rivalries among and between the old and the new merely set the stage for a major policy dilemma." See Judith Kildow, Deepsea Mining.

44. The last four of these points are also raised by Kildow and Dar, "An Unusual Resource Management Problem," in Deepsea Mining.

45. Ann L. Hollick, "United States and Canadian Policy Processes in Law of the Sea," San Diego Law Review 12 (April 1975): 518-552.

46. Ann L. Hollick, "Seabeds Make Strange Politics," Foreign Policy 9 (Winter 1972/73): 148-170.

47. Ibid, p. 154.

48. Ann Hollick, "Bureaucrats at Sea," in Hollick and Osgood, New Era of Ocean Politics, pp. 1-3 and 15-40.

49. Ibid, p. 1-4 and pp. 52-64.

50. Kildow and Dar, "An Unusual Resource Management Problem," in <u>Deepsea Mining</u>.

3
Mining the Deep Seabed:
A Complex and Innovative Industry

INTRODUCTION

This chapter is concerned primarily with the nature, concerns, and interests of the deep seabed mining industry in the United States. The issues--technical, financial, economic, legal, and political--help illustrate the ways domestic and international aspects of ocean mining are interlinked.

High costs, technological uncertainties, and a complicated legal morass have led representatives from United States ocean mining companies to exert pressure on Administration and Congressional leaders in Washington, D.C. to help secure a favorable operating environment for the industry. These efforts have complicated United States relations with many other countries at the Third United Nations Conference on the Law of the Sea (UNCLOS III).

Only the highly industrialized countries will be able to pursue seabed mining operations in the foreseeable future; a fact of considerable importance when discussing the attitudes of the developing nations towards the exploitation of manganese nodules. Nations directly involved in nodule mining ventures include: Belgium, West Germany, France, Italy, Great Britain, Holland, Japan, and the United States--all members of the Trilateral and OECD (Organization of Economic Cooperation and Development) group of nations. UNCLOS III received a good deal of publicity in 1981 when the Reagan Administration dramatically replaced the top United States negotiators and called for a total review of the proposed Treaty. These changes effectively scuttled the possibility of signing a Draft Treaty in 1981. The President's actions were welcomed and influenced by representatives of the deep seabed mining industry.

A study made by the U. S. Geological Survey indicates that the development of alternative sources of energy, whether nuclear, coal gasification, geothermal,

solar or others, will make great demands on the supplies
of metals such as nickel, copper, and cobalt. Mining the
deep seabed may one day provide a viable supply of those
metals. The following statement nicely summarizes
industry's viewpoint:

> Since it takes a considerable length of time
> to build up a sizeable industry, perhaps twenty to
> thirty years or more, we cannot afford to wait.
> Furthermore, ocean mining promises to produce the
> nickel, copper, and cobalt with less energy than
> the equivalent land ores. Therefore, the United
> States should encourage industry to develop the
> manganese nodule resource.
> From industry's point of view the most
> immediate need to reduce the risk of development
> of this great resource is the passing into law of
> the pending interim legislation. [Which became
> law June 28, 1980, PL 96-283.] This will provide
> a reasonably predictable legal environment under
> which to make the necessary investment when the
> business conditions dictate.[1]

THE NATURE AND MAKE-UP OF THE OCEAN MINING INDUSTRY

Early Developments in the Industry

Dr. John Mero was one of the first scientists to
recognize nodules as a potential resource, study the
worldwide distribution and metal contents of nodules, and
assess feasible recovery and processing techniques.[2]
He also designed and patented the hydraulic-lift system
of raising manganese nodules from the seabed to surface
containers. Mero probably initiated the first international consortium when his company, Ocean Resources,
Inc., joined forces with Japanese mineral interests in
the late 1960s--eventually negotiating formation of the
Continuous Line Bucket (CLB) consortium.

After the pioneering efforts of Mero in late 1962,
Newport News Shipbuilding and Dry Dock Company (NNSDDC)
began a study of the technical aspects of nodule exploitation. Within two years it had acquired a 300-ton cargo
vessel and begun converting it to the Research Vessel
Prospector for nodule exploration. The man in charge of
NNSDDC's efforts in the field of marine mining was Jack
Flipse, and he became president of the corporate subsidiary known as Deepsea Ventures when Tenneco Inc., (a
diversified industrial complex with interests in manufac-
turing, natural gas, pipelines, oil, chemical packaging,
and land use) acquired NNSDDC in 1968.

Deepsea Ventures, Inc. was composed mainly of
scientists and engineers. Under Flipse, the firm started

to develop the technology necessary to mine, process, and market metals found in seabed manganese nodules. By mid-January 1970, the R/V Prospector had been converted to a prototype ocean mining vessel, outfitted with winches, wires, dredge components, a number of underwater cameras with videotape, a chemical laboratory and other scientific instruments. The Prospector's mission was to view, sample, and determine the characteristics of the seafloor deposits and the ocean environment down to depths of 18,000 feet. Deepsea Ventures, Inc., is currently the service contractor to, and is owned by, Ocean Mining Associates.

Tenneco was not the only firm interested in seabed mining operations. The Kennecott Copper Corporation of the United States and the International Nickel Corporation of Canada (INCO) also turned their attention to manganese nodules beginning in 1962. Besides the several nodule survey cruises which were completed by these firms, various other economic feasibility studies and some pilot plant operations were initiated in the 1960s. By 1972 company spokesmen were predicting that the commercial mining of manganese nodules from the ocean floor was only a few years away. They were wrong.

Several other industrial groups became actively interested in deep ocean mining within a few years after the initial NNSDDC and Kennecott studies. In 1965 Ocean Resources, Inc. began preliminary cooperative studies with Japanese groups. In 1969 West German commercial interest in nodules began. About the same time, Japanese and French groups also started to explore the commercial recovery of manganese nodules. Simultaneously the Soviet Union conducted several surveys of the seabed with the plain intent of eventually recovering the deepsea minerals. Information about the progress of the Russian development of that industry, however, remains minimal.[3]

In 1969 the Summa Corporation, with Lockheed and Global Marine, commenced its own program, later to be revealed as a guise for attempts to recover a sunken Russian submarine, although genuine nodule research was carried out at the same time. Since 1973 a number of other potential domestic and foreign mining competitors have been active in planning for the exploitation of manganese nodules.

Commercial exploitation of manganese nodules may not begin before the mid 1990s. Thus far, the many millions of dollars that the industry has spent have been for research and development on the various technologies needed for ocean mining exploration and exploitation. The technology is very sophisticated and in some cases sounds like something Jules Verne might have imagined.

The Technology of Mineral Exploitation

The technology of deep seabed manganese nodule

mining can be separated into four basic activities. The first task involves surveying and prospecting for the nodules on the deep seabed. Once that has been accomplished, the nodules must be gathered and lifted to the ocean's surface. The third stage is to transport the nodules to a processing area--most likely on land. The final step is to chemically process the nodule material to extract the contained metals. The total mining operation is highly capital-intensive and technically complex.

Prospecting techniques have become extremely sophisticated, with optical searches using closed-circuit television, and geophysical tests using sensitive magnetic and acoustical systems. Acoustical systems, including sonar scanning and seismic tests, help map the topography of the ocean floor in terms of depth from the surface, thickness of substrata and composition of the seabed itself. The ultimate geological data, however, are derived from actual sampling, with mechanical devices such as grabs and dredges employed to recover the nodules themselves. These activities generally require special prospecting ships. All potential mining firms have undertaken research and prospecting cruises.[4]

Mechanical and hydraulic systems have been devised to gather and lift nodules from the ocean floor. What makes these technological achievements so revolutionary is that they enable recovery of nodules lying on the deep seabed under a variety of ocean conditions. (For a description of mining technologies see Appendix 5.)

The most technically advanced system is the self-propelled submersible "robot" method being developed by the French government/industry group AFERNOD. (See Appendix 6.) This example of a second generation system is planned to allow for the collection of nodules without pipelines or buckets. The mining unit will be self-propelled and will sweep an area of the seabed, rise to the surface to deposit its load in a container vessel, and return to the bottom for more mining. The payload of this system is relatively small, but other French groups are studying systems which involve up to one hundred of these robot miners servicing several ore carriers.

If the robot system works it could be the most efficient mining method. In the long run such a method might indeed be cost effective vis-a-vis the more conventional methods outlined in Appendix 5. For example, conventional mining ships are estimated to cost between $300 to 500 million dollars for a 360,000 ton ship. Such a ship would be ten times larger than the Glomar Explorer. There are also many technical difficulties involved in dynamically positioning such large ships--which might require satellites to provide a three-point positioning technique.

Whether a conventional method is used, or one involving submersible robots, a great deal of technological sophistication and capital will be required before ocean mining begins on a full-scale basis. While the submersible system is highly technical and expensive, the more conventional systems would cost a great deal as well. In sum, ocean mining is not just a simple matter of plucking nodules up off the seabed and turning them into a usable resource overnight, as some Third World countries think.

The third phase of operation is transportation. First generation ore carriers are unlikely to do more than transport the nodules, perhaps in crushed or dried form, to land-based processing facilities. They are likely to be separate from mining vessels, and the nodules will probably be transferred to them from hoppers in mining ships. Second generation transportation vessels might conduct partial processing so that waste material such as silica are separated at the mine site and not transported to shore. Processed ore could then be shipped directly to industrial centers.[5]

Once the nodules have been mined at sea and transported to land, they would be delivered to the processing plant via slurry pipeline from the port facilities and stored wet. There are four major processes for smelting. These are briefly described in Appendix 7.

Because manganese nodules differ in physical form and chemical composition from all terrestrial ore now being mined, a unique processing sequence must be developed to extract metals from nodules; one which fully meets the requirements of feasibility, reasonable production size and environmental standards within an overall economic concept.[6] The choice of a process depends partly upon which metals are deemed worthy of marketing. For instance, the consortia led by Kennecott and INCO, before they drastically cut their funding for ocean mining R&D, had planned to recover only nickel, copper, and cobalt. Ocean Minerals Company does not intend to process for manganese either. Ocean Mining Associates intends to recover manganese as well, perhaps because U.S. Steel is a major participant in that consortium. Ultimately the choice of a process will reflect the need to balance metal recovery efficiencies and volumes against amount of capital investment for the processing plant.

The main physical and technical conditions needed to sustain a manganese nodule mining operation can be summarized as follows. First, the site must have a sufficient concentration of nodules of suitable grade. Only nodules with a combined copper and nickel assay of near 2 percent currently are considered economic. Second, the topography, dredging, and lifting equipment must be such that there is at least 20 percent efficiency in nodules swept and brought to the surface. The factors governing this efficiency rate are complex; second generation methods will no doubt bring about an improvement to 30 to 50 percent. Third, the tonnage of nodules recovered should be such as to enable the plant to process one to three million metric tons a year, depending on the particular metals sought and the operating type. Fourth, the distance from the processing plant to industrial markets should not be excessive, so that shipping costs are minimized. Second generation operations might involve processing at sea with transporation of ore directly to industrial areas. Finally, the operation needs to be maintained over a sufficient span of time (20 to 25 years) to justify investment costs in plant and equipment. Figures of slightly over $1 billion are currently cited as the amount required to bring a three million ton project into operation.

THE COSTS TO THE CONSORTIA

There are basically three stages in developing an ocean mining program. The consortia have spent approximately $50-120 million each to finance the first phase of initial research and development and exploration. The second, or "pilot" stage will involve expenditures of about $250 million over a four to five year period. None of the consortia have yet fully entered this stage of development. The third, "final plant," phase, when full-scale ocean mining is under way, will involve an outlay of approximately $1 billion. Both Ocean Minerals Company and Ocean Mining Associates have refrained from committing funds to the second phase because of investment uncertainties caused by several unacceptable ocean mining provisions in the Law of the Sea Treaty text and lack of grandfather rights protection.[7] It remains to be seen whether foreign ocean mining companies will proceed to the second phase of development if the LOS Treaty text does not allow more access guarantees to private or states' parties.

There are uncertainties associated with economic projections for ocean mining. An important one involves estimating the project operating cash flows based on uncertain long-term escalation factors for the different components, particularly energy costs. Another is the assessment of environmental risks and the costs of conforming to regulations for waste disposal. An additional unknown is the impact of the regulatory agencies to be set up by the Law of the Sea Treaty governing seabed mining activity. Yet another uncertainty is the depletion allowance which the Internal Revenue Service would permit mine operators to deduct from their taxable income. This is a percentage of the total revenues less royalties attributed to mining based on the ratio of operating costs plus depreciation for mining to those of the entire project.

A particularly valuable economic feasibility study of ocean mining using the discounted cash flow technique

and modern finance theory was conducted by John Black in
1980.[8] (Several of his findings, which were also used
in the October 1981 report to the National Science
Foundation by Charles River Associates (1981 CRA report),
are summarized here.) The manganese and cobalt markets,
which are essential aspects of the feasibility of an ocean
mining project, were analyzed with a view to the impact
of a large supply influx from ocean nodules on demand and
price.

The following conclusions are useful in understanding some of the basic components and factors involved in
determining the economics of ocean mining.

First, the cost of a three million ton nodule
recovery project for all four metals is approximately
$1.5 to $1.7 billion in 1980 dollars for whatever metallurgical process is chosen. The cost for a one million
ton project of four metals was estimated at $700 to $800
million. Operating costs for each size plant were
respectively estimated to be $350 to $450 million and $160
to $225 million per year.[9]

Second, the three metal process (not processing
for manganese), with all equity financing, gave a higher
net present value (NPV) than the equivalent four metal
process, assuming the economy avoids severe shocks and
recovers only slightly from its long run equilibrium
growth path with inflation returning to lower levels.
The study determined that the addition of a manganese
production facility actually lowered profitability
compared with processing for just three metals.[10]

Third, once ocean mining does prove technically
and economically feasible, debt financing probably would
become available, and creative ways could be found to
finance such a large venture. For example, a company
could obtain capital in credit markets once investments
look profitable. This, in turn, would help overall
profitability for the ocean mining company.

Fourth, the key issue that will determine if the
consortia decide to recover manganese from the nodules is
whether there will be a market to absorb the large
quantities of manganese that could be mined from just
three or four ocean mining projects. An analysis of new
applications of manganese base alloys and alloys with
increased manganese content indicates that the most important prospects for such usage are in the steel, stainless
steel, and aluminum industries. Although manganese alloys
have already been developed, they have not been used
widely. The study estimated that materials engineering,
which emphasizes application and design optimization, will
be crucial for the promotion of manganese, in preference
to the development of new alloys.[11]

Fifth, using a system dynamics simulation model
for the world cobalt market, the feasibility study tracked

the historical behavior of cobalt price up through the end of 1979 and showed that the price would gradually decrease about $5 per pound by 1993 without the impact of nodule supplies. Black concluded that the price of cobalt will come down after 1990 due to capacity expansion stimulated by the higher prices existing in the early 1980s. Zaire's increased cobalt capacity, along with cobalt from nodules, should maintain a supply/demand balance without a future price rise above $5 per pound at least until 2010.[12]

The 1981 CRA report concluded that the price of nickel would have to be substantially higher by 1990 (perhaps double 1981 prices) if new investment in the ocean mining industry is to be encouraged. Different price scenarios were developed which indicated that the most "realistic" scenario was one with higher nickel prices, despite strong possibilities of long-term low prices. The report concluded that the economic impacts of ocean mining on the world economy would be beneficial overall, but that the costs would be borne mainly by developing land-based producers, while benefits would be experienced principally by consuming nations.[13]

J.D. Nyhart et al. updated their 1978 M.I.T. study on the economics of deep seabed mining in 1981. The more recent study attempts to correct previous assumptions that had been challenged as misleading and provide a more accurate and up-to-date economic analysis. The new figures are generally very close to the ones found in the studies cited above.[14]

The greatest difficulties in ocean mining appear to lie in the pronounced economic uncertainties of prices in the next ten to thirty years, the uncertainty of energy costs involved, and the unknown capital equipment and construction costs in six to ten years. Tables 1 and 2 show overall capital costs and annual operating costs of a manganese nodule recovery venture for four metals at a three million metric tons per year (dry) nodule capacity. These tables provide a good overall picture of the costs involved in a first generation nodule project.[15]

A major factor affecting the metals market is the substitutability of nickel and cobalt. If the price of cobalt increases drastically because of long-term supply disruptions from Zaire, then nickel, because it is cheaper, will be substituted wherever possible. In addition, full-scale ocean mining operations may reduce the price of nickel by 5 to 10 percent and of cobalt by 25 to 50 percent.

One of the primary reasons the oil companies have invested in ocean mining is that the metals industry is a promising long-term business venture. Although metal prices are still moderate, they will probably climb higher over the next twenty years. Atlantic Richfield Corporation (ARCO), for example, purchased Anaconda Copper at a time

TABLE 1

Overall Capital Costs of Manganese Nodule Recovery Venture for
Four Metals at 3 Million Metric TPY (Dry) Nodules Capacity (In
Millions of 1979 Dollars)

Sector	Cost
1. Research and Development Expense	$100.0
2. Capital Costs:	
Prospecting and Exploration	19.9
Mining	120.8
Transport	65.5
Subtotal:	$206.2
Mining Working Capital (8 per cent assumed)	$ 9.7

3. Processing	INCO	CUPRION	SULFURIC ACID	HYDROCHLORIC ACID
Ni, Cu, Co Recovery	$ 711.3	$ 510.4	$ 665.2	$1355.5
Extra Pollution Control Cost	(50.0)[1]	--	--	--
FeMn and SiMn Production	442.1	547.0	547.0	--
Total Fixed Investment: (2 + 3)	$1359.6 ($1409.6)	$1263.7	$1418.5	$1561.7
Total Project Working Capital:	$ 183.9	$ 169.8	$ 193.2	$213.0

Source: John Black, The Recovery of Metals from Deepsea Manganese Nodules and the Effects on the World Cobalt and Manganese
Markets. (Boston, Charles River Associates) 1980.

[1] Parentheses indicate that additional costs are necessary in
some states.

TABLE 2

Overall Annual Operating Costs of Manganese Nodules Recovery
Venture for Four Metals at 3 Million Metric TPY (Dry) Nodules
Capacity (In Millions of 1979 Dollars)

Sector	Cost
1. Mining	$ 25.2
2. Transport	15.9

3. Processing	INCO	CUPRION	SULFURIC ACID	HYDROCHLORIC ACID
3-Metals	$ 199.6	$ 144.7	$ 164.5	$ --
Mn Recovery	188.8	224.7	224.7	290.0
Total	$ 429.5	$ 410.5	$ 430.3	$ 331.3
Startup Costs in Year 1	$ 50.0	50.0	50.0	50.0

Source: John Black, "The Recovery of Metals from Deepsea Nodules."

when copper prices were in a worldwide slump. Unfortunately for ARCO, the price of copper has not yet risen significantly since the mid 1970s. Several oil concerns have bought controlling shares in other mineral companies as well. One of the more publicized mergers was the offer by Standard Oil of Ohio (SOHIO) to buy Kennecott Corporation for $1.77 billion in March 1981. The influx of oil money in certain ocean mining consortia has enabled those consortia to maintain relatively high levels of funding for research and development.[16]

The 1981 CRA report used seven price scenarios in analyzing the profitability of ocean mining. The scenarios were dependent on different market assumptions and the possible extent of ocean mining in the 1990s. Each of the four major processing options was assessed from a profitability perspective. (John Black's figures were used for part of this analysis, see Tables 1 and 2.) The report found that each of the processes affected profitability in a similar fashion, and concluded that ocean mining might provide adequate incentives for private investment if international regulations are not too burdensome, and if nickel prices double in real terms by 1990. Higher prices are needed to attract new investment from land-based producers. If nickel prices do not increase substantially, then ocean mining will be less attractive. The report also found that proposed international regulations concerning royalties and site selection decrease the estimated real, after-tax internal rates of return by almost one percentage point.[17]

Finally, because of the high costs and uncertainty of short-term metals prices it is possible that the United States government will eventually mine the deep seabed on a COMSAT type basis with private industry. Operational responsibility in COMSAT--the Communications Satellite Corporation--is shared by the United States government and the private sector. France, West Germany, and possibly Japan may set an example in this area and help put competitive pressure on the United States for a similar approach to ocean mining. The processing stage of a seabed mining operation might then be made available to a private company.[18] This type of quasi-public arrangement may be a harbinger of things to come for resource-related industries in the United States if American companies cannot compete with joint business-government efforts in other countries.

Both business and government recognize the high costs associated with the development of an ocean mining industry. The large amount of capital required has led to the formation of several consortia to carry out exploration, mining, and processing research. It has been estimated that six United States based companies have already spent approximately $200 million to investigate various aspects of nodule mining, and that by the late

1980s the total investment may reach $3 billion.[19] The principle organizations that have been pursuing nodule exploitation are listed in Table 3.

The costs of deep seabed mining are so great and involve so many uncertainties that the ocean mining industry has been aggressively lobbying the United States government for the past decade to protect its interests at the Third United Nations Conference on the Law of the Sea. However, many of the ocean mining companies in the United States are no longer spending as much money on research and development as they did throughout the last decade. The industry faces considerable economic risks and uncertainties.

Bank Loans: Unavailable

Difficulties in obtaining bank loans have curtailed activities by American companies. In any type of new corporate venture that requires massive sums of front-end capital investment, banks play an important role in determining the pace of development. Particularly in the case of deep seabed mining, very large capital expenditures are required to meet development costs. Given the high costs and expected poor rate of return on investment due to the poor metals market, no bank has thus far made major loans to the principal consortia for ocean mining develoment. Why? Banks traditionally have insisted on some form of assurance before making large capital loans. Unfortunately, the ocean mining industry has been unable to provide the type of assurance the banks have required. The banks have refused loans because the ocean mining industry does not yet possess a license giving sufficient rights to the resource.[20] United States unilateral ocean mining legislation offers some legal assurances regarding access, but it does not guarantee the companies investment protection from potential losses due to actions of the International Seabed Authority. A better legal arrangement must be found for investment protection.

ELUSIVE PROFITS

Each of the major consortia has invested a great deal of money ($50-120 million each) during the last decade in developing technology to make recovery of nodules possible.[21] Most of the consortia have developed test devices that have brought nodules from the deep seabed to the surface. During that time many economic analyses of ocean mining have been published. An examination of these efforts shows a wide range of estimated costs and profitability. One of the more elaborate economic studies was made in 1978 at the Massachusetts Institute of Technology. The study used a computer model

TABLE 3
Major International Deep Sea Mining Consortia

Consortium	Country	Stake (%)	Mining Technology	Processing Technology	Current Plans (1982)
1. Ocean Mining Associates			Dredge device with airlift	Hydrochloric acid leach	1-2MM tons of dry nodules/yr. after 1989. Capital investment: $1.5 billion required.
U.S. Steel	U.S.	25			
Union Miniere	Belgium*	25			
Sun Oil Co.	U.S.	25			
SAMIN	Italy	25			
(Note: Deepsea Ventures, Inc., is the service contractor and is owned by OMA partners.)					
2. Ocean Management, Inc.			Dredge device with hydraulic or airlift	Pyrometal- lurgical	Not expected to mine commercially before 1990-2000, if at all. AMR and DOMCO groups doing separate studies.
INCO	Canada	25			
SEDCO	U.S.	25			
AMR group:	West				
Preusagg A.G.	Germany	25			
Metallgesllshaft A.G					
Salzgitter A.G.					
DOMCO Group (led by Sumitomo)	Japan	25			
3. Ocean Minerals Co.			Dredge device with hydraulic lift	Unspecified	Not expected to mine commercially until 1990; eventually 2.75MM tons per year.
Lockheed	U.S.	30			
Standard Oil of Indiana (AMOCO Minerals)	U.S.	30			
Royal Dutch Shell (Billiton Intl. Metals)	UK/Holland	30			
Royal Bos Kalis Westminster	Holland	10			

*Participation through subsidiaries incorporated in the U.S.A.

No.	Consortium / Participants	Country	%	Mining Method	Processing	Status / Comments
4.	**Kennecott Consortium**			Dredge device with hydraulic lift	Ammonia Leach	Reduced activities to very low levels and may no longer proceed.
	Kennecott Copper Corp.	U.S.	40			
	Noranda Exploration, Inc.	Canada	12			
	Consolidated Gold Fields	U.K.	12			
	Rio Tinto-Zinc, Ltd.	U.K.	12			
	British Petroleum	U.K.	12			
	Mitsubishi Corporation	Japan	12			
5.	**Afernod****			Unspecified-- studying dredge and continuous line bucket; possible future use of robot submersibles	Unspecified	Says ocean mining is currently not economic. For present no plans to go beyond pilot-plant tests. Strong government support.
	Centre National pour l'Elploitation des Oceans (CNEXO)	France				
	Commissariat a l'Energie Atomique (CEA)	France				
	Bureau de Recherches Geologiques at Minieres	France				
	Societe Metallurgique Nouvelle/Societe Le Nickel	France				
	Chantiers de France Dunkerque	France				
6.	**Deep Ocean Minerals Association (DOMA)**** An association between Japanese industry and government. Includes 35 Japanese companies—three from Mitsubishi Group, four from Mitsui Group, six from Nippon Group, four from Mitsui Group, six from Nippon Group, four from Sumitomo Group and C. Itoh, Dowa Mining, Furukawa, Kanematsu-Gosho, Kyokuyo, Marubeni, Nichimen, Nissho-Iwai and Toyo Menka.	Japan		Exploration carried out by Metal Mining Agency, a semi-commercial entity linked to MITI of the Japanese government; co-operative arrangement with Geological Survey to use vessel Hakurei-Mauru; survey on southern Hawaiian seas.		Extensive exploration using ship launched in 1980.

*Participation not publicly available.

Sources: Based on figures from J.K. Amsbaugh, Ocean Mining Associates, H. Enzer, U.S. Department of the Interior, and industry correspondence.

to develop a deterministic financial simulation of ocean mining. But even this analysis was challenged on its basic underlying assumptions by a German study in 1979 which was critical of the technology and the cost estimates used.[22]

Several analysts agree that with careful management and minimal or no royalty impositions paid to an International Seabed Authority, first generation ocean mining projects may realize a profit. The size of that profit is not likely to be as great as projections anticipated just five years ago. Technological improvements in both mining and processing should enable subsequent projects to meet even more severe profitability criteria. But technological advances alone will not determine the profitability of deep seabed mining.

For the past three years most deep seabed mining companies have markedly slowed their expenditures for research and development. During that time SEDCO and International Nickel Company of Canada (INCO), have backed off from further ocean mining activities. In addition, Kennecott's ocean mining investment is down and most of its engineering activities have stopped.

At first glance it appears that the industry cut back on R&D due to its stated reason, that of a need for political and legal protection by the government. While the lack of such protection may have been a factor in declining R&D in the early 1970s, expenditures actually grew in that period. Closer analysis shows that low prices on the international metals market throughout most of the 1970s simply did not make ocean mining a profitable venture. Consequently, most United States ocean mining consortia have--for both political/legal and economic/market reasons--reduced their expenditures for R&D over the past three years (1979-1982), and expect a slow growth pattern over the next three to four years. It is likely that Ocean Mining Associates has maintained previous absolute levels of R&D funding, due in part to the participation of a new Italian partner (SAMIN) in the consortium.

The International Metals Market: Low Demand

The early 1970s set the stage for the international metals market and the general conditions of the mining industry throughout the decade that followed. In 1970 most mining companies had expectations of higher copper and nickel prices, which led to early incentives for ocean mining research and development. However, compliance with new federal environmental regulations within the copper industry cut into profits. Furthermore, the trend in prices throughout the decade did not fulfill profit expectations.

The United States' primary demand for nickel has remained fairly constant over the last decade: from 174.7

thousand short tons in 1970 to 199.2 thousand short tons in 1979, with peaks in 1973 and 1974. The price of nickel has risen only slightly over the same period with highs of slightly over $2.20 per pound in 1976, $2.41 in 1979 and $3.45 in April 1980.[23]

Quoted cobalt prices have risen from $1.50 per pound in 1964 to $25.00 per pound in February 1979. The $25.00 price reflected supply disruptions that occurred in Zaire in 1978. (Zaire supplies approximately 60 percent of the world's cobalt.) Attempts to maintain that price have not been successful. Due to increased supplies from sources outside Zaire and Zambia, and greater substitution, the free market price declined to just under $15.00 per pound in the fourth quarter of 1981--which is about $10.00 per pound in 1978 dollars. Producer prices at the end of 1981 were in the $13.00 to $15.00 range. These price fluctuations were not anticipated by the U.S. Bureau of Mines in their 1980 reports, which found that from 1974 to 1980 prices had risen nearly exponentially.[24] From 1976 to 1981 the United States primary demand for cobalt was fairly constant, at approximately 18,000,000 pounds per year. The average demand for the previous four years, 1972 to 1976, was closer to 20,000,000 pounds per year.[25]

The primary demand for manganese in the United States has remained fairly constant as well, at approximately 1,350,000 tons per year. The price for manganese in metallurgical ore has risen gradually since 1975. In that year the price rose from an average of $.65 cents per long-ton unit (over the previous four years), to approximately $1.55 from 1975 to 1980. The price in 1980 was $1.70 per long-ton.[26] See Tables 4 and 5.

These figures indicate that while price and demand for manganese, cobalt and nickel increased somewhat during the 1970s, it was not a strong enough increase to entice the ocean mining companies to go beyond their current stage of development. In some cases the unexpectedly poor growth rates led some companies to severely curtail any further R&D activities. Corporate expectations for higher profits in the years ahead are indicated by increased take-overs of mining companies by the large oil companies and by the participation of oil companies in the major deep seabed mining consortia. The growing costs of production for mining land-based ores and compliance with environmental regulations, in addition to a worldwide recession which decreased demand (due in large part to increased OPEC oil prices), have lowered mining profits below those anticipated in the early 1970s. Ocean mining, therefore, has not offered a sufficient return on investment to warrant high capital expenditures for research and development beyond the first phase of development, which by now has been successfully completed by most groups.

TABLE 4
Salient Statistics: Nickel, Cobalt, Manganese, Copper
-Salient nickel statistics
(Short tons)

	1976	1977	1978	1979	1980
United States					
Mine production [1]	16,469	14,347	13,509	15,065	14,653
Plant production:					
Domestic ores	13,869	12,897	11,298	11,691	11,225
Imported materials	20,070	25,000	26,000	32,500	33,000
Secondary [2]	13,273	12,449	12,304	13,201	11,338
Exports (gross weight)	47,166	39,412	36,293	50,810	56,675
Imports for consumption	188,147	194,770	r234,352	r177,205	189,168
Consumption (primary)	162,927	155,260	180,723	196,203	156,299
Stocks, Dec. 31: Consumer	31,690	18,581	20,443	r19,248	15,398
Price, cents per pound	220	241,208	210,193	193,320	320,345
World: Mine production	r873,357	r886,738	r727,936	r753,214	850,366

r Revised.

[1] Mine shipments.

[2] Nonferrous scrap only: does not include nickel from stainles or alloy steel scrap.

-Salient cobalt statistics
(Thousand pounds of contained cobalt)

	1975	1976	1977	1978	1979
United States					
Consumption--------------	12,787	16,482	16,577	19,994	17,402
Imports for consumption--------	6,608	16,487	17,548	19,029	19,998
Stocks, Dec. 31: Consumer-------	1,801	3,180	3,738	4,387	3,390
Price: Metal, per pound[1]--------	$3.75-$4.00	$4.00-$5.40	$5.20-$6.40	$6.40-$20.00	$20.00-$25.00
World production, mine[1]---------	r47,600	r47,218	r48,168	55,662	62,874

rRevised.

[1]Based on estimated recovered cobalt.

TABLE 4 (cont'd)
-Salient manganese statistics in the United States
(Short tons)

	1975	1976	1977	1978	1979
Manganese ore (35% or more Mn):					
Imports, general--------	1,574,045	1,316,812	930,947	547,820	499,782
Consumption--------	1,818,983	1,600,873	1,358,811	1,281,479	1,372,190
Manganiferous ore (5% to 35% Mn):					
Production (shipments)--------	159,225	256,633	215,893	312,124	240,695
Ferromanganese:					
Production--------	575,809	482,662	334,134	272,530	317,102
Exports--------	32,300	6,789	6,051	9,433	25,344
Imports for consumption--------	397,212	537,409	534,423	680,399	821,213
Consumption--------	881,527	896,299	886,299	985,623	976,482

Sources: U.S. Bureau of Mines Minerals Yearbook, 1980, United States Department of the Interior. Nickel data compiled by Scott F. Sibley; Cobalt data by Sibley; Manganese by Gilbert L. DeHuff; copper by W.C. Butterman.

-Salient copper statistics

Salient Statistics--United States:	1976	1977	1978	1979	1980[e]
Production: Mine	1,457	1,364	1,358	1,444	1,175
Refined Copper: Primary	1,396	1,357	1,449	1,515	1,255
Secondary	340	350	420	498	500
Imports for consumption: Total[1]	426	396	532	282	520
Refined	346	351	403	204	385
Exports: Total[1]	156	114	178	185	210
Refined	102	47	92	74	15
Shipments from Govt. stockpile excesses			N o n e		
Consumption, refined (reported)	1,807	1,982	2,189	2,158	1,870
Consumption, apparent (primary and old scrap)	2,036	2,035	2,333	2,350	2,032
Price: Average (cents per pound):					
Domestic producer	69.6	66.8	65.5	93.3	101.2
London Metal Exchange	63.9	59.4	61.9	90.1	100.2
Stocks: Producer (refined), yearend	172	212	153	64	40
Employment, mine and mill[1]	29,700	29,400	26,700	28,800	27,000
Net import reliance[2] as a percent of apparent consumption	12	13	20	12	14

[e]Estimate.
[1]Includes ores and concentrates, matte, blister, refined, and unalloyed scrap.
[2]Net import reliance = imports − exports + adjustments for Government and industry stock changes.
[3]Duty on waste and scrap suspended by Public Law 95-508 until June 30, 1981.

Source: Mineral Commodity Summaries, 1981. U.S. Bureau of Mines, Department of the Interior.

TABLE 5

Stockpile Status, 11/30/80 (Government Programs)

Material	Goal	Total Inventory	Authorized For Disposal	Sales, 11 Months
Nickel (short tons)	20,000	--	--	--
Cobalt (short tons of metal)	42,700	20,402	--	--
Manganese (thousand short tons, gross weight)				
Battery: Nat'l ore	62	195	57	14
Synthetic dioxide	25	3	--	--
Chemical ore	170	221	--	--
Metallurgical ore	2700	2410	--	(35)[1]
Ferromanganese:				
High carbon	439	600	--	--
Medium carbon	0	29	--	--
Silicomanganese	0	24	--	--
Electrolytic metal	0	14	--	--
Copper (thousand metric tons)	907	26	--	--

Source: Mineral Commodity Summaries, 1981. (U. S. Bureau of Mines, Department of the Interior).

[1] Cancellation of earlier sale.

The commodity markets show that demand for the four major metals in manganese nodules has been satisfied by available domestic and import supply. As the figures in Table 6 illustrate, the percentage imported is substantial. Imports as a percentage of total United States supplies is lower, but it is significant. Over the past five years a considerable amount of the total United States supply of nickel, cobalt, and manganese has gone into industry and government stockpiles. Stable consumption patterns, due in large part to modest economic growth over the past five years in the United States and world economies, has resulted in extensive industry stockpiles. It will be twenty years or more before it is necessary to secure access to new supplies of manganese, nickel, and cobalt, unless severe supply disruptions occur. Because most United States imports of nickel come from Canada and Norway, the likelihood of major supply disruptions is small. Cobalt, however, is imported mainly from Zaire, which may experience internal political problems that adversely affect U.S. supplies. Hence there is a need to maintain and perhaps increase government stockpiles of this mineral. In the fall of 1981 the Reagan Administration sold reserve stockpiles of silver. The money obtained from that sale was used to purchase additional and higher grade cobalt from Zaire (for $15.00 per pound) to increase government stockpiles of that mineral. Potential supply disruptions of United States imports of manganese ore are also a possiblity. Gabon and South Africa supplied the United States with 68% percent of its manganese ore requirements in 1979. Australia and Brazil may be somewhat more secure suppliers of manganese, but ore quality and availability in those two countries may decrease significantly by the year 2000. It is likely that the United States government could obtain sufficient supplies of manganese and cobalt on the world market to meet stockpile demands. This is especially true given recent market prices and trends where supply has exceeded demand for manganese, cobalt, and nickel. The Administration's proposed plans to provide a government guaranteed price for cobalt would become necessary only if stockpile needs could not be met from current world surpluses. Price supports might still be forthcoming if the government deems it sufficiently important to provide financial support to a United States ocean mining industry that in ten to fifteen years could meet all or most domestic requirements for the strategic minerals in manganese nodules. There are, of course, short-term social and economic costs involved in guaranteed government prices for minerals. A minimum government guaranteed price for cobalt would certainly be welcomed by the mining industry. Such guarantees, however, would help make ocean mining a more economically viable venture. The cost benefit ratio of government price supports is

TABLE 6
U.S. Consumption - Supply Relationships, 1979

	Nickel (thousand tons)	Cobalt (thousand lbs.)	Manganese (thousand short tons, Mg. content)	Copper (thousand metric tons)
U.S. Consumption:				
Total industrial "demand"	256.6[1]	18,805[6]	1,250[11]	2,408[16]
Total U.S. primary "demand"	199.2[2]	17,635[7]	1,250[12]	1,834[17]
U.S. Supplies:				
Domestic	267.7[3]	7,189[8]	1,106[13]	2,505[18]
Imports	183.7[4]	19,998[9]	952[14]	215[19]
Total U.S. Supplies	451.4[5]	27,187[10]	2,058[15]	2,720[20]
Imports as a % of U.S. Total Industrial Demand	71%	106%	76%	9%

Sources: Table compiled from figures in U.S. Bureau of Mines, Mineral Facts and Problems, 1980 edition and Mineral Yearbook, 1980. U.S. Department of the Interior: Nickel, Cobalt, Manganese

Notes:

1. Includes: Transportation, Chemicals, Petroleum, Fabricated metal products, Electrical, Household appliances, Machinery, Construction, other.

2. Industrial demand less secondary (re-cycled).

3. Includes: domestic mines, secondary, shipments of government stockpile excesses, industry stock, Jan. 1.

4. Major sources: Canada (61% of total U.S. imports for consumption of Ni metal; 83% of oxide and oxide sinter); and Norway (14% of total U.S. imports for consumption of Ni metal, and 18% of powder and flakes).

5. Distribution of U.S. supply: Industry stock, Dec. 31, 146.9; Exports 47.9; Industrial demand 256.6.

6. Includes: nonmetal (paints, chemicals, ceramics and glass) 4,937; and metal (transportation: aircraft, electrical, machinery, coating and plating, and other) 13,868.

7. Total demand less secondary supply. Total U.S. demand for primary metal: 12,698.

8. Includes secondary (1,170), and industry stocks, Jan. 1. (6,019).

9. Major sources: Zaire (8,801, 44%), Benelux (2,206, 11%), Scandinavia/Finland (2,032, 10.8%), and Canada (878, 4%).

10. Distribution of U.S. supply: Industry stocks, Dec. 31., (7,656); Exports, 726; Industrial demand 18,805.

11. According to Mr. G. DeHuff of the U.S. Bureau of Mines, there is no secondary demand for manganese.

12. Includes: Construction, Transportation, Machinery, Cans and containers, Appliances and equipment, Oil and gas industries, Chemicals, Batteries, and other (which includes processing losses).

13. Includes domestic mines, shipment of government stockpile excesses, and industry stocks, Jan 1.

14. Imports: ore (244) and alloy and metal (708). Major sources of manganese ore: Gabon (29%--45% in 1978); South Africa (23%); Australia (22%); and Brazil (21%).

15. Distribution of U.S. supply: industry stocks, Dec. 31 (749); exports, ore (29); exports, alloy and metal (30); and industrial demand (1,250).

16. Includes: electrical (1,082); construction (309); machinery (230); transportation (180); endurance (156); and other (103).

17. Industrial demand less old scrap/secondary.

18. Includes: Refined production, old scrap (unrefined), and industry stocks, Jan. 1.

19. Imports of refined: Major sources, Canada (23%); Chile (27%); Zambia (16%); Peru (13%); other (21%). Figures are for 1976-1979.

20. U.S. supply: Industry Stocks, Dec. 31, (491); Exports, (refined: 182); Industrial demand (18,805).

difficult to determine at this time, though a 1981 report prepared for the National Science Foundation by Charles River Associates (1981 CRA report) attempted to quantify the effects of United States government capital subsidies to the ocean mining industry.[27]

Two major criteria will determine the profitability of deep seabed mining: the future price of the minerals contained in the nodules and the capital and accrued costs associated with mining technology, transportation, and processing; and the nature of the ocean mining regime-- the rules and regulations of mining in international waters. Questions about profitability should consider the following issues: Are miners subject to international taxation and, if so, at what rate? What are the prospects for the security of investment in terms of exclusive mining claims to mineral deposits in areas outside the limits of national jurisdiction? Will miners be subject to any regulations in terms of determining an efficient level of production or in terms of marketing their output? What type of costs will be involved for environmental regulations?[28] This chapter does not attempt a detailed economic analysis of the profitability of deep seabed mining. Highlights of recent studies are given and interested readers are provided with references to them.[29]

Although manganese is the most abundant mineral in ocean nodules, most of the revenue derived from the mining of the deep seabed should come from the sale of cobalt, nickel, and to a lesser extent, copper. Manganese itself has a more limited market due to large and available land-based supplies. The United States Bureau of Mines (Mineral Facts and Problems, 1980 edition) estimates that the "total" probable average annual growth rate in the demand for manganese between 1978 and 2000 is 1.4%; nickel 4.0% (total primary and secondary demand); copper 3.0% (total primary and secondary demand); and cobalt 2.9% (total primary and secondary demand).

Industry spokesmen and many Congressmen believe that ocean mining will be critical to the United States in the future because, in spite of the present excess productive capacity and large stockpiles of copper and nickel, there are uncertainties about long-term supply. An indication of the Reagan Administration's concern about the nation's supply of crucial minerals can be seen in the President's 1981 proposal for $100 million to be allocated for the stockpiling of cobalt in anticipation of politically motivated supply disruptions. There is also a distinct possibility of consumption increasing at a more rapid rate towards the end of the century, as many of the Third World countries increase their industrial development, particularly if the economies of the advanced nations begin to grow more rapidly again.

More recent analyses, however, indicate that the need of the United States for access to the minerals is not as crucial as previously thought. In addition to increasing doubts about the profitability of ocean mining in the 1990s, there is a belief that substitutability, technological developments, and better mining techniques will ensure an adequate supply of manganese, copper, nickel, and cobalt for several decades. One study, based on various economic analyses, concluded that deep seabed mining is presently not an economic or strategic necessity, though it would provide some economic benefit to the United States.[30] On purely economic grounds it may not be necessary to acquire minerals from manganese nodules over the next fifteen to twenty years.

RISKS

Industry claims that it is the risks that have the greatest impact upon the deep seabed mining program. According to Conrad G. Welling, Vice President of Ocean Minerals Company (Lockheed), deep seabed mining does have the potential of becoming financially rewarding: "provided not only that our feasibility studies prove to be reasonably correct but more important that many of the potential risks we face can be reduced to manageable proportions."[31] Industry faces four types of mining risks: technical, political/legal, environmental and economic. This chapter is concerned primarily with economic risks.

If the risks can be reduced to reasonable levels in the next two or three years, then the investment climate will be favorable for the large capital expenditures required. Current projections of profit levels over the next ten years are not sufficient to attract significant investments, especially without some form of grandfather rights protection. For example, most land based miners seek a return on investment (ROI) of around 15 percent; but most economic analyses of ocean mining operations have found that they will have only an 8 to 10 percent profitability factor at projected costs and metals prices.[32] These factors have forced some deep seabed mining groups to shelve development plans or leave the industry.

Ocean mining is uniquely risky precisely because there is a lack of prior experience to provide a guide to solving the numerous problems that will be encountered. Nor can the problems themselves be precisely identified. Most knowledge of ocean mining is limited to estimates based on scale models which are one-fifth the size of expected commercial equipment. Kinks in the overall program are certain to occur when full scale operations are in effect.

Table 7 lists the principal economic risks associated with ocean mining, many of them similar to

TABLE 7

Economic Risks

Revenue Forecast:
 -nickel, copper, cobalt, manganese markets
 -nodule abundance, grade, accessibility, deposit

Investment Cost Estimate:
 -land lead fixed assets pricing
 -engineering design changes
 -program scheduling

Operational cost estimates:
 -system configuration
 -energy (fossil fuel) costs

Policy Impact:
 -environmental system
 -domestic taxation/international fund
 -depletion
 -depreciation
 -investment credit
 -maritime aids
 -production control
 -technology transfer

Source: Conrad Welling, Ocean Mineral Company.

those in other mining development programs.
If risks can be reduced and returns on investment increased, ocean mining may attract the necessary investment capital if the international metals market picks up in the near future. If metals prices do not increase significantly over the next five years, U.S. ocean mining groups will put increasing pressure on the Administration to provide some form of "grandfather rights" provisions in domestic legislation and in the Law of the Sea Treaty text; provisions of government financial guarantees for corporate losses due to actions taken by an International Seabed Authority. Such guarantees would help obtain investments from banks and other sources and would guarantee access and ensure tenure for ocean mining ventures.

NEED FOR STRONG GOVERNMENT SUPPORT

The question, then, is whether the United States government should become more directly involved with an infant resource industry that faces stiff competition from foreign ocean mining groups that have the economic support of their governments. It is unlikely that there will be direct participation in the ocean mining industry by the United States government, particularly with a conservative Republican Administration and Senate in the early 1980s. On the other hand, the Reagan Administration has provided various tax breaks and other forms of indirect support for industry, especially industries involved with minerals vital to the nation's security. It was, after all, the United States government that was the first to pass legislation on deep seabed mining for which the ocean mining industry had lobbied approximately ten years.
The Deep Seabed Hard Minerals Resource Act, became law (PL 96-283), on June 28, 1980. It established an interim procedure for the orderly development of hard mineral resources in the deep seabed, pending adoption of an international legal regime related to the development of deep seabed mineral resources.[33]
According to industry spokesmen, however, domestic legislation has not provided enough legal certainty to encourage expansion beyond the initial R&D phase. The next phase, which requires significant engineering scale-up to prototype development, is considered too costly to risk continued high levels of investment without guaranteed access to the resources under conditions similar to domestic resource programs.[34]
The Deep Seabed Hard Minerals Resources Act and the current draft Law of the Sea Treaty text are basically two different approaches to the mining of manganese nodules. One is a centrally planned framework with production limits that seems to deter private sector investments; the other is a free market approach designed to encourage investment and production. Industry spokesmen

claim that the only way the two approaches can be linked, as is anticipated in the Act, is by the incorporation of grandfather rights (nondiscriminatory, assured access and security of tenure), in a Law of the Sea Treaty.

Industry has been reluctant to accept direct subsidies from government, as the consortia would like to minimize government interference in their operations as much as possible; neither the United States government nor industry has favored outright subsidies. On the other hand, the industry has lobbied long and hard for the government to provide a legal and economic framework that meets most, if not all, of its needs. Like many other industries in the United States, the ocean mining companies have sought to have the government set the rules of the game in such a way that helps maximize profits while minimizing government control of actual operations.

In August 1981, James L. Johnston of the new Marine Minerals Panel within the National Advisory Committee on Oceans and Atmosphere (NACOA) stated that the ocean mining industry was in favor of government support that permits its "natural development." Johnston, of Standard Oil Company of Indiana, told the Panel that the industry did not favor a government policy that "fosters" or "over-promotes the industry." He urged the Panel to identify regulations that do not artificially stimulate development, "but on the other hand do not artificially retard it." These recommendations are somewhat different in tone from the policy goals of Public Law 96-479, the National Materials and Minerals Policy, Research and Development Act of 1980, (October 21, 1980). This Act, among other provisions, declares that the President shall support basic science and technology for the exploration, discovery, and recovery of nonfuel materials, and promote and encourage private enterprise in the development of economically sound and stable domestic materials industries. If the ocean mining industry favors more direct forms of support from the United States government at a later date, then PL 96-479 and PL 96-283 should provide a legal means to do so.

Most American deep seabed mining companies have retrenched--but those of other nations are expanding. The German group AMR, the French AFERNOD/CNEXO group, and the three major Japanese groups (Mitsubishi, Sumitomo and Mitsui), have continued their R&D efforts and are potentially major competitors with American interests. The Japanese Ministry of International Trade and Industry (MITI) has decided to develop nodule mining technology as part of a major National Research and Development Program. This exclusively Japanese effort will invest about $100 million for R&D in ocean mining from 1981 to 1988. The French government/industry group, AFERNOD, has had the financial and technical support of the French government in the development of a submersible system. In 1980 the

government of Norway also formed a national effort called
the Deep Ocean Nodule Mining Project. The project's goal
is to analyze and outline the possibilities of Norwegian
industry and shipping participation in the exploitation
of manganese nodules.[35] The steady progress of foreign
ocean mining enterprises is due in large part to the
substantial economic support they have enjoyed from their
governments.

   In the United States, the Lockheed group (OMC) was
one of the first to raise sufficient funds to carry out
all its first phase development goals. Government
guaranteed loans in 1971 and a continuation of aircraft
and ocean related government contracts has not only saved
Lockheed from going bankrupt but has provided a base from
which it now leads in ocean mining development in the
United States. One of the most important reasons Ocean
Minerals Company (OMC) is a leader in the development of
a deep seabed mining program is that Lockheed Ocean
Systems has received millions of dollars in defense
contracts to develop underwater technology for the United
States Navy. These contracts have given Lockheed an
advantage over ocean mining groups that lack funds and
ocean technology know-how. Lockheed has been quite
successful in transferring much of its defense related
ocean systems research into civilian programs.

   In November of 1980, however, Lockheed spokesmen
told the State Department's Law of the Sea Advisory Group
that the consortium would decrease the size of its program
and curtail most of the "technology proving" activities
necessary for a successful pilot demonstration program.
Lockheed announced that the consortium would continue to
collect prospecting and environmental data that would be
required for domestic licensing procedures. Spokesmen
said that the consortium would cease all at-sea tests of
its equipment, restricting itself only to what is needed
to obtain an exploration license from the National Oceanic
and Atmospheric Administration (NOAA).[36] The reason
given for the cutbacks was that the Law of the Sea Treaty
does not guarantee United States citizens nondiscriminatory access to the hard minerals resources of the deep
seabed. Ocean Minerals Company and Ocean Mining
Associates--the two leading American-based groups--fear
that the Treaty will not provide the necessary security
to attract investments for viable economic operations.

   An interesting feature of the present ocean mining
consortia is that not one of the groups is an entirely
American owned operation. The make-up of the individual
consortia indicates that companies with a specific area
of expertise and those with financial capital for investment were drawn together in the early stages of ocean
mining development. By including participants from Europe
or Japan in consortia, American ocean miners have
increased the likelihood that the governments of these

countries will favor an open access regime at UNCLOS III and generally support United States unilateral action. As more foreign companies break away from a slowed down American industry, companies from the United States can point to strong foreign competition as a bargaining chip with the federal government when seeking additional legislation or more government assistance. This lack of an entirely American owned consortium seems to have occurred because early American interests sought partners with technological sophistication and/or investment capital in all the highly industrialized nations.

One of the reasons French, German, and Japanese ocean mining companies are still committed to research expenditures is that they have yet to complete their basic exploration and development programs. They continue at high research and development spending levels because business groups are more willing to make less than the American cut-off level of approximately 15-20 percent that is considered an acceptable profit on most ventures--including deep seabed mining. Lower profit levels are more acceptable because the governments of these countries have provided varying degrees of direct subsidies to their ocean mining industries to help ensure future access to critical minerals.

As first phase operations in these companies reach completion there will be increased pressure on their governments for some form of legislation similar to that passed into law in the United States. A reciprocating state arrangement between the "like-minded" nations would be very helpful to settle potential claim disputes and to offer the legal framework necessary for commercial activities. German deep seabed mining legislation was passed in July 1980. A useful comparison between the United States and West German legislation was made by D. Caron in 1981. The provisions in the West German legislation are very similar to those contained in PL 96-283.[37] In the fall of 1981 the French government, too, passed a similar deep seabed mining law. British legislation was passed in August 1981. The Japanese government has yet to pass deep seabed mining legislation. In comparison with the deep seabed mining legislation of other countries, PL 96-283 and the final ocean mining rules and regulations published by NOAA in September 1981 have the most thought out and detailed provisions for protection of the marine environment. Section 118 of PL 96-283 states that the provisions for the protection of the environment found in that law should be implemented by other "reciprocating states."

INDUSTRY'S EFFORTS TO INFLUENCE U.S. OCEAN MINING POLICY

Much of the United States' domestic legislation and its negotiating positions at the LOS Conference

concerning deep seabed mining have reflected the orienta-
tion of ocean mining interests based in this country.
There are three reasons industry has had such a large role
to play in ocean mining policy. First, most research to
date on deep seabed mining has been undertaken by private
industry. Second, because of the knowledge that industry
possesses, it has been called upon by Congress and the
Administration to supply investment figures and research
data. And third, the industry has spent large sums of
money to retain law firms to lobby and present testimony
to the Government for specific coporate interests. These
interests are almost always presented in a way which
reflects "national interests."

As early as 1970, the American Mining Congress
(AMC) had expressed concern about United States policy
for the seabed beyond national jurisdiction. The AMC
suggested that it might be in the best interest of the
United States for a Law of the Sea Conference to fix the
limits of jurisdiction and that interim arrangements for
mining should be based on the 1958 Geneva Convention.
This Convention was actually four conventions which were
based largely on existing customs and activities.

Lobbying action by the AMC led to the introduction
of bills in 1972 and 1973 to promote the conservation and
orderly development of hard mineral resources of the deep
seabed. Throughout the 1970s, several Congressional
committees held hearings on United States oceanography
and related international issues. Most receptive to the
views of the industry in the early part of the decade was
the Subcommittee on Mines, Minerals, and Fuels, chaired
by Senator Lee Metcalf of Montana, under the Senate
Interior and Insular Affairs Committee.[38]

The early attempts of industry to influence ocean
mining legislation centered on efforts to get Congress to
grant United States' entrepreneurs immediate 15-year
mineral exploration licences in blocks up to 40,000 square
kilometers on the ocean floor in areas beyond national
jurisdiction. These licences would be exclusive for all
persons subject to United States jurisdiction. Bills such
as S.1134 in the early 1970s, provided that the licences
might also be exclusive with respect to other states that
entered into reciprocal agreements with the United States
during this interim period. The same concept appeared in
the ocean mining bills which finally became law in 1980--
PL 96-283.

In November of 1974 Deepsea Ventures filed a
"Notice of Discovery and Claim of Exclusive Mining Rights"
with the Secretary of State and requested diplomatic protection for the claimed investments in a tract of seabed
in the East Central Pacific ocean. This was the first
time an ocean mining company had filed such a claim. It
brought to a head the issue of legal jurisdiction and the
specific meaning of the common heritage concept for

American interests in international waters. The State
Department did not grant the requested claim. Secretary
of State Henry Kissinger believed and hoped that an
overall agreement at UNCLOS III would be more likely if
the United States did not aggravate the Third World by
accepting Deepsea Venture's claim of exclusive mining
rights--a concept diametrically opposed by the Group of
77.

An analysis of Congressional seabed mining testimony clearly shows that industry has been very successful
in both the House and Senate in building support for most
of its major goals regarding ocean mining legislation and
policy, except for the key one--complete grandfather
rights protection.[39] There was only minimal opposing
testimony in Congressional hearings on the Deep Seabed
Hard Mineral Resources Act (PL 96-283). Environmental
groups focused on particular aspects of unilateral
legislation having to do with marine life and the general
guarantees of the maintenance of the ocean's ecosystems.
Groups such as the United Methodist Law of the Sea Project
had some influence in shaping the legislation. The
Methodist group organized meetings across the country to
demonstrate their opposition to the unilateral legislation
that they claim goes against the common heritage of mankind principle. Although the United Methodist Project
and other public interest groups presented testimony to
Congress throughout the 1970s on deep seabed mining, they
could not stop passage of domestic ocean mining legislation. They did, however, succeed in facilitating informal
dialogues between the United States and several key heads
of delegation from the Group of 77 on some difficult
negotiating issues.[40]

It would be inaccurate to conclude that all of the
industry's interests are represented in PL 96-283. It is
safe to say, however, that the goal of open access to
manganese nodules in international waters, and the desire
to begin American mining as soon as possible, are shared
by the industry and government.

CONCLUDING REMARKS

With a strong policy commitment from the Reagan
Administration to support American ocean mining companies,
it is likely that legal detriments to mining will be
minimized. The form of that commitment will necessarily
include a domestic licensing regime that is favorable to
the industry and an international arrangement that satis-
fies the industry's need for open access to the nodules.
It is probable that this type of support will continue
throughout the Reagan Administration.

If commercial ocean mining is to begin by the mid
1990s, it will also be necessary for banks to provide vast

front-end capital for continued research and development
for mining techniques, processing research, and ships.
The banks will do so only if government actively supports
industry and if the price of manganese, nickel, copper
and cobalt increases in the international metals market.
With an increase in prices, corporations and investors
will see ocean mining as a profitable venture. Should
that happen, commercial seabed mining may commence by the
mid 1990s.[41] If prices stay low, the present slowdown
in R&D expenditures by ocean mining companies will
continue. Prices will have to increase considerably for
the investment climate to improve, particularly if interest rates on bank loans are in the 20 percent range and
money market funds and other forms of low risk investment
continue to be offered at around 15 percent return.

The nature of the consortia will change a good deal
over the next ten to fifteen years. The companies providing technology and equipment development in the United
States groups may opt to remain partners or become service
contractors once full-scale commercial exploitation is
underway. The remaining companies comprising the consortia will reflect more direct metal mining, processing,
and marketing interests.

As more governments of free market economies work
closely with their resource and high technology industries
in order to secure access to resources, pressure will
increase for changes in the traditional ties between
United States government and corporate interests. In the
past, industry has been fairly successful in having the
United States government "defend the national interest"
in various locations around the world when foreign pressure was put on American businesses overseas.[42] A clear
distinction, however, has remained between business and
government interests. The role of ideology, and promotion
of capitalism for its own sake, has been of less importance over the past decade. The government's interest
increasingly has been in securing resources. Corporate
interests have been, and remain, in making a good return
on investment. The ocean mining industry's lobbying
efforts on the Deep Seabed Hard Mineral Resources Act
stressed that the importance of access to minerals such
as the ones in manganese nodules was not new or unusual.
Given the possibility of declining availability of supply
around the turn of the century for cobalt, nickel and
manganese, their arguments have struck at the core of the
nation's long-term national interests. Those resource
interests may create a larger role for the state in
promoting industries that are essential to the nation's
security.

FOOTNOTES

CHAPTER 3

1. Conrad G. Welling, "The Economics of Marine Mineral Production: A Private Sector Profitability Analysis," paper delivered at the Marine Sciences and Ocean Policy Symposium, University of California, Santa Barbara, June 17-20, 1979.

2. John L. Mero, "Manganese," North Dakota Engineer 27 (1952): 28-32; John L. Mero, "The Mining and Processing of Deep-Sea Manganese Nodules," unpublished Ph.D. dissertation, University of California, Berkeley, Institute of Marine Resources, 1959. See also John L. Mero, The Mineral Resources of the Sea, (Amsterdam, Elsevier Press, 1965).

3. The ocean mining interests of the Soviet Union are allied with those of the other developed nations. The Soviets have been opposed to the establishment of an International Seabed Authority to regulate deep ocean mining for several years. Their desire to maintain the goodwill of the Third World countries, however, has caused them to reluctantly accept an Authority at UNCLOS III. See Ruth M. Linebaugh, "Ocean Mining in the Soviet Union," Marine Technology Society Journal 14 (February/March 1980): 20-24.

4. Surveying and prospecting activities are required for the selection of a prime mine site. Such a site is described as being topographically smooth, with a dense concentration of nodules with small variations in size, content, and specific gravity. The mineral content of the nodules should be high in specific minerals whose extraction is likely to yield high revenue. In the current situation, miners are primarily interested in deposits with high nickel and cobalt content. See U.N. A/Conf. 62/25 (May 22, 1974) for details on these points and on prospecting and research cruises by industry. For an entertaining description of much of this type of technolgoy, see Ian Slater, Sea Gold, (New York: Bantam, 1979), one of the first novels based on the mineral resources of the deep seabed.

5. Interviews with Mr. Jay Agarwal, Boston, June 1980. Agarwal now works with Charles River Associates. He was a key figure in Kennecott Copper's ocean mining efforts in the 1970s when that company was actively

pursuing research and develpment for deep seabed mining.

6. See Krueger, Joachim, and Karl-Heinz Schwarz, "Processing of Manganese Nodules," in Manganese Nodules-- Metals from the Sea, Metallgesllschaft A.G., Rev. Activi- ties, Edition 18, 1975, pp. 36-43.

7. Industry spokesmen have repeatedly stressed their desire for an eventual Law of the Sea Treaty--but one considered to be realistic, workable, and beneficial for an operational deep seabed mining project. Spokesmen from Ocean Minerals Company (Lockheed), pointed out in September 1981, that the lack of "grandfather rights" provisions in U.S. legislation has also worked to hold back additional funds for R&D beyond the initial phase of development.

8. John R.W. Black, The Recovery of Metals from Deepsea Manganese Nodules and the Effects on World Cobalt and Manganese Markets, (Boston: Charles River Associates, Inc., 1980.)

9. A sensitivity analysis done on cobalt prices indicated the APV was sustained positive by an average cobalt price remaining at or above $5 per pound in real terms. Black assumed figures of $4 per pound for nickel and $1.25 per pound for copper in real terms. He con- cluded that: "If the economic environment is a little less favorable in the future with sharper rises in energy and materials costs, the APV would easily turn negative for the four metal process recovering ferromanganese." Black, op cit. p. 272.

10. Ibid. Black determined that, "the addition of a manganese production facility actually lowered APV by -$140 million to -$190 million, meaning the ferromanganese and silicomanganese production in itself was a negative net present value operation."

11. Ibid.

12. Ibid.

13. Analysis of Major Policy Issues Raised by the Commercial Development of Ocean Manganese Nodules, Final Report prepared for the National Science Foundation by Charles River Associates, Incorporated. Report No. 383, October 1981, concluded that: "In the aggregate, consum- ers will gain more from lower prices than producers will lose. The problem, of course, is that the major benefits of lower prices will be realized by the industrialized countries, and many costs will be borne by less developed countries that are major producers. Lower nickel prices

will primarily affect Canada, New Calendonia, and Australia, but many LDCs will suffer as well. Zaire will be the biggest loser from lower cobalt prices. Should manganese prices fall with ocean mining, South Africa and Australia will be two of the major countries affected, but Gabon, Brazil, and other less developed countries will be hurt as well. If manganese from the deep seabed simply replaces South African capacity, (a distinct possibility) then the other manganese producers will not be affected by ocean mining." See Chapter 1, p. 7.

14. J.D. Nyhart et al. Update of 1978 MIT Economic Study on Deep Seabed Mining, 1982.

15. For an idea of the processing costs see Black, op cit., pp. 111-120.

16. See, New York Times, March 16, 1981. Business section D.1., "Mineral Takeovers Critized," "Oil Companies' Mineral Offers." See also, Newsweek, March 23, 1981, p. 57.

17. The October 1981 CRA report, op cit., found that: "Ocean mining at moderate levels (four operations in 1990 and one additional operation every two years thereafter) is likely to cause a 10 percent drop in the nickel price and possibly a 60 percent drop in the cobalt price, from long-run levels. It also might cause up to a 15 percent drop in the ferromanganese price, depending in particular on the response of production in South Africa. Rapid ocean mining, at twice this rate, is likely to cause a 15 percent fall in the nickel price and possibly a 75 percent fall in cobalt price. Ocean mining seems unlikely to be sufficiently profitable over the next 25 years to occur at this rapid rate. It may well not be sufficiently profitable to occur at the moderate rate, either, over the next 25 years." See chapter 1, p. 6.

18. These ideas were suggested by ex-Kennecott executive Jay Agarwal in an interview, June 1980. Mr. Agarwal is a consultant at Charles River Associates in Boston.

19. These figures, and many of the viewpoints expressed by industry spokesmen in this chapter are based on consultation with Conrad G. Welling and Edward Dangler of Ocean Minerals Company, J.K. Amsbaugh, Ocean Mining Associates, Marne Dubs, Kennecott Copper and A.P. Statham, INCO Ltd. Correspondence from 1979 to February 1982. (Hereafter cited as consultation with ocean mining industry.) Estimated expenditures by consortia, as of September 1981, are as follows: Ocean Mining Associates (OMA): prior to formation of OMA expenditures were in excess of

$20 million and since formation of OMA $60 million; Kennecott Copper: $50-60 million; Ocean Minerals Inc. (OMI): $45-50 million; Ocean Minerals Company (OMC): $120 million; AFERNOD/CNEXO (France): $45 million ($38 million between 1980 and 1982); Continous Line Bucket System (approximately 20 companies from 6 countries): $1.5 million. These figures are from J.K. Amsbaugh, President of Ocean Mining Associates, "The Ocean's Contribution to the Solution of the U.S. Strategic Materials Crisis." A paper presented at an American Metals Society Meeting, September 22, 1981.

20. Consultation with ocean industry, op cit. For a good overview on the type of information modern banks want when corporations go to them for loans see, George H.K. Schenck, "Investment and Financial Analysis: An Update," Coal Mining and Processing, June, 1978.

21. Ibid. For a discussion of the type of technology being developed for deep seabed mining see, Conrad G. Welling, "The Massive Technology for Ocean Mining," Stockton's Port Soundings, September 1980, pp. 8-11.

22. See, Deep Ocean Mineral Mining: A Computer Model for Investigating Costs, Rates of Return, and Economic Implications of Some Policy Options, revised edition, The M.I.T. Marine Industry Collegium Opportunity Brief #12, July 1, 1978. M.I.T. Sea Grant Program. This economic study was led by Professor J.D. Nyhart and attempted to develop a deterministic financial simulation model of the deep ocean mining of manganese nodules. Also see, Franz Diederich, Wolfgang Muller, and Wolfgang Schneider, Analysis of the MIT Study on Deep Ocean Mining--Critical Remarks on Technologies and Cost Estimates, (Aachen: Research Institute for International Technology-Economic Co-operation, Technical University, March 1979). In addition see, Arthur E. Capstaff Jr., "Profitability of the Industry and Competition," in Edward Miles and John King Gamble, eds., Law of the Sea: Conference Outcomes and Problems of Implementation, Proceedings of the Law of the Sea Institute, Tenth Annual Conference, June 22-25, 1976, (Cambridge: Ballinger, 1977), pp. 327-341.

23. Nickel, in particular, has a high income elasticity of demand. Nickel is consumed primarily in capital goods (65%) and consumer durables (35%). Consumers will delay purchases of these items when the economy is depressed. Because nickel demand is sensitive to the business cycle, it is difficult to forecast demand accurately. For figures on nickel supply and demand see, U.S. Bureau of Mines, Bulletin 671, Mineral Facts and Problems: Nickel, U.S. Department of the Interior, 1980.

24. See, <u>Mineral Facts and Problems,</u> Cobalt, op cit., Department of the Interior, 1980. One of the most important relationships in the cobalt market is cobalt's byproduct relationship with either copper or nickel, and the consequent relative price inelasticity of supply under normal conditions. Over the long-term, the price of cobalt will be governed by production of nickel and copper, and therefore is likely to settle to an equilibrium of two to three times the price of nickel or seven to eight times the price of copper.

25. Ibid.

26. Ibid., Manganese.

27. The October 1981 Charles River report, op cit., see chapter 5, p. 5-24.

28. These questions underline some of the basic issues which both developed and developing countries have been concerned with at UNCLOS III.

29. See John R.W. Black, <u>The Recovery of Metals from Deepsea Nodules,</u> op cit.; <u>Analysis, Commercial Development of Ocean Manganese Nodules,</u> 1981 CRA report, op cit.; Joel P. Clark and Marian R. Neutra, "Potential Economic and Environmental Consequences of Mining Deep Sea Manganese Nodules," unpublished paper, MIT, November, 1981; and the 1982 updated M.I.T. study by J.D. Nyhart et al., op cit.

30. J. Clark and M. Neutra, "Consequences of Mining Deep Sea Manganese Nodules," op cit. Clark and Neutra conclude that the effects of a disruption in cobalt supplies from Zambia and/or Zaire "would not have a measurable effect on the national security of the United States." They believe that increased prices would result in significant substitution away from cobalt in "nonessential" uses. They point out, however, that there would be a time delay, and that it would be necessary to release a "small amount of cobalt from the government stockpile for one or possibly two years." They conclude that there would be an economic cost to the United States resulting from a supply disruption due to the loss in consumer surplus. The cost of such a disruption, they say, "could be substantial but would be short-lived because of the downward pressure on the price." See also, <u>Analysis, Commercial Development of Ocean Manganese Nodules,</u> 1981 CRA report, op cit.

31. Ibid.

32. John R. W. Black, <u>The Recovery of Metals from Deepsea Manganese Nodules</u>, op cit.

33. A brief summary of the Purposes of the Deep Seabed Hard Mineral Resources Act, clearly shows that the Act is concerned with the orderly, safe, and equitable exploitation of deep seabed nodules. Briefly summarized, the Purposes of the Act are to: encourage successful conclusion of a comprehensive UN Law of the Sea Treaty which will give legal definition to the idea that hard mineral resources of the deep seabed are the common heritage of mankind, (hard mineral resources refers only to manganese nodules as the legislation is currently written); provide for an international revenue sharing fund (drawn from taxes based on 3.75% of the imputed value of the resource involved); establish an interim program to regulate exploration for and commercial recovery of deep seabed hard mineral resources by U.S. citizens; accelerate the program of environmental assessment of exploration and production and assure that those activities are conducted in a manner which will encourage the conservation of such resources to protect the quality of the environment; and encourage continued development of technology necessary to recover those hard mineral resources. Another Purpose of the Act addresses international objectives: The Act states that while the U.S. has jurisdiction over its citizens and vessels in the exercise of high seas freedom to engage in exploration for and production of hard mineral resources in accord with accepted principles of international law recognized by the U.S., it does not assert sovereignty or exclusive rights or jurisdiction, or ownership of any resources or areas of the deep seabed. PL 96-283 also emphasizes that the regimes to be established under its authority are transitional pending the coming into force of a superseding international agreement. It outlines the minimum conditions necessary for such an international agreement to be acceptable. Specifically, it states that an international agreement should provide assured and non-discriminatory access to the resources of the deep seabed and that there be a provision for security of tenure. The U.S. government has stressed this last point as there are no "grandfather rights" provisions in the Act itself. The legislative history of the Deep Seabed Hard Mineral Resources Act goes back to S.2801 as introduced by the late Senator Lee Metcalf on November 2, 1971. Legislation was introduced in the House soon after. The Senate eventually passed S.493--a bill very similar to its predecessor of the 95th Congress, S.2053. S.493 was passed December 14, 1979 by the 96th Congress. The House passed HR 2759 June 6, 1980. Although both bills lacked specific "grandfather rights" provisions contained in earlier draft legislation, the American ocean mining

industry was happy to see the creation of PL 96-283 on
June 28, 1980. Industry spokesmen are still seeking some
form of "grandfather rights" protection--either added to
U.S. legislation and/or added to the proposed Law of the
Sea Treaty text.

34. These concerns are understandable given current
projections of poor returns on investment and low metals
prices. Based on consultation with Ocean Minerals
Company, May 1981.

35. J.K. Amsbaugh, "The Ocean's Contribution to the
Solution of the U.S. Strategic Materials Crisis," Paper
presented at American Metal Society Meeting, September
22, 1981.

36. The Deep Seabed Hard Mineral Resources Act
establishes NOAA as the agency from which industry will
obtain ocean mining licenses. The Office of Ocean
Minerals and Energy (OME), has been established within
NOAA to carry out the intent of the Hard Minerals Act
(and the Ocean Thermal Energy Act). OME published Deep
Seabed Mining Regulations for Exploration License: Final
Rules, September 1981; a Final Programmatic Environmental
Impact Statement (Vols. I and II); and a Final Technical
Guidance Document, both published in September 1981. The
rules became effective October 15, 1981. NOAA expects to
receive license applications from U.S. Steel, Lockheed,
Kennecott, SEDCO, Sun Oil, and Standard Oil of Indiana,
among others. The cost of the license is $100,000.

37. For a good comparison of U.S. and West German
deep seabed mining legislation, see D. Caron, "Deep seabed
mining: A comparative study of U.S. and West German
municipal legislation," Marine Policy, January 1981.

38. Gerard Mangone, Marine Policy for America,
(Boston: Lexington Books, 1977), see especially Chapter
5.

39. For an excellent summary of the ocean mining
legislation, and some of the major arguments given for
and against it, see Congressional Record, House, June 9,
1980, pp. H4641-2667. This document includes viewpoints
from industry, Ambassador Richardson, and Congressmen both
for and against the legislation. There is a good discussion of the type of legislation the industry wanted and
the Preparatory Investment Protection plans proposed by
the State Department. Specific references to legislation
are: U.S. Congress, House, Committee on Merchant Marine
and Fisheries, Deep Seabed Mining, Hearings before a
subcommittee of the House Committee on Merchant Marine
and Fisheries on H.R. 1270, H.R. 6017, H.R. 11879, 94th

Cong., 1st sess., 1976; U.S. Congress, Senate, Joint Hearings, Mining of the Deep Seabed, Hearings before the Committee on Energy and Natural Resources, and the Committee on Commerce, Science, and Transportation, on S.2053, 95th Cong., 1st. sess., 1977; U.S. Congress, House, Committee on Merchant Marine and Fisheries, Oceanography Miscellaneous Part 2, Hearings before a subcommittee of the House Committee on Merchant Marine and Fisheries on the Law of the Sea Conference Briefings, 95th Cong., 1st and 2nd sess., 1977 and 1978; U.S. Congress, House Committee on International Relations, Deep Seabed Mineral Resources Act, Hearings before a subcommittee of the Senate Committee on Foreign Relations on H.R.3350, 95th Cong., 2nd sess., 1978; U.S. Congress, House, Committee on Ways and Means, The Deep Seabed Hard Mineral Resources Act, Hearings on H.R. 3350, 95th Cong., 2nd sess., 1978; U.S. Congress, Senate, Joint Hearings, Deep Seabed Mineral Resources Act, Hearings before a subcommittee of the Senate Committee on Energy and Natural Resources and the Committee on Commerce, Science and Transportation, on S.493, 96th Cong., 1st sess., 1979; U.S. Congress, House, Committee on Merchant Marine and Fisheries, Report together with Dissenting Views before the House Committee on Merchant Marine and Fisheries on H.R. 2759, statement by Mr. Murphy of New York, 96th Cong., 1st sess., 1979; U.S. Congress, House, Committee on Foreign Affairs, Briefing on the Eighth Session of the Third United Nations Conference on the Law of the Sea, before a subcommittee of the House Committee on Foreign Affairs, 96th Cong., 1st sess., 1979.

40. Lee Kimball has long been a leading spokesperson for the United Methodist Law of the Sea Project, and is actively involved in the organization, Citizens for Ocean Law. She was very helpful in gathering information for this book.

41. Based on consultation with ocean mining industry, op cit.

42. See Stephen D. Krasner, Defending the National Interest: Raw Materials Investments and U.S. Foreign Policy, (Princeton: Princeton University Press, 1979).

4
UNCLOS III, The Group of 77, and the New International Economic Order

INTRODUCTION

Complex deep seabed mining negotiations at the international level have been made especially difficult because the Group of 77 has made many attempts to link ocean mining with Third World goals of attaining a New International Economic Order (NIEO). The Group of 77 has succeeded in obtaining many concessions from the developed nations on seabed mining that will help set precedents for the exploitation of other resource commons favorable to the lesser developed countries (LDCs). The Group of 77 would, for example, like to see agreements for the transfer of ocean mining technology, a commitment of the industrially advanced states to finance the creation of an international Enterprise for mining manganese nodules, and a favorable structure for the International Seabed Authority, serve as examples for future efforts in shaping a NIEO. Leaders of many Third World countries believe that only with a NIEO will the opportunity exist for LDCs to obtain more of the world's wealth and resources and become less dependent on the advanced nations of the North for economic development.

With approximately 120 member countries, the Group of 77 is comprised of the Latin American, African, and Asian negotiating groups. Within this group there are considerable diversities of interest, capabilities, geographical location and natural endowments. The group is based, however, on an assumed commonality of interests of all "have nots" against all "haves". Consequently, there are tensions within it between the ideological dictates of maintaining group unity and the varying and often incompatible perception of delegates of their countries' interests on the issues being negotiated.[1]

Much time is therefore consumed in within-group bargaining. In addition, the Group must stay at the level of general principles in order to retain unity since it could not hope to negotiate successfully on details. Most American officials associated with the Law of the Sea negotiations concur that the Group of 77 has formally adopted a full set of extreme positions and associated texts. Although many countries in the Group may have accepted the texts for only tactical reasons, it is difficult for them formally to moderate their positions. At times individual members of the Group informally agree to moderate positions, but then cannot "deliver" the Group as a whole. At best, they can prevent it from formally rejecting a possible compromise.

One observer suggests that the members within the Group of 77 enforce a rule of unanimity among themselves which gives veto power to a relatively small number of extremists.[2] State Department officials participating in the Law of the Sea negotiations point out that many Third World countries believe they have no interest higher than the Group of 77 solidarity and therefore instruct their delegations simply to "vote with the 77." When they do, efforts of reaching an overall agreement are severely hampered. Spokesmen from the State Department also point out that there is a significant split within the Group of 77 between a group of pragmatists and a group of ideological purists.[3] The pragmatists have been led by a few land-based producers (of the marketable minerals in ocean nodules) who are willing to compromise on some issues of principle in exchange for extreme production controls of manganese nodules. (Interestingly enough, Canada, as a major land-based producer--especially of nickel--has been one of the leading proponents of production control.) The ideological purists are led by a few individuals whose countries have no direct economic interest in a Law of the Sea Treaty and who are free to insist on their principles to the end.[4]

The Group of 77 has used the seabed negotiations as a means to further their objectives in establishing a New International Economic Order. Many of the demands are purely ideological, such as those to establish a quasi-government seabed Authority to mine the seabed and exclude private miners without the Authority's consent. A Seabed Authority of this nature presents a threat to the concept of free access to resources in international waters. Some of the demands represent legitimate aspirations to which the United States government has tried to offer accommodation. Such aspirations include the desire of the lesser developed countries to have a significant voice in the Seabed Authority and their desire to participate directly in the exploitation of the seabeds rather than leaving such exploitation to the few companies or countries which happen to have a technological advantage.[5] M.C.W. Pinto, Ambassador, Special Representative of Sri Lanka to UNCLOS III, has frequently reviewed the concerns of the LDCs in Law of the Sea negotiations, and has tried to demonstrate many times how these goals are consistent with more general political and economic objectives formulated in the Declaration on

the Establishment of a New International Economic Order.
He believes the new order of the oceans will do much to
pave the way "for the meek to inherit the earth."[6]

ATTEMPTS TO SHAPE A NIEO

How has the Group of 77 used UNCLOS III in an
attempt to shape a New International Economic Order? In
order to fully understand the process it is necessary to
briefly examine past attempts by the LDCs to create a new
world economic order.
Changes in the international economic order have
been demanded by developing countries for almost two
decades. These demands were the main topic of the first
United Nations Conference of Trade and Development
(UNCTAD) meeting in 1964. It was at that meeting that
the developing countries who joined together to form the
Group of 77 issued a declaration hailing the establishment of UNCTAD "as a significant step towards creating a
new and just world economic order".[7] In addition, the
Charter of Algiers of 1967 and the International Strategy
for the Second United Nations Decade of 1970 dealt with
reordering the world's economy.
In April of 1974, the first of the recent series of
demands entitled "Declaration on the Establishment of a
New International Economic Order" was approved by the
Sixth Special Session of the United Nations General
Assembly.[8] It pointed to the widening poverty gap
between rich and poor nations; cited the importance of
international cooperation in an increasingly interdependent world; asserted the right of all nations to exercise
sovereignty over their natural resources and economic
activities, including the right to regulate multinational
corporations; and demanded better terms of trade, more
aid, more resources of the International Monetary Fund,
and transfer of science and technology on more beneficial
terms. It is important to note that the United States
and several other Northern, industrially advanced,
nations did not approve of this Declaration.
In October 1974, the United Nations Environment
Program held a joint symposium with UNCTAD at Cocoyoc,
Mexico at which the Cocoyoc Declaration was issued. This
declaration criticized rich nations for wasting cheap but
precious resources; cited the unequal distribution of
income internally as well as internationally; and complained of biases of international market mechanisms. It
also endorsed the call approved at the April 1974 UN
session for a new international economic order.[9] In
December 1974, the UN General Assembly adopted the
"Charter of Economic Rights and Duties of States".[10]
Besides duplicating many aspects of the other two
relevant declarations of 1974, the Charter asserted the

rights of states to organize associations of primary commodity producers.

In February 1975, the developing countries held an official conference on raw materials in Dakar, Senegal. The declaration which followed criticized the existing world economy in which developing countries, dependent on raw material exports, see their terms of trade deteriorate and are condemned by economic forces to remain dependent on the unfair structure of world trade and investment.[11] The Dakar Declaration called for a change in negotiating tactics: instead of presenting a list of requests, it declared that LDCs should work together to obtain the strength necessary to win their demands for basic changes in the economic order.

The views and goals of the developing countries with respect to a NIEO can be divided into four main categories.[12] The first is Monetary: Developing countries want more control of the system and a greater share of the international assets created by the monetary system. Trade is another concern: LDCs have suggested that commodity producers organize in order to negotiate with more clout and (with OPEC's help) demand better and more stable prices, indexed to protect the real value of those prices from deteriorating with general inflation. The Group of 77 has demanded that actions be taken to help developing countries export more manufactured goods and suggested that LDCs de-link their trade from such exclusive reliance on OECD countries and instead encourage more intro-LDC trade. A third area focuses on Resource Transfers: The Group of 77 claims that since aid commitments are not being met, "automatic" types of resources should be developed--such as taxes on non-renewables, sharing revenues from ocean exploitation, and more generous debt relief. The fourth category is Participation in International Decision-Making: The Group of 77 hopes to achieve this by shifting more decisions to United Nations forums where developing countries have more influence, and by changing weighted voting formulas in other forums.

The developing countries are essentially making demands for two kinds of change in the institutions that make up the international economic order: (1) more LDC influence in operation of international systems, and (2) more benefits for the LDCs from the operation of those systems. These demands have not been heard more loudly or more persistently than they have at UNCLOS III.

Some Northern critics have asserted that even if the industrialized nations of the North gave the countries of the South every change demanded the development problems of the South would not be solved. Difficulties would persist to a large degree because external factors probably are not as important as internal ones (i.e. elite structures and values) in determining the success of development. But real reforms of the international economic system could result in major increases in the resources and revenue available to developing countries from areas considered the common heritage of mankind.[13] The efforts of resource-poor developing countries to improve their access to resources from other nations and the international commons are worthwhile as long as they are not seen as a substitute for wise internal economic policies.[14]

Where UNCLOS III is concerned, there is a deepening and somewhat more sophisticated perception among both developed and developing countries that the issue of a seabed regime represents interests more fundamental than the immediate economic benefits envisioned. As the negotiations have progressed, the stakes in the process of "who gets what, when and how" have been considerably enlarged and elevated.[15] The issues at UNCLOS III are no longer simply confined to pragmatic questions of State practice and jurisdiction but rather encompass more issues of State's principles. In 1978 one Carter Administration expert correctly asserted that the mandate at UNCLOS III has evolved from the technical design of a regime for deep seabed mining to the "architectonic construction of the contours of a future international legal, economic, and political order."[16] The struggle is no longer for the codification of international law but a competition for the control of future global institutions and commons resources.

In this context, it is not surprising that national interests are increasingly defined in ideological terms: centralization versus decentralization; private enterprise versus Authority control; resource policies versus free market principles; unitarianism versus pluralism; and equity versus efficiency.[17] This trend explains not only the increasing politicization of the negotiations but also the critical nature of the hard bargaining and slow progress that took place on the last few remaining issues of a final overall agreement.

The Group of 77 is aware of the significance of a Seabed Authority and is doing much to shape its legal framework and have it set precedents in other areas of international system building. The world community is involved in the development and modification of global institutions for the increasing number of problems perceived to require global treatment. The struggle ranges from development of conventions for the governance of air waves, Antarctica, and outer space and the Moon, to the increasingly complex set of institutions associated with the United Nations system.[18] For a large number of developing countries the same individuals participating in the LOS Conference are also involved in the wide range of institution-building efforts associated with the overall United Nations system--indicating a close connection between UNCLOS III and other resource/economic related UN activities.

Elisabeth Mann Borgese has been concerned with the connections between the NIEO and UNCLOS III for many years.[19] In the following statement she succinctly points out the relationship between the Law of the Sea and the efforts of the underdeveloped nations to restructure the world political and economic order:

> It cannot be stressed enough that the adoption of the [common heritage] principle by the General Assembly as a norm of international law marked the beginning of a revolution in international relations. It must and it will become the basis of the new international economic order, of which the Law of the Sea convention, whether one likes it or not, is both a forerunner and an essential part.[20]

Statements like this give hope to the Group of 77 for a NIEO, and stir confusion and fear among leaders of governments and industry in the developed industrialized nations of the North.

The developing states view the prospect of a new free-market seabed mining industry as a threat because it would create competition for existing minerals industries in a number of developing states, possibly reducing their export earnings. Furthermore, a free-market ocean mining industry would give the developed world alternate sources of raw materials, thereby reducing the credibility of any developing states' threat to cartelize or withhold such materials. The developing states have always felt that a free-market industry would allow the developed nations to dominate another lucrative high technology industry, to the exclusion of their interests.[21]

Ocean miners in the developed countries, however, need legal clarity and certainty before they will commit further large sums of money which are needed to enter into full scale production. The need for legal certainty (which is in part due to the demands of the Third World for an International Seabed Authority), has provided the LDCs with a real bargaining opportunity as their acquiescence is needed for a regime that appears "reasonable" to United States interests. The opportunity presented at UNCLOS III was one not merely to slow or even temporarily stop a widening of the economic gap. Rather, it is seen by the Group of 77 as a chance to create an entirely new system to exploit nodules that would be a working example of the type of economic system that the LDCs consider just.[22]

How has UNCLOS III served as a test for the efforts of LDCs to construct a NIEO? To begin with, they saw UNCLOS III as a forum where they could demonstrate the proper way to manage some of the world's raw materials—especially those to be exploited in areas designated the common heritage of mankind. In particular, the negotiations offer a chance to create a seabed institution that would be conscious of the needs of the developing countries and thus alter aspects of the world economic institutional framework. The LDCs also perceive UNCLOS III as an opportunity to gain experience in controlling, and limiting dependence on, multinational corporations (MNCs) by having an independent international Enterprise that would mine the deep seabed for the benefit of developing countries. In addition, a LOS Treaty would offer a test case for the efficacy of production controls--an important control mechanism among many LDCs. The Group of 77 hopes that an International Seabed Authority would enable the developing countries to demand mandatory technology transfer to help close the technology gap. By demanding that ocean mining technology be transfered to the Enterprise from the industrially advanced nations, the Group of 77 would be setting a precedent for technology transfers in other areas. Finally, the developing countries would like to ensure that the revenues earned from a successful seabed Authority would be set aside primarily for aid to LDCs. The Group of 77 is aware that in the long-term, precedents set at UNCLOS III will influence LDC participation in the exploitation and revenue sharing of Antarctica and other global commons resources.[23]

Given these considerations, general theories which apply to the treatment of the oceans as a commons area are also relevant to matters with a more direct and pervasive effect on the distribution of global wealth (which is after all the reason why the Group of 77 has called for a new international economic order). The institutional character of an International Seabed Authority would affect international commodity arrangements, international financial development and monetary agreements. The decision-making structure of the Authority would establish the relative influence of member States in matters concerning the acquisition and distribution of deep seabed wealth. The immediate source of such wealth will be manganese nodules. Later, technology of the twenty-first century may see developments allowing oil drilling in much deeper waters, exploitation of polymetallic sulfide ore deposits, and various types of energy production from the ocean in international waters.

As reflected in the negotiating texts and the dominant trends of the Conference, several economic features of the demands of the Group of 77 for the deep seabed regime can be pinned down. The LDCs would like to see a mandatory transfer of technology from private and State holders to the Enterprise, and possibly to developing countries.[24] They also hope to impose a ceiling on seabed mineral producers.[25] The LDCs want to ensure representation by the International Seabed Authority in international commodity arrangements.[26] They have made demands for quotas or similar measures to establish limits on the number of mine sites which may be held by each State and its public or private enterprises.[27] The Group of 77 wants a future moratorium on ocean mining of manganese nodules by State and private enterprises, pending successful renegotiation of the deep seabed regime.[28] In addition, they demand revenue-sharing with the Authority by private and State enterprises for the direct benefit of the Enterprise and developing countries.[29] The LDCs desire immunity of the Enterprise from national taxation,[30] state funding of the Enterprise shortly after the Treaty becomes effective, and a banking system through which State and private operators would be required to provide prospected or explored mine sites to the Authority for the direct benefit of the Enterprise or developing countries.[31] The Group of 77 would also like to obtain a moratorium on development of non-manganese nodule minerals, pending establishment of an agreed regime for them.[32]

To summarize: The developing countries insist that they must control the mineral resources of the deep seabed and that they must direct the actions of global institutions. In order to achieve a fundamental redistribution of wealth a restructuring of the global system of public order is required to establish a lawmaking democracy of nations.[33] An important step toward the realization of this New International Economic Order is control of the vitally important mineral resources of the deep seabed. Supporters of unilateral American legislation would like to ensure that the Group of 77 does not shape the nature of that control to the detriment of United States business and supply interests. In the long-run, however, those interests will be more secure if international agreement can be reached on the uses of the oceans. Highlights of the United Nations Conference on the Law of the Sea from 1958 through 1982 are presented in Appendix 8.

TECHNOLOGY TRANSFER

According to some observers of North-South relations the issue of technology transfer will become a major item on the international policy agenda of the 1980s, occupying the central role which aid, trade, and multinational corporations filled in previous decades.

How important an issue it actually proves to be will be determined to a large degree by the final wording of technology transfer provisions of a United Nations Law of the Sea Treaty. Current LDC pressures in the technology area are predominately political in nature and to varying degrees reflect an expectation that changes in the international availability of technology will help solve some

of their development problems. An overview of the economics of technology transfer indicates that LDCs can
usually obtain technology from more than one source, thus
putting pressure on suppliers of technology (i.e. MNCs)
to be price-competitive. LDC governments, however, have
interfered in some cases in the market mechanism by
specifying royalty fees to the exporting firm at a level
closer to the firm's marginal cost than at more profitable levels. The motivations for such action may have
been to improve the position of the LDC (in the eyes of
the government), or to improve the personal position of a
particular governing elite. Regardless of the motives,
such action, in addition to no guarantees that technology
supplied to one LDC firm will not end up in the hands of
unauthorized or non-paying users, tends to cut back on
the technology exporting firms will offer.

The political dimension of LDC demand for technology
transfer is important for intergovernmental relations on
other political, military, and economic levels and therefore has several implications for United States foreign
policy. Some analysts of technology transfer argue that
current technology and international technology measures
cannot be expected to have much effect in resolving the
LDC's growth and unemployment problems.[34] LDC governments are also uncertain about the effectiveness of past
transfers of technology. The usual goal of LDCs has been
the transfer of advanced technology to their countries
for economic development. Transfers of this type make
available to indigenous producers the requisite know-how
to reduce production costs or to produce certain goods in
order to raise productivity and living standards.[35]

Over the past ten years, however, the objectives of
technology transfer have been broadened.[36] A second
goal of LDCs now focuses on possession of, not just use
of, advanced technology. The concern here is to reduce
the duration of the contract periods during which they
pay license fees and to reject MNC restrictions in regard
to the "leakage" of technology to unauthorized users.[37]

A third LDC objective reflects a desire to increase
their domestic capacity to generate technology indigen-
ously. By doing so, the LDCs hope to break away from
their reliance on technology developed in the advanced
countries which places them in a state of neo-colonial
dependency. As a result, many LDCs are eager to enhance
their internal technological capabilities by placing a
greater emphasis on domestic research and development
rather than on imported know-how.

Because of the multiple policy objectives of most
developing countries, the different goals may require
trade-offs rather than total agreement on what is the
most appropriate form of technology to be transfered from
the North. Policies which effectively deal with one goal
may do so only at the cost of lower performance with

respect to the other technology/development policy objectives. This situation puts the United States in somewhat of a "no-win" situation. If it attempts to satisfy one area of LDC concern for technology transfer it will be difficult to avoid LDC criticism on the other two goals.

Fruitful dialogue between LDCs and the United States on technology transfer is possible only when participants share common premises. This condition is not always satisfied in the transfer-of-technolgy issue. Over the last five years, in fact, there has been an increase in the number of Third World leaders who consider know-how a free good, the heritage of all humankind. Most industrial technology is in the hands of trilateral-based corporations, and most governments of those nations lack the means to control techology-tranfer decisions by those firms. Given these conditions technology transfer may not be a promising issue for the United States to cultivate in its relations with the developing countries.

The United States may not be able to avoid the technology transfer issue with the LDCs. Up to 1970 the transfer of technology was mentioned only occasionally in the discussions of the committee on the Peaceful Uses of the Seabed and the Floor beyond the Limits of National Jurisdiction as one of the measures by which it might be possible to bridge the gap between developed and developing countries. It is surprising that direct provisions concerning the transfer of technology are not in the Declaration of Principles Governing the Seabed and Ocean Floor and the Subsoil thereof beyond the Limits of National Jurisdiction.[38] The Declaration does, however, contain some basic principles concerned with the transfer of technology.[39]

It was recognized only in 1972 that technology transfer issues within the United Nations system had to be dealt with separately from scientific research. In the early stages of negotiations at UNCLOS III, the transfer of technology issue was intended to favor only single States. In the course of discussion this approach slowly lost importance. The new approach adopted for the transfer of technology favored the Enterprise.[40] The proposed Treaty contains aspects of both approaches--much to the consternation of several State Department officials, policy makers on Capitol Hill, and their counterparts in several other Northern nations with corporations involved in ocean mining.

There were two sources that provided the impetus for the demand that the transfer of technology should favor the Enterprise. Beginning with the 1974 Caracas session of the LOS Conference, some developing countries emphasized that the discussion of the riches of the seabed was a part of the worldwide struggle for a new international economic order.[41] This trend appeared in the 1974 Charter of Economic Rights and Duties of States[42] and

has resulted, with respect to the seabed, in demands by
the Group of 77 for an Authority which had the right not
only to control deep seabed activities but also to
participate directly therein. Consequently, it was
necessary to furnish the Enterprise with the technology
needed to begin deep seabed mining. If the technology
and necessary capital were not forthcoming, the Authority
would have no chance to participate effectively in deep
seabed activities.

The second impetus for technology transfer favoring
the Enterprise came from another source. The United
States offered to furnish the Enterprise with the necessary technology to achieve a parallel system which would
allow States' parties and private corporations, as well
as the Authority, to take part in deep ocean mining.[43]
The United States' offer was essentially a bargaining
proposal: transfer of technology for partly free access.
The developing countries, after some hesitation, accepted
this approach without committing themselves to a solution
regarding access. Some American analysts argue (somewhat
incorrectly), that this was just one in a series of concessions the United States delegation made that gained
nothing for American interests. As a result, the question
of technology transfer became one of the main issues in
the discussions at UNCLOS III.

The regulations regarding the transfer of technology
depend on how the questions concerning access will be
resolved. One of the basic provisions of the transfer of
technology is found in Article 144 of the proposed Treaty.
It obliges the Authority and States' parties to encourage
the transfer of technology through the development of
programs in which the Enterprise and all States benefit.
The text states that the Enterprise and the developing
countries shall receive the technology under fair and
reasonable conditions. To many policy makers in the
United States this provision seems unsettling if not
unclear. One aspect of Article 144 that may offer ways
for reaching agreement between the goals of the
developing countries and ocean mining companies is
paragraph 2(b). It states that:

> measures directed towards the advancement of the
> technology of the Enterprise and the domestic
> technology of developing states, particularly by
> providing opportunities to personnel from the
> Enterprise and from developing states for training
> in marine science and technology and for their full
> participation in activities in the area.

Some United States based companies have expressed a
willingness to participate in training programs.

The Treaty raises three technology transfer issues.
First, the relationship between Article 144 and Article

274 of the treaty text is not solved. Article 144 deals
with the transfer of technology concerning deep seabed
mining, while the scope of Article 274 is broader and
covers scientific research as well. Second, Article 144
does not state what is meant by "progress for transfer of
technology." The difficulty here is that in the western
industrialized countries, the private companies--not the
States--are the owners of the relevant technology. Third,
one has to ask whether Article 144 creates a monopoly of
the Authority in the coordination of the transfer of technology, which would force the States' parties to invoke
the Authority if they seek cooperation in this field.
While the wording of Article 144 may not appear to tend
in this direction, one German analyst feels the development of the provision makes it likely that it is
intended to create such a monopoly of the Authority.[44]

A second way of transfering technology is provided
in Articles 150 and 151. Under these provisions the
Authority may require the Contractor to make available to
the Enterprise the same technology to be used in the
Contractor's operations on fair and reasonable terms.

There are three characteristic attributes of this
system based on the draft Treaty. First, the negotiations
on the transfer of technology take place after the applicant has already received a contract. As a result,
the sanction is severe because the contractor may lose
his investment. Second, this method of transfering technology benefits only the Enterprise. Third, the proposed
Treaty gives the Authority the right to connect the
negotiations on the transfer of technology with the
negotiations concerning a contract which would open the
access to the deep seabed area. If no agreement on the
transfer of technology is reached, the applicant will not
receive a contract. In this case the decision of the
Authority basically cannot be reconsidered by the Seabed
Dispute Chamber.

The industrialized states of the North maintain that
seabed mining technology would be available to the
Enterprise and developing countries through normal operation of the international marketplace.[45] The United
States delegation has conceded mandatory transfer "on
fair and reasonable commercial terms and conditions" to
the Enterprise, but not to individual developing
countries.[46] Spokesmen for the United States
delegation argue that the mandatory transactions can be
commercially fair and reasonable; that technological
innovation can be protected; and that the deep seabed
regime represents a unique situation lacking significant
precedential effects. Some mid- to high-level officials
in the Department of State, however, have indicated that
precedents may be set and that there is thus a need to
have a very carefully worded, fair, and workable Treaty
on these issues.[47]

Congressman John Breaux and other seabed policy analysts argue that the South's fear that mining technology might not be available to the Enterprise or to developing countries under normal conditions is unfounded. Based on discussions with industry and State Department spokesmen, his assessment appears correct. In fact Global Marine Development Incorporated will reportedly be eager to sell such technology (so long as it is not under proprietary restrictions by a company requesting its development) to whomever wants it in the near future. Much of the technology required to manufacture sophisticated seabed mining equipment will be available to all nations (including the Enterprise) from Global Marine Inc. In addition, States that are parties to the Treaty will provide the Authority with funding for the purchase of seabed mining technology. Also, because State and private enterprises seeking licenses would provide the Authority with its choice between two equally attractive mine sites and because most ocean mining technology is site-specific, mining companies would sell their technology to the Authority or developing countries to maximize profit.[48]

The conclusion that mandatory transfer of technology cannot be on fair and reasonable commercial terms and conditions is questionable. The United States delegation has agreed that it could be--at least with regard to the Authority. There may eventually be competition among the corporations in the few nations that have the technology to develop seabed mining operations; this will help provide access to technology for all parties on the open market. If the scale of technology is not profitable, then companies such as Global Marine will not pursue their efforts in that area. They would not be involved in this venture unless they felt a market existed to make a good return on investment.

It is wrong to think that technological innovation cannot be protected. The United States delegation to the Law of the Sea believes that it can be. It is unlikely that there will be adverse commercial consequences inherent in mandatory transfer which would necessarily discourage technological development. If there are research corporations willing to sell their ocean mining know-how, there is absolutely no reason why this should influence other technological developments among the major ocean mining consortia.

It is very likely that mandatory transfer of technology would have significant precedential effects. Only if both the North and South accept it as such, will the deep seabed regime be a unique situation. The Group of 77, though, has repeatedly asserted that mandatory transfer of deep seabed technology is only one aspect of the LDCs right to advanced technology. The Group of 77 stance on technology transfer has been articulated in the negotiations to conclude an International Code of Conduct on

Transfer of technology. The Group of 77 has asserted the following:

> Technology is part of universal human heritage and that all countries have the right to access to technology, in order to improve the standard of living of their peoples.[49]

> Technology transfer is an effective instrument for the establishment of a New International Economic Order.[50]

> An international legally binding instrument is the only form capable of effectively regulating the transfer of technology.[51]

The United States delegation to the Code of Conduct negotiations rejects these positions because capitulation to the Group of 77 would have negative effects on the international sale and the domestic development of technology.

The problem of technology transfer is aggravated by Third World resistance to effective protection of proprietary rights--both in UNCLOS and the Code of Conduct negotiations.[52] The Group of 77's position at UNCLOS III in this area is directed toward a wider goal than just seabed mining technology. What worries American negotiators as well as policy makers in all the developed nations is that a concession by the North in LOS negotiations would be a precedent for future arrangements concerning LDCs' rights to advanced technology. Those in the United States who object to technology transfer concessions made at UNCLOS III believe that acceptance of the Third World position could be very costly for the United States--a nation which relies on the development and sale of technology for a substantial portion of its foreign earnings and its gross national product. Interfutures, a 1979 report by the Organization for Economic Cooperation and Development (OECD), concluded that high technology will play a larger role in the economies of the United States and other highly industrialized nations throughout the 1980s.[53]

In a 1979 informal working paper to members of the National Ocean Industries Association, NOIA president, Charles Matthews listed examples, drawn from "practices firmly established in commercial licensing agreements and transactions in technology transfer," of what he considered to be fair and reasonable commercial terms for ocean mining technology transfer. NOIA does not believe it possible or appropriate to set out in advance what would be fair and reasonable in all circumstances, or for all transactions. Rather, the list compiled represents

examples which, in light of commercial practices in
relevant trades, are generally considered fair and reasonable means to protect the technology being transfered,
to ensure fair compensation to its owner and to protect
the recipient of the technology. In light of these guidelines it is important to remember how "technology" is
defined in the proposed Treaty:

Technology means the equipment and technical
know-how, including manuals, designs, operating
instructions, training and technical advice and
assistance necessary to assemble, maintain and
operate a system for the exploration for and
exploitation of the resources of the Area and the
non-exclusive legal right to use these items for
that purpose.

The eleven provisions which NOIA felt important to
ensure fair and reasonable technology transfer are listed
in Appendix 9. The National Ocean Industries Association
attempted to influence United States technology transfer
policy at UNCLOS III by corresponding directly with
Ambassador Elliot Richardson and other key policy makers
in United States ocean policy. NOIA has more than once
expressed its preferred policy on technology transfer and
asserted that if ocean mining companies are not satisfied
that their interests will be adequately protected, development of a regime for seabed mining may be a "fruitless
academic exercise."

IDEOLOGICAL DIFFERENCES BETWEEN THE FIRST AND THIRD
WORLD NATIONS

Against this background, we can now turn to an
analysis of the major ideological differences between the
First and Third World regarding deep seabed mining and
changes in the international economic system. The debate
at UNCLOS III over an acceptable structure for the control of the deep seabed represents the Conference's own
version of the North-South dialogue. The philosophical
tenets of the Third World's theory of a NIEO are the basis
of discussion regarding the development of deep ocean
minerals. That the negotiations are focused on the
resources of an area of the earth which is beyond the
jurisdiction of any nation, points to the unique dimension
of this dialogue at UNCLOS III. The Conference also opens
up the much larger political issue of the management of
other common resources.
Some Congressmen believe that the debate at UNCLOS
III did not emphasize the traditional NIEO issues such as
increased trade, underwriting Third World projects, loans,
grants, or the types of terms usually associated with the

World Bank or the International Monetary Fund.[54]
Evidence indicates that the position taken by the Group
of 77 at these negotiations, however, includes these
demands. For example, the industrialized nations are
being asked to provide funds and technology to realize a
Third World goal of developing a supra-national Enterprise
for the mining of manganese nodules through an International Seabed Authority. In addition, the Authority
will set the requirements for access to those resources
for private industry from the industrialized nations. It
is not surprising, therefore, that these negotiations have
taken so long to reach final agreement.

There are two major reasons for explaining the long
struggle at the Conference. First, there are radically
different economic ideologies between the industrial
nations that are developing mining technology and the
developing world. Second, there has been a feeling on
the part of most nations at the Conference that the industrial world would continue to delay full scale ocean
mining activities until UNCLOS III reached a successful
conclusion. This last point explains the push for United
States unilateral legislation. The result of such action
was to speed up the negotiations by forcing the Group of
77 to be more realistic in some of its demands. With
respect to the different ideologies represented at the
Conference, it would be misleading to categorize the
struggle as one between capitalism and socialism. This
is so because each country has a different economic mix,
including those within the industrial bloc, and positions
on any given issue are based on a myriad of factors. But
when the industrialized countries and the Group of 77 face
each other the individual differences and similarities of
each state tend to fade as the ideological stance taken
by both sides as a group become more pronounced.

Several key supporters of American unilateral ocean
mining legislation believe that the industrialized
nations, in general, accept the premise that one shares
in the benefits of society largely to the extent that one
shares in the cost. One Congressman, for example, has
suggested that this is fair, and that it is also the way
a nation improves its standard of living: "by investing
in ventures today that will lead to increased national
wealth at a later time."[55] The problem with this perspective is that it tends to exacerbate the North-South
economic inequalities that already exist, i.e. the "haves"
possess the means and capital to invest, while the "have
nots" do not. The goals of the developed and developing
countries at UNCLOS III with respect to the deep seabed
issue are, therefore, fundamentally different. (Possible
areas of agreement and alternative approaches to a comprehensive LOS Treaty are discussed in the next chapter.)

The Group of 77 advocates the establishment of a
unitary structure for the control and management of seabed

FIGURE 1

INTERNATIONAL SEABED AUTHORITY

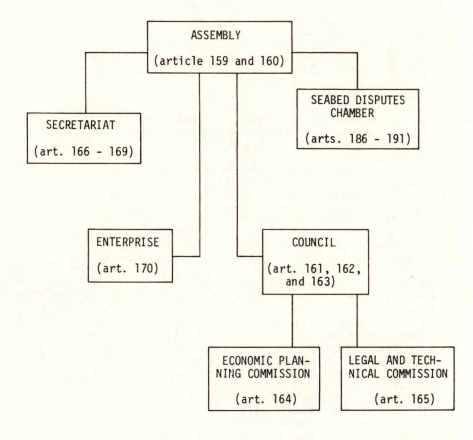

development. The membership of the governing unit of the structure, the International Seabed Authority, is to be based on a one nation, one vote scheme and, thus, would be controlled by the numerically superior developing world. The United States, on the other hand, wants the mineral resources of the deep seabed developed rapidly and efficiently with due regard to the protection of the marine environment and to the interests of other nations. It is deemed important that individual States, and organizations sponsored by States, should have nondiscriminatory and assured access to mining sites, with security of tenure. This view reflects American awareness that rapid and efficient development of the mineral resources of the deep seabed will require the participation of the private mining industry, which has developed the technological capability for the task at a considerable cost.[56] At question is whether that means only those countries with the capability may exploit resources that have been declared the common heritage of mankind, or if the technology should be shared so that the developing countries, with assistance from the industrialized North, will have the opportunity to gain access to ocean minerals and other commons resources in the future. Exploitation should be carried out by both the Enterprise and private or state run ocean mining concerns. The framework for assuring the success of a "joint venture" or "parallel" access is a difficult political issue centered on the make up of the Authority.

The structure of the actual governing body of the International Seabed Authority has remained one of the most difficult negotiating issues between the North and South. A description and analysis of the Authority is therefore needed to more fully understand the ideological nature of the arguments in the negotiations.

The proposed Authority is to be composed of a supreme body known as the Assembly, an executive arm known as the Council with subsidiary specialized organs, and an operating arm known as the Enterprise. In addition, the Authority is to have a Secretariat, to handle administrative matters, and a Seabed Disputes Chamber, which would have judicial power over individual cases between states or between a nation and the Authority. See Figure 1.

The Assembly is to establish the general policies for determining the rights and duties of states in areas beyond national jurisdiction, including (1) electing members of various Authority bodies, (2) establishing subsidiary organs, (3) considering problems related to resource exploitation in the area, and (4) ensuring fair distribution of economic benefits derived from activities in the area. (See Appendix 10, Powers and Functions of the Assembly.)

Members of the Authority are to have one representative in the Assembly, and determinations are to be made under a one nation one vote concept. It is this voting arrangement that has disturbed the United States, because control over Assembly actions are to be in the hands of a two-thirds majority of nations--a majority which would probably consist of nations who consider themselves members of the Third World. This eventuality creates the possibility that actions of the Authority may steer guidelines, as set forth in the Treaty, toward actions which the United States may consider to be inimical to its interests. Owing to the sheer number of developing countries, it would be difficult for the United States to mobilize enough support on key issues in the Assembly; thus the United States would have to look elsewhere within the Authority to have its voice heard--i.e. the Council.

The Council, as the executive body of the international seabed regime, would establish specific policies on activities in the area under international jurisdiction in conformity with the Treaty and general policy guidelines adopted by the supreme organ of the Council--the Economic Planning Commission, the Technical Commission, and the Rules and Regulations Commission. The Council is to play a critical role in regulating the activities of contractors in the area under international jurisdiction. As a prerequisite for a contract either to explore or exploit seabed resources, a contractor would file with the Council a detailed plan of work describing his proposed operations. The Council would then forward the plan to the Legal and Technical Commission for its review.

Council decisions may be considerably influenced by the conclusions of the Legal and Technical Commission. For this reason, there was much concern about the possibility that this Commission would become a political, executive entity rather than an advisory, technical body. The Council would, however, be the final arbiter of contractor plans. If a plan is rejected, all contractor activities must cease. If it is not rejected within sixty days, it is considered approved.

The composition and voting procedures of the Council would therefore be critical in determining the types of activities that may be undertaken by contractors. As outlined in the proposed Treaty, the Council is to be composed of thirty-six members drawn from several interest groups--seabed miners, major importers of minerals found in nodules, major exporters of such minerals, and developing countries--as well as regional representatives. Although the Treaty text specifically calls for three East European seats on the Council, there is no mention of the United States (by name) in any of the categories. The United States, being a major importer and exporter of some of the metals in the nodules as well as a developer of ocean mining technology, falls under several categories for Council membership--but is not guaranteed a seat. The composition of the Council was one of the areas United

States Ambassador Malone raised for re-negotiaton in 1981.
The Group of 77 considers the Council's role to
implement Assembly policies: i.e. to rule on day-to-day
matters. Thus, the primary direction of the members would
be to carry out Assembly policies and only secondarily
would it represent particular economic and regional interests. The developed nations, on the other hand, look
to the Council to counterbalance the Assembly by representing producer and consumer, as well as regional interests. For this reason, the United States and other
Western nations have introduced weighted voting proposals.
Instead of requiring a three-fourths overall majority,
the United States proposed that Council decisions require
concurrent simple majorities in three of the four special
interest categories or four of the five total categories.
The proposal, however, was rejected by the developing
countries who considered the principle of weighted voting
discriminatory and recommended instead that the requirement be reduced to a two-thirds or simple majority.
Assuming an overall majority of one kind or another is
the requirement adopted, the United States and other
developed nations would be confined to blocking actions
for their voice to be heard. If this issue is not resolved, ratification of a possible LOS Treaty by the
United States Senate appears unlikely.

The Enterprise is designed to undertake commercial
exploitation in a manner similar to that of private
corporations or state parties. Partially explored
minesites would be given to the Enterprise and it would
receive technology, transferred at "fair market price,"
to be able to enter into production and to compete effectively. Financing would be made available to the
Enterprise, either directly or through the Authority, to
allow it to enter into production at an early date.

The primary concern of the United States has been to
ensure creation of a parallel system of access to the deep
seabed which would make exploitation of seabed resources
economically feasible for both private contractors and
the Enterprise. The Authority could also turn over one
of the "banked" minesites to developing nations for
exploitation. Thus, seabed resource exploitation would
be open to private contractors and individual states as
well as the Enterprise. With respect to the resources
themselves, this system is workable in that there are
ample opportunities for all who may wish to mine in a
regime of parallel access. Available data indicates that
ocean manganese nodules are sufficiently vast and dis-
persed to support mining operations by multiple parties.

To summarize: the major obstacles to Senate ratification of the LOS agreement are likely to be ideological
and economic in nature, with the two often joined. The
ideological debate has centered on the role of the international seabed area as a "new" area, to be developed on

a basis agreed to by all nations. It has been contended from the early 1970s, that since the area is the "common heritage of mankind," and exploitation has not yet begun, the opportunity should be seized to create the means whereby the area would be used for the benefit of as large a group as possible--particularly for the developing countries.[57] Participants at UNCLOS III have agreed in principle that the exploitation of seabed resources should be carried out in such a way that the LDCs are fully associated with the development of the relevent technology and industrial exploitation and that financial revenues should go to the poorest countries, including those land-locked producers directly affected by ocean mining.

Initial negotiations emphasized that seabed exploitation could help fill the technological gap between developed and developing countries. It was also felt that seabed mining could provide benefits which did not depend, like normal technical assistance, on the economic "bounty" of the rich nations. In later discussions the focus shifted. For the past few years the accent has been put on the realization of the NIEO--the exploitation of an agreed common resource was to proceed on a basis where profit for some was not the guiding principle. One analyst has nicely summarized this developing country viewpoint:

> The matter had to be seen, it was said, in the context of wider change in international economic relations, and hence the argument for exercise of 'control' or 'discretion' by the Authority and its participation in direct operations.[58]

The developed countries--especially those with companies involved in ocean mining--have agreed to some of the points demanded by the Third World.[59] The notion that the deep seabed is the common heritage of mankind has also been agreed to--although the exact meaning and implementation of that concept has yet to be fully agreed upon. Still to be worked out are the means to be used for implementation of the principle and the extent of their application. There is also still a basic difference over ideological premises of the common heritage concept.[60]

It is unlikely that an International Seabed Authority, with a huge bureaucracy and problems of internal politics, will be better able to "share the wealth" of the seabed than a simple tax collected by a less complex Authority from the revenues of ocean mining consortia. The money would then be distributed to the poor and most affected nations. Similar tax structures exist in many countries host to multinational mining companies. The major difference would be that the recipients of the money generated would be much more broadly based. The amount of the tax should be carefully set to ensure that mining companies still have an incentive to invest and carry out operations.

The attempts by the Group of 77 to create a favorable International Seabed Authority and Enterprise for the mining of ocean nodules are very understandable. Both political/ideological and economic arguments have been used by the Group of 77 to achieve their goals. Unfortunately the political/ideological elements of the Group when acting as a body tend to outweigh the more calm, rational and economic self-interest approach of many, if not most, individual Third World countries.

POLITICAL AND ECONOMIC CHANGES IN THE INTERNATIONAL ENVIRONMENT

The international political and economic context within which the New International Economic Order was proposed has changed a great deal over the past decade. It is important to understand these changes so that we can predict what, if any, consequences they may have on LOS-type negotiations between the First and Third World over commons resource management. First, positions on policies vis-a-vis the developing countries within the United States have shifted. Because of continued stagflation (stagnant economic growth in a time of inflation) and the prospect of generally poor economic conditions in the technologically advanced nations, American policy makers have lost most of the interest they may have had in the cost-raising measures of the NIEO. In fact, the main hope of officials in the United States Administration with a pro-developing outlook, is now to prevent new barriers to the LDCs from being erected which would restrict their exports to the United States--not the dismantling of old ones.

Another important change concerns ideological shifts within the United States. These have undercut much of the philosophical basis for the massive American resource transfers which were an integral part of the NIEO proposals. Many supporters of LDCs in the United States have belatedly decided that it is important for Third World aspirations, and for American relations with the Third World, to reduce developing-country dependence. There is also recognition of the inherent inconsistency between a large United States developmental role and a reduction in LDC dependence. As the reality of the "aid as imperialism" has become clear, the position of Senate liberals has moved closer to the position of Daniel Moynihan of "benign neglect."[61] The change in American political values toward a more conservative pro-business attitude reflected in the 1980 Presidential victory of Ronald Reagan and the Republican control of the Senate has already raised hopes in many Third World nations. Most governments in the lesser developed countries are now actively encouraging MNCs to open operations because of their capacity for investment and export promotion. In broader terms, however, the position taken by the United States during the Carter Administration and the even more conservative stance of President Reagan hardly provides the political basis for a vigorous American commitment in support of the NIEO proposals.

Positions have also changed within the Group of 77. Different views have developed as the higher-income LDCs, such as Brazil and South Korea, have done better in surmounting economic difficulties than have the poorer ones. The issue of an international debt moratorium has brought out the differing positions between these two groups of developing countries. Lack of unanimity, as compared with the 1972-1976 period, has also appeared as individual LDCs have scrambled for international investment and export markets. The major splits within the Group of 77 at UNCLOS III have been between coastal and land-locked states. All agree as a group, however, of the need for a strong Authority--despite domestic economies that will not benefit significantly for many years by having the potential revenues generated from ocean mining and the minerals themselves made available to them.

It has become increasingly clear to oil-importing LDCs that the function of the NIEO issue in international diplomacy is now different from what they first expected. Given the present tenuous state of the world economy--particularly among the developed countries--the prospects for carrying through anything like a comprehensive NIEO program are very doubtful, if they were ever really seriously considered by the developed countries. It also seems doubtful, that even if there is an eventual LOS Treaty creating an Enterprise as it is currently envisioned, the lot of Third World countries will significantly, if at all, improve for several decades. But efforts must be made toward that goal. The various parts of the Treaty text taken individually would not be satisfactory to individual countries, but taken as a whole the Treaty would seem to be generally acceptable--including for the United States once the last few remaining issues were worked out. The developing countries had many issues at stake in the UNCLOS III negotiations; such as the definition of the continental shelf and the international seabed, as well as various resource and navigation issues.62

Increased political, economic, and social disruption in the Third World can only create future problems for the entire world community. UNCLOS III will be long remembered for attempting to achieve two broad goals beyond a comprehensive ocean treaty. These are its goals of restructuring the world economic balance and of developing an international mechanism for sharing of the global commons.

FOOTNOTES

Chapter 4

1. Edward Miles, "The Structure and Effects of the Decision Process in the Seabed Committee and the Third United Nations Conference on the Law of the Sea," International Organization 31 (Spring 1977): 159-234. See the entire issue, which is devoted to UNCLOS III.

2. Ibid.

3. Interviews with Arthur Kobler, Ray Meyers, and Milt Drucker of the Department of State. Interviews were made in March and October of 1979, and June 1980 and March 1981 in Washington, D.C.

4. Richard Darman, "The Law of the Sea: Rethinking U.S. Interests," Foreign Affairs 56 (January 1978): 373-395.

5. Arthur Kobler, "Government Treatment of Ocean Mining Investment," in Judith Kildow, ed., Deepsea Mining: Selected papers from a series of seminars held at MIT in December 1979 and January 1979, (Cambridge: MIT Press, 1980).

6. M.C.W. Pinto is Ambassador, Special Representative of Sri Lanka to the Third United Nations Conference on the Law of the Sea and Chairman of the Delegation. See, M.C.W. Pinto, "The Developing Countries and the Exploitation of the Deep Seabed," Columbia Journal of World Business 15, no. 4. (Winter 1980): 30-41. Also see, Declaration on the Establishment of the New International Economic Order, UN General Assembly resolution 3201 of the Sixth Special Session adopted May 1, 1974.

7. United Nations, UNCTAD, Final Act and Report (Proceedings of the U.N. Conference on Trade and Development, Geneva, 23 March-16 June 1964), p. 1.

8. United Nations, Centre for Economic and Social Information, Problems of Raw Materials and Development: Declaration and Programme of Action (Declaration CES 1.E21 adopted by the Sixth Special Session for the U.N. General Assembly, 1 May 1974).

9. U.N. Environment Programme, The Cocoyoc Declaration (Declaration A/C 2/292 adopted by the participants in the UNEP/UNCTAD Symposium on "Patterns of Resource Use, Environment and Development Strategies," Cocoyoc, Mexico, 8-12 October 1974).

10. United Nations, Charter of Economic Rights and Duties (OPI/542-75-38308), February 1975).

11. Problems of Raw Materials and Development, U.N. General Assembly, 1974.

12. James W. Howe, "Power in the Third World," Journal of International Affairs 29 (1975): 113-127.

13. Ibid.

14. Ibid.

15. Patsy T. Mink, Assistant Secretary of State, Bureau of Oceans, International Environmental and Scientific Affairs, in the "Forward" to the Law of the Sea X, San Diego Law Review 15 (April 1978): 357-364.

16. Ibid.

17. Richard Darman, Foreign Affairs 56.

18. These connections will be more closely examined in chapter 6 of this study.

19. See Arvid Pardo and Elisabeth Mann Borgese, The New International Economic Order and the Law of the Sea, Occassional Paper No. 4, International Ocean Institute, Center for the Study of Democratic Institutions, Santa Barbara, California, 1976.

20. Elisabeth Mann Borgese, "A Constitution for the Oceans: Comments and Suggestions Regarding Part XI of the Informal Composite Negotiating Text," San Diego Law Review 15 (1978): 371, 375-76.

21. Robert L. Friedheim and William J. Durch, "The International Seabed Resources Agency Negotiations and the New International Economic Order," International Organization 31 (Spring 1977): 343-384.

21. Ibid. p. 352.

23. These points are discussed Friedheim and Durch, International Organization 31.

24. Informal Composite Negotiating Text (ICNT), articles 144, 151 (8), annex III para. 4; Alternative Texts, articles 144, 150, annex II, paras. 4 and 5.

25. ICNT, article 150 (I) (g) (B).

26. ICNT, article 150 (I) (g) (A).

27. ICNT, annex II, para. 5 (I).

28. ICNT, article 153 (6).

29. ICNT, articles 169 (4), 173, annex II, para. 7, annex III, para. 10.

30. ICNT, article 184, annex III, para. 11 (e).

31. Ibid, annex II, para. 4 (j) (i).

32. ICNT, article 150 (I) (g) (c).

33. John Breaux, "The Diminishing Prospects for an Acceptable Law of the Sea Treaty," Virginia Journal of International Law 19 (Winter 1979): 257-297.

34. See for example, Nathaniel H. Leff, "Technology Transfer and U.S. Foreign Policy: The Developing Countries," ORBIS 23, (Spring 1979): 145-165. See also, Journal of International Affairs 33 (Spring/Summer 1979): entire issue.

35. Leff, ORBIS 23.

36. See Simon Teitel, "On the Concept of Appropriate Technology for Less-Industrialized countries," Technological Forecasting and Social Change 11, (April 1978): 349-369.

37. Leff, ORBIS 23.

38. United Nations, A/Res, 2749 (XXV) 17 December 1970.

39. Principle 9 reads: "The regime shall, inter alia, provide for the orderly and safe development and rational management of the area and its resources and for expanding opportunities in the use thereof and ensure the equitable sharing by States in the benefits derived therefrom..." Principle 10 states: "...States shall provide international cooperation in scientific research exclusively for peaceful purposes:...(c) By cooperation in measure to strengthen research capabilities of developing

countries, including the participation of their nationals in research programs...."

40. The ICNT mentioned the developing countries as the principal beneficiaries of the transfer of technology.

41. United Nations, Honduras Doc. A/Conf. 62/SR 25; Morocco Doc. A/Conf. 62/SR 28; Chairman of the Committee I, Paul Engo (Cameroon) Doc. A/Conf. 62/D, 1/L 16; opposed by France in general Doc. A/C. 2/SR 1650 para. 8.

42. United Nations, A/Res. 3281 (XXIX) 12 December 1974; Articles 8 to 13 emphasize the demand for a higher degree of organization in the field of international ecomomic relations.

43. Henry Kissinger, Department of State Bulletin LXXV: 395; Edward Miles, "An Interpretation of the Caracas Proceedings," in Edward Miles, ed., Law of the Sea: Conference outcomes and problems of implementation: Proceedings, Law of the Sea Institute, Tenth annual meeting, June 22-25, 1976, (Cambridge, Mass.: Ballinger, 1977).

44. C. Rudiger Wolfrum, University of Bonn, "Transfer of Technology," in Alternatives in Deepsea Mining, Proceedings of the Workshop on Alternatives in Deepsea Mining, December 1978, Ka'u, Hawaii, Law of the Sea Institute Workshop, Scott Allen and John P. Craven, eds.

45. United States Congress, House, Committee on Merchant Marine and Fisheries, Hearings before a subcommittee of the Committee on Merchant Marine and Fisheries, Oceanography Miscellaneous Part 2, 95th Cong., 1st and 2nd sess., 1977/1978.

46. Ibid, pages 57, 60-62, 125.

47. Ibid, at 61, 88, 89, 124.

48. John Breaux, Virginia Journal of International Law 19, op. cit.

49. United Nations Conference on Trade and Development (UNCTAD), Report of the Intergovernmental Group of Experts on an International Code of Conduct on Transfer of Technology on its Fifth Session, Annex 1, U.N. Doc. TD/AC. 1/15 (1978, preamble, art. 2).

50. Ibid, preamble, art. 4.

51. Ibid, preamble, art. 13.

52. John Breaux, <u>Virginia Journal of International Law</u> 19, op. cit.

53. Interfutures, <u>Facing the Future: Mastering the Probable and Managing the Unpredictable</u>, (Paris: Organization for Economic Cooperation and Development, 1979).

54. John Murphy, "The Politics of Manganese Nodules: International Considerations and Domestic Legislation," <u>San Diego Law Review</u> 16 (April 1979): 542. Special Law of the Sea issue.

55. Ibid, p. 543.

56. Ibid, p. 544.

57. See, Michael Hardy, "The Implications of alternative solutions for regulating the exploitation of seabed minerals," <u>International Organization</u> 31 (Spring 1977): 313-342.

58. Ibid, p. 329.

59. The United States, United Kingdom, West Germany, Japan, Canada, the Netherlands, Belgium, and Italy.

60. Hardy, <u>International Organization</u> 31 p. 329.

61. See, Nathaniel Leff, "Changes in the American Climate Affecting the NIEO Proposals," <u>The World Economy</u> 2 (January 1979): 91-98. Also see, Roger D. Hansen, <u>Beyond the North-South Stalemate</u>, (New York: McGraw-Hill, 1979).

62. Hasjim Djalal, "The Developing Countries and the Law of the Sea Conference," <u>Columbia Journal of World Business</u> 15 no. 4. (Winter 1980): 22-29. Dr. Djalal is Minister/ Deputy Chief of Mission at the Indonesian Embassy in Washington, D.C., and a Vice Chariman of the Indonesian Delegation to the Law of the Sea.

5
Complex Interdependence
and the Political Process
of Ocean Politics

INTRODUCTION

What is the nature of international ocean resource management and what role do international organizations have in shaping national ocean policy? When considering these questions it becomes evident why some experts in the United States charged with formulating a national ocean policy have examined alternatives to a comprehensive Law of the Sea Treaty. Due to the complexities of multi-level interactions between nation states (e.g. interdependence) on economic, political, military, and resource issues, it is possible that a ratified comprehensive LOS Treaty will not be attained until the late 1980s. Therefore, alternative regime structures should be considered and perhaps put into operation to ensure the orderly development and use of ocean resources until an acceptable treaty enters into force for the United States. After examining the role of interdependence in ocean politics this chapter will evaluate some possible alternatives to a comprehensive Treaty.

THE INTERDEPENDENT NATURE OF INTERNATIONAL
OCEAN RESOURCE MANAGEMENT

To more fully understand the politics of deep seabed mining it is necessary to examine the role of interdependence in ocean resource issues. Even more than monetary politics, ocean politics in much of the twentieth century has conformed very closely to Robert Keohane and Joseph Nye's criteria of "complex interdependence."[1] Three conditions have to be met to satisfy this condition. These are: (1) a minor role for military force; (2) the presence of non-hierarchical, multiple issues; and (3) multiple channels of contact among societies.[2] By examining each of these factors we will be better able to gauge the degree of interdependence in ocean politics.

The role of force is always in the background in ocean negotiations. Of the three conditions Keohane and

133

Nye establish for "complex interdependence," the expanding role of force in ocean issues suggests that their model may not hold as strongly as they suggest in explaining international ocean policy formation.

The United States could, of course, use the Navy to defend deep sea mining operations or scientific research studies--but force must be weighed against other sources of influence peculiar to conference diplomacy, broad political goals, and economics. This is particularly so in an era of North-South conflict and debate over systemic economic structures and balances. The use of force, and the United States' negotiating strategies at international conferences on resource management, will become even more delicate as the full importance of resource access and ownership is realized.

The conclusions to be drawn about trends in the use of force in the oceans are complex. The oceans remain strategically important, which affects bargaining on issues of ocean space and resources. Military force, for example, continues to directly affect these issues, although there has been a marked change in its use. Traditionally, great powers have freely used their navies to reinforce regimes. In recent years there has been an increase in the use of force by small states. The growing number of nations that use various types of force has eroded the established free seas regime by extending national jurisdiction, and is well illustrated by the now more common occurrence of small countries taking on past naval giants. The "Cod War" of the mid 1970s between Iceland and the United Kingdom over British fishing rights and economic zones off the coast of Iceland serves as a prime example.

According to Keohane and Nye force is often useful in particular circumstances, but it is not the predominant factor determining outcomes--except, of course, in times of outright war. There are major exceptions to that observation, however. The seizure of United States tuna boats off the west coast of South America in the early 1970s is an example of the use of force (by Peru) leading to a change in ocean resource policy. The United States government did not recognize Peru's claims of a 200-mile fishing and economic zone. That policy was changed to a large degree because of Peru's active use of force in detaining United States boats until large fines were paid for fishing in its waters. The United States tuna industry suffered major financial losses because of restricted access and large fines. In addition, the Soviet naval build-up, which began on a large scale in the mid-1970s, has caused worry in the U.S. Department of Defense about the security of different ocean regions. With an increasing Soviet naval presence and the likelihood of greater American efforts to check that growth over the next ten years, complex interdependence may explain

less than pure power politics in understanding the role
of force in international ocean management.

The ocean as a political arena has <u>not</u> exhibited a
consistent <u>hierarchy of issues</u>. Coastal interests, for
example, were strong and had substantial international
influence during the 1930s and 40s which led to the 1945
Truman proclamations. And although security concerns were
dominant during the Cold War, the hierarchy of goals has
been challenged by new issues that different actors regard
as more important. The Navy's desire for minimal constraints on mobility (e.g. narrow state coastal jurisdiction), for example, has not always had higher priority
than economic interest in exploiting ocean resources or
ecological concerns about pollution.[3]

Over the past ten to fifteen years fishing, oil,
gas, shipping, environmental, military, mineral, and
political ocean issues have become more closely interrelated. As more government agencies have become involved
in ocean policy formulation there has been a large
increase in the number of agencies concerned with solving
ocean related problems. In 1968 for example, the
Interagency Task Force on the Law of the Sea consisted of
three departments: Defense, Interior, and State. By 1975,
thirteen agencies were involved. The two major reasons
for the growth and linkage of issues are technological
change and international regime change. The growth in
the number of agencies involved in ocean issues is an
indication of the many and varied interests of United
States ocean policy. A much greater appreciation of the
value of ocean resources has steadily increased over the
past decade.

Increased Administration and Congressional concern
has led to many new pieces of legislation directly tied
to ocean use and resources. For instance, an Executive
Order, in 1970, established the National Oceanic and
Atmospheric Administration. In 1972, the Federal Water
Pollution Control Act was amended to include coastal
waters, the Marine Protection, Research, and Sanctuaries
Act was enacted to establish a regulatory system for the
dumping of materials in the ocean and the marine sanctuary
program, and the Coastal Zone Management Act was signed
into law. Additional Acts signed into law throughout the
1970s included the Marine Mammal Protection Act, the
Fishery Conservation and Management Act, the Outer
Continental Shelf Lands Act Amendments, the Deep Seabed
Hard Minerals Resources Act, the Ocean Thermal Energy
Conversion Act, the Deepwater Port Act, and a number of
other single purpose laws designed to deal with ocean
resource problems.[4]

Another criteria of complex interdependence is
<u>multiple channels of contact</u>. Before 1945, the major non-
governmental interests concerned with issues were
fishermen and shipping firms; the latter being organized

transnationally into liner conferences and other cartel-like arrangements. Since 1945, however, multi-national oil companies and mining firms, as well as transnational groups devoted to science, environmental regulation, and world order, have joined traditional shippers and fishermen both in using the oceans and in making political demands on governments. This has resulted in a rapid growth and diffusion of transnational activity in the oceans.[5]

From 1946 to 1966, transnational activity became more extensive. Oil companies, for example, worked through their lawyers' membership in the International Law Association, which influenced the International Law Commission's work on draft conventions for the 1958 Law of the Sea Conference. Also during this period, scientists organized transnationally in the Scientific Committee on Oceans Research (SCOR) and successfully pressed their governments to create the International Oceanographic Commission (IOC) to coordinate large-scale oceanographic research. The United Nations has also worked transnationally to promote a stronger international regime.

There has been even more political activity by transnational organizations since 1967. Oil and mining companies, for instance, have lobbied in various countries for their specific policy preferences. In addition, the International Law Association has taken stands very close to the positions of these two industries. Furthermore, multi-national ocean mining consortia have been formed in order to broaden their political support in major countries as well as to spread their economic risks. The similar nature of ocean mining legislation in the United States, Great Britain, France, and West Germany is a good example of multiple channels of influence in action. Scientists, too, have lobbied to influence national and international ocean policy goals. Also, groups promoting goals of world order, such as the Trilateral Commission, have often organized unofficial conferences to disseminate their views.[6] Table 1 summarizes the changes in complex interdependence that have occurred for ocean issues from the 1920s through the 1970s.

In sum, two aspects of Keohane and Nye's "complex interdependence" model accurately reflect conditions in ocean resource politics: multiple issues and multiple contacts and levels of influence. The role of military force, however, frequently plays more than a minimum role in determining the outcome of ocean use and resource issues. Over the past two decades, multiple issues and multiple channels of contact among societies have increased. As a result, there have been increases in: (1) politicization; (2) bargaining linkages among issues; (3) opportunities for small states; and (4) involvement of international organizations in ocean issues. For the past

TABLE 1

Changes in Complex Interdependence for Oceans Issues, 1920-1970s

Dimensions of complex interdependence	How closely does the situation correspond to the complex interdependence model in the 1970s?	Have the patterns changed over time toward the complex interdependece model?
Negligible role of force	Weak approximation to complex interdependence; role of force still significant	Yes, with qualifications: Now used more by the weak nations, but force is not effective on many issues, especially for the great powers
Lack of hierachy among issues	Close approximation to complex interdependence; hierarchy difficult to maintain	Yes
Multiple channels to contact	Close approximation to complex interdependence	Yes

Source: Robert O. Keohane and Joseph S. Nye, Power and Interdependence, (Boston: Little, Brown, and Co., 1977).

twenty years in particular, interdependence has increased as a result both of greater societal interdependence and of increasing awareness of indirect interdependence. Problems of interdependence in ocean use have been especially noticeable when unilateral claims of jurisdiction or control have been made. Consequently, the political process has become increasingly complex, with more government agencies involved, and more opportunities for transgovernmental relations.[7]

THE ROLE OF INTERNATIONAL ORGANIZATIONS IN SHAPING OCEAN POLICY

There has been a marked increase over the past two decades in the number of newly independent Third World nations and their participation at international conferences on economic and resources issues. These states have demanded new means for dealing with North-South economic inbalances (e.g. commodities agreements, loan deferals, structuring ocean resource regimes, and transfers of technology) which affect both developed and developing countries. There have also been several attempts in the last ten years by global-oriented "trilateralists" and others in the United States, to maintain world harmony, and passivity in the Third World, while insuring continued prosperity in the industrially advanced states. One of the mechanisms central to this task has been to include key Third World nations in international conferences devised to negotiate the more radical demands of the developing nations and to formulate new acceptable structures for an increasingly interdependent world.

Twenty years ago, basic economic and resource decisions were made by a handful of industrially advanced nations with no real concern for the non-developed states. At that time there was no need for including developing countries in systemic related negotiations. The ties with European colonial countries existed, but the degree of economic interdependency was still low. With the increase in interdependency and newly independent, ideologically vocal, Third World states in the 1960s, international organizations and conferences such as the United Nations and the Law of the Sea Conference have become major influences in determining resource access and Third World cohesiveness. Consequently, multilateral conferences have frequently witnessed several demands from the Third World for economic and technology transfer concessions from the developed to the developing nations. The influential role of the Latin American, African and Asian groups at UNCLOS III is testimony to this situation. Group cohesiveness at these conferences, as exhibited by the Group of 77, has also frequently become a much more important source of influence than country capabilities or global status. This has been especially true in the negotiations for an International Seabed Authority.

Because there has been an increase in the number of ideologically motivated Third World countries participating in international conferences, the bargaining position of the the United States has been weakened in international forums. The loss of power to dictate terms is well illustrated by the many concessions the United States has made on deep seabed mining at UNCLOS III to the Group of 77. When that Conference began in 1974 the full importance of resource ownership was just beginning to be fully appreciated. As that appreciation increased, the American concessions appeared more and more a mistake in purely economic terms.

Another aspect of international organizations is that subgovernmental agencies' interests are, at times, more like those within another country than those of competing domestic agencies. For example, the agencies involved with securing access to the deep seabed in the United States, France, Great Britain, Japan, and West Germany frequently have more in common than do those agencies and their respective counterparts in agencies seeking to ensure passage through international straits. At international conferences, personnel assigned to agencies promoting deep seabed mining work closely with their foreign counterparts in an attempt to obtain the most open access for ocean miners.

UNCLOS III and other international conferences have provided the physical contact and legitimacy for some of these potential transgovernmental coalitions to become active. Keohane and Nye claim that American fallback positions in bargaining were often disclosed in advance at UNCLOS III negotiations. There had been, for instance, lobbying by the United States Interior Department and oil company officials with LDCs in favor of broad coastal state jurisdiction over the continental shelf (contrary to then official United States policy) at the Geneva sessions of the Seabed Committee.[8] In addition to lobbying governments at international conferences, transnational oil and mining companies have frequently formed joint ventures with partners from several countries to affect governments' perceptions and definitions of their interests in new resource policy areas. An obvious example of this was the success of American and British oil companies in the Middle East up to 1973 in influencing the oil policies of the OPEC nations. Another example is the success of American mining companies in several Latin American countries (such as Chile) up to the early 1970s, in influencing both resource policy and perhaps the outcome of attempted government coups.

Of major importance in coming to terms with the highly interdependent nature of international ocean resource politics, then, is the need to appreciate the role

played by international organizations. The international
organization model offers an analytical framework for
understanding the complexities involved in international
resource management by focusing on the role and significance of international actors and organizations and their
cross-national interdependencies. The role of international organizations in the determination of access to,
and ownership of, resources beyond land-based sovereignty
may increase in the future. If international organizations are not used for negotiating differences, then there
will be increasing instances of individual nations
settling their resource or economic differences by military means.

The likelihood of the Northern states successfully
working together to ensure access to resources is not very
high. For example, during the Middle East oil embargo of
1973/74, and the years which have followed, the OECD
countries have been unable to plan and operationalize a
united stance against OPEC political pressure because of
the cartel's monopoly of oil supply to the western
industrialized states. The major oil companies, however,
did effectively work out distributional problems of the
1973/74 oil boycott by reallocating oil while at sea. In
response to this successful effort the OPEC states are
developing their own oil tanker networks, and are
insisting more frequently on shipping in their own
"bottoms." A future boycott would be more effective
because the OPEC countries would control the resource and
a greater percentage of its shipment/trade.

On the one hand the technologically advanced
nations of the North have been attempting to negotiate
resource policy in different international forums--both
official and unofficial. On the other hand, individual
nation states are finding such negotiations and international organizations inadequate in providing guarantees
for resource supply. They are therefore pursuing bilateral arrangements with land-based mineral supplying
states. Mindful of the dynamics of international organizations in explaining the United States' concessions at
UNCLOS III, policy planners should better understand
potentially similar negotiating advantages and pitfalls
for determining other resource commons access.

During the process of multinational negotiations
at international organizations, certain trends have
emerged which have troubling implications for other
problems on the global agenda.[9] The first has been an
erosion of "global-interest" and "international-interest"
themes in favor of more specific "special-interest" and
"national-interest" proposals. This is well illustrated
by the ever-expanding territorial claims of coastal
states. Because this trend has been legitimized in the
proposed Law of the Sea Treaty the original theme of the
"common heritage of mankind," which was based on the

concept of narrow territorial waters and narrow national economic zones, has been all but lost to the national and special-interest scramble for greater access to the resources of the ocean.[10]

A second trend concerns the continuing conflict between developed and developing countries. The degree of LDC distrust of United States foreign policy initiatives has become very strong within organizations designed for negotiating international issues. As a result, initiatives of the United States are frequently rejected automatically by the developing states--which, as at UNCLOS III, have acted as a remarkably solid unit on many issues. Furthermore, many LDCs with coastal waters abundant with fisheries and continental margins rich in minerals have successfully exploited the developing countries' distrust of United States policy initiatives. These Machiavellian LDCs have grievously injured the common heritage principle.

But UNCLOS III has also demonstrated a third trend: the tenative nature of Third World cohesion. Many times the Group of 77 alliance has been stressed to the breaking point over several issues. This was particularly so over the questions of the right of land-locked and shelf-locked Third World states to some of the benefits of other developing states' coastal economic zones.

A fourth trend, implicit in the first three, concerns the extraordinary difficulties of reaching optimal solutions, or any solution for that matter, to the problem of international ocean resource management. UNCLOS III has made clear the difficulties inherent in a conference where over 150 countries are attempting to negotiate an international issue with hundreds of distinct sub-issues. It has also demonstrated several problems with the present mode of international negotiations. For instance, domestic interest groups frequently formed both national and transnational alliances to support, modify, or defeat national positions on specific issues. As in all foreign policy issues, it is therefore necessary to reconsider the linkages between domestic interest groups, national governments, and the process of multilateral diplomacy in general. There have been too many issues and interests at UNCLOS III for it to have finished its work in less time. Given a less ambitious undertaking, not only would the results have been quicker, but probably also better for the United States and a new acceptable ocean regime.

Despite the limitations of international organizations, they do offer hope that conflict can be reduced by offering the opportunity to discuss issues of increasing international interdependence in a global forum. Governments of all nations will be looking closely at the success or failure of the proposed Law of the Sea Treaty process.

ALTERNATIVES TO A COMPREHENSIVE LAW OF THE SEA TREATY

The political dynamics of international organizations and the increasing amount of interdependence between states on numerous policy issues surrounding deep seabed mining and ocean resource management in general suggest that a comprehensive Law of the Sea Treaty may not emerge for several years. It would therefore be helpful to evaluate Treaty alternatives and possible interim arrangements that have been suggested by policy analysts over the past five years.

The main goal of these alternatives (some of which offer different structures within the proposed LOS Treaty framework) has been to attain the best possible ocean use framework for the United States. Unfortunately, what is best for one nation--even the United States--is not always in the best interests of the international community as a whole. Consequently, the long-term interests of the United States would not be served if some of the alternatives discussed here were implemented in such a way that caused a threat to world or regional order. This is particularly so for United States-Third World relations.

Maintaining friendly ties with Third World countries would be made even more difficult if, for political reasons, the OPEC countries put pressure on the United States and its industrially advanced allies to make concessions to the Group of 77 on the issue of international resource commons management. But given the varied political, economic, and ideological differences between the developing oil exporting countries and other less developed countries, it is unlikely that a significantly unified effort could succeed in putting pressure on the United States to make major shifts in its commons resource policies. If a viable international legal regime for the use of ocean space and resources is really the goal of United States policy, then the various alternatives offered can be seen as possible tools towards reaching a working international comprehensive agreement-- not as absolute alternatives to it.

In order to properly assess the alternatives it is necessary to understand the objectives sought by the United States. There are two basic goals: enhancement of world order and protection of United States economic security interests. Essentially, enhancing world order means securing a stable and predictable regime governing ocean transit and the exploitation of ocean resources. A regime of this nature should also help minimize conflict over fisheries jurisdiction and the control of ocean pollution. A stable and predictable regime that the United States and its industrially advanced allies might create should help ensure environmental controls and open access to the ocean's resources beyond a nation's territorial or economic jurisdiction. Additionally, it should allow for rational future planning of the oceans, since under stable conditions expectations about future conduct are more likely to be realized.

A deep seabed mining regime that was limited to six or seven industrially advanced nations would not ensure world order. In fact, the likelihood of potentially volatile disputes would increase between those nations within the regime framework and those outside it. Therefore, the first task of American ocean policy makers is to work for an acceptable Law of the Sea Treaty. If that is not possible then effort should be directed at the creation of a limited treaty--either within or outside the auspices of the United Nations.

Of equal importance for the assurance of world order is the protection of United States security and economic interests. This objective is not questioned. What is open for debate is a definition of the national interest. Is the public interest regarding international resources of the oceans the same as the national interest in terms of economic and national security? Security interests include both physical security from external attack and protection of coastal and marine interests from impairment by pollution, for example. Economic interests include the extraction of living and nonliving marine resources and of various forms of energy from adjacent waters.

Both security and economic interests extend beyond the coastal waters of the United States (and any economic zone over which it has jurisdiction) to the protection of naval mobility necessary for the implementation of American foreign policy. The influence of ocean mining companies in economic areas thus frequently becomes entwined with the broader question of international security. This type of interdependence means that protection of national economic and security interests has both global and parochical components. Because national interests are often cited as reasons for the United States position on ocean mining and other resource related policies it is crucial to question just how those national interests are determined. Table 2 points out the major domestic and foreign policy interests of the United States pertaining to ocean mining.

The best way to achieve access goals for ocean resources through alternatives to an LOS Treaty will vary according to the particular resource in question. For example, an alternative that is considered optimal with respect to securing supplies of seabed mineral resources may be politically or economically infeasible when applied to protection of distant-water fishing interests. Thus, the basic practical alternative to a Treaty for the United States appears to be limited to the following.[11] The United States could acquiesce in all unilateral, bilateral, and multilateral regimes established by other

TABLE 2

Ocean Mining: Major Domestic and Foreign Policy Interests
of the United States

Domestic

(1) Secure supply of strategic mineral resources obtainable
     from manganese nodules

(2) Assure access to the deep seabed for American-based
     ocean mining companies

(3) Maintain American technological advantage in ocean re-
     search and mining

Foreign

(1) Maintain world order

(2) Obtain an international legal framework for the uses
     and resource exploitation of the oceans

(3) Support geopolitically important and resource-rich
     nations of the North and South

nations or groups of nations.[12] Or, the United States could, in order to avoid the adverse effects of acquiescence, use military force to assert its ocean policy objectives. Alternatively, the United States or its citizens could negotiate for, or purchase from other nations or groups of nations, the authority to conduct certain activities where a regime established by others conflicts with national policy objectives. The negotiation or purchase could occur at either the governmental or private level.[13] Another alternative would be for the United States to create bilateral and multilateral arrangements with affected or like-minded nations to achieve its security and economic objectives. The rationale for entering into such arrangements would be to solve immediate problems such as boundary or fishery conservation matters, and to serve as models or catalysts for the development of new international law. Or, as a variant of the domestic legislative action already taken, the United States might simply proceed to make whatever uses of the marine environment it feels are in its interests--for example, it might initiate deep seabed mining--and determine subsequent courses of action in response to the reactions of other nations. Finally, there is the possibility of a flag of convenience option which would establish a United States-owned mining operation in a willing small state.

With respect to seabed mining, the commencement of extractive activities would appear at first glance to be a viable option. But action of this sort does pose international legal problems. It is likely, for example, that an international court would hold the resources of the deep seabed to be subject to the 1970 United Nations moratorium on ocean mining in international waters.[14] Courts of the industrially advanced nations with interests in seabed mining would probably declare ocean mining legal. If the United States and other reciprocating states (i.e. states that have passed ocean mining legislation or laws with frameworks similar to the American), came to agreements for site location and other controls, then it is unlikely that the efforts of a Third World legal deterrent to ocean mining would carry much real weight.[15] If, on the other hand, international courts held that there should be a moratorium on deep seabed mining until there was an international agreement, the industrial ocean mining states might decide to wait. Because the international courts do not have power to enforce their decisions it is unlikely that they would have much impact on ocean mining by the industrial states if those nations wanted to mine. But it would be in the long-term interests of all states to abide by an international court's decision in order to help maintain some semblance of law and order in international relations. It is uncertain, however, the extent to which international courts would get involved with ocean mining disputes between nations in international waters.

It is possible that the practices established during the conduct of mining operations limited to the like-minded nations prior to the coming into force of an acceptable comprehensive treaty could form the basis for a workable legal regime outlined in the LOS Treaty. The United States ocean mining legislation is written so that in the event of Senate ratification of the Treaty, the Treaty would take precedence over the legislation. If a Treaty does not enter into force for the United States, then the legislation would provide an excellent framework for an ocean mining regime with reciprocating states. From a purely economic perspective, such an arrangement would be attractive to the ocean mining industry and the United States government. Politically, many problems would arise between the Group of 77 and the individual countries involved in mining operations. If the mining were to be carried out in a nation's exclusive economic zone there would be minimal political or legal objections. Since most nodules are located in international waters, however, the impetus will be to consistently pressure for mining rights beyond the 200-mile EEZ.

In the absence of a widely accepted, comprehensive Treaty, there are a number of alternatives which, if used together and where most appropriate on specific issues, could provide the framework for a reasonably stable regime for the oceans. United States security and economic interests could be sufficiently protected through a combination of unilateral action/domestic legislation, limited treaties, purchase of rights, and the "occasional application of force." (Even the occasional use of force, however, would prove increasingly costly over time.)

Alternative solutions for regulating the exploitation of seabed minerals have consequences for both non-agreement and acceptance of an LOS Treaty. For example, unilateral action by industrialized states with respect to the seabed, unlike resource exploitation in a 200-mile EEZ, would run counter to the view which prevails at UNCLOS III and would provoke a strong political reaction by the Group of 77. If the American action had not been revised to prohibit commercial exploitation until January 1, 1988, it is possible that the Group of 77 would have decided to adopt an international treaty among themselves, embodying their approach in its full form. This would have created two sets of legal norms for the exploitation of the ocean's resources.[16] Such action would create enormous problems for effective management of all uses of the ocean in international, and possibly national, waters.

If the Treaty does not enter into force the restraints on coastal states within their economic zones (EEZs) would probably be eroded. If that happened there would be increased pressure to claim the economic zone as

territorial sea--an area in which coastal states' rights
were paramount in all respects, not just resources. An
extension of territorial rights would create many problems
for maintaining pollution control and research freedom in
the oceans. If the Treaty is not ratified the seabed will
become another example of doctrinare conflict that
threatens to eventually lead to direct confrontation. In
a world divided on seabed mining and on so many other
issues, maritime rights in general would be the source of
increased friction and disputes among states.[17] If, on
the other hand, the Treaty does enter into effect then
the result would be one from which all major groups stand
to obtain certain advantages. Because the main consumer
countries are more prosperous than LDCs, they have a
general interest in political and economic stability along
with their desire to ensure that seabed minerals are
exploited and are available for international commerce.
Similar broad considerations apply in the case of developing countries. Besides the special case of land-based
producers, LDCs seek to have seabed resources developed
in a manner which brings them economic benefit and
establishes an exemplary method of international resource
management.[18]

Another alternative for reaching an acceptable
agreement calls for a "Phased Authority" framework which
would incorporate the objectives of both the Northern and
Southern states.[19] There would be two phases in this
plan. The first phase would allow Authority officials,
on the basis of experience, to work out a subsequent stage
of the Authority's operations. The initial phase would
also generate funds to provide a firm financial backing
for the Authority. During this period various compensation mechanisms could be established for land-based
mineral producers as insurance against negative impacts.

From a purely economic perspective it makes little
sense to compensate land-based producer nations. It is
mainly for political reasons, though, that they will
receive compensation. The best type of assistance would
be to help the LDC producers create other industries so
that they are not heavily reliant on the export of one or
two minerals for foreign income. (Unfortunately, this
runs counter to the history of developed countries'
exploitation of Third World countries.) The period of
time that such nations should receive compensation should
be minimized so that the economic and social benefits
derived from exploitation of manganese nodules is maximized. Article 150 (g) of the proposed Treaty states the
need for the protection of developing countries from
adverse effects to their economies or their export earnings caused by a reduction in the price of an affected
mineral, or in the volume of that mineral exported, to
the extent that such reductions are caused by activities
in the Area.

Proponents of the Phased Authority approach assume the LDCs would accept the first phase if they are guaranteed--in the Treaty itself--that they would possess greater control in the subsequent phase (or phases) of the Authority's existence. Advocates of this approach believe the common heritage principle will prevail and that a "vigorous program" of technology could take place, enabling the Authority to gradually obtain the skills and know-how to participate directly in mining. The transfer of needed technology may take less time than was originally thought. For example, several high-level members of ocean mining companies based in the United States have opened their own consulting firms with the goal of selling their expertise. In addition, some developers of mining technology and equipment will want to market their system designs.[20] There is little reason why Third World states or the Authority could not benefit by these services.

The second phase would initiate direct Authority control and participation in ocean mining. According to this plan, mining companies would be required to conclude a contract with the Authority for mining, and it would be left to the Authority's discretion whether to enter into a joint venture, service contract, or various other arrangements with the companies. Under this scheme, miners would be able to retain control over their initial site selections. Furthermore, the Authority would not have the jurisdiction to completely prevent national or private mining companies from exploiting the deep seabed. This suggestion would most likely run into serious opposition from the Group of 77.

Proponents of a Phased Authority would allow the Authority to retain direct and effective control over the nature and pattern of all seabed mining in a joint venture arrangement. The Authority would also be permitted to retain the power to conduct a designated percentage of exploration and exploitation on its own. Evidence indicates that the Group of 77 would not accept this privilege in lieu of decreased jurisdictional control. Depending on many factors, including overall patterns of North-South relations and the availability of various crucial raw minerals, these factors could change in a very short space of time contingent on security of supply questions and a possible shift in political attitude and/or Administrations of the United States and its allies toward a much more forceful and stringent policy vis-a-vis the Group of 77 and its demands.

Many ocean mining analysts believe that the seabed is sufficiently large and nodules sufficiently diffuse that all interested mining entities--private, national, multinational or international--can be accommodated in the foreseeable future. If this is accurate (some analysts do believe otherwise), then a strong prohibitive

Authority may force most major ocean mining consortia to seek mine sites in national waters where they have legal access to all economic uses of the seabed, water column, and surface. Such areas might include the Blake Plateau off the Florida coast and around islands in the Pacific Ocean. If most of the mining for nodules were carried out in EEZs, the Authority would be left in the position of having jurisdiction over international waters where little ocean mining was being conducted. This scenario is unlikely, as most of the known economically exploitable nodules are found in international waters. A revenue-sharing plan based on various taxation methods of a more moderate Authority, however, could be implemented during the second phase that would both finance the Authority and also raise development funds for distribution to the nations most adversely affected by ocean mining (Zaire, Zambia, and other land-based producers) and the least well-off of the developing countries.[21]

The "Phased Authority" proposal is designed to accommodate the many divergent interests expressed at UNCLOS III. It is possible that the LDCs would be willing to see these common heritage resources exploited during Phase I with minimal international jurisdiction if clear legal assurances were given that the second phase would commence at a definite future date. This could be accomplished by including a framework for Phase II in the Treaty with details to be worked out later. Unless there is a major change in the ideological nature of the bargaining stance taken by the Group of 77, though, this plan will not work. It is possible that the mining companies would continue to mine in the second phase, despite greater Authority power, as long as they make a "reasonable profit" in Phase I and are assured of doing so in the second phase. Unfortunately, there are too many important "ifs" in this proposal for it to work successfully when current and likely negotiating positions of the technologically advanced nations wanting to mine the seabed with a minimum of Authority control are counterposed with the positions of the Group of 77 which demand maximum control by the Authority.

Yet another alternative to the approach actually followed by the United States combines aspects of those already discussed. It is an alternative that is more centralized, less comprehensive, and less universal than the United States has thus far followed in negotiations at UNCLOS III. Like domestic legislation already passed, this less comprehensive approach contains provisions to encourage developing country participation in deep seabed mining consortia. Advocates of this approach say this could be done by diverting revenue sharing payments in the near-term to subsidize interest on LDC debts obtained for the purchase of equity interests in joint ventures with miners from developed countries. This proposal is offered, "in part for reasons of equity, in part for reasons of practical merit, and in part for reasons of politics and appearance."[22] The plan also calls for the encouragement of reciprocating agreements and harmonious domestic legislation among developed country mining states. Finally, the plan calls for the vigorous encouragement of selected developing country participation in the joint arrangements contemplated by the other parts of the plan--to assure that the arrangements are not merely for appearance.[23] The criteria for selection would probably depend upon several factors, including: how technically advanced the LDC was, how much capital it could raise, the location of the country (e.g. proximity to the minerals, or important straits), or selection would be made for purely political reasons.

Three Scenarios

For purposes of analysis it will be useful to briefly examine three scenarios (some of which have been mentioned earlier) as possibilities for the legal future of deep seabed mining. Obviously, time and events will narrow the options. The first can be called an extralegal Law of the Sea legal regime. There are four variables to this scenario. First, the United States alone would design its own legal framework for ocean mining without a Law of the Sea Treaty. (PL 96-283 would serve as the basis for such a possibility.) Second, the United States, Great Britain, West Germany, and France would form a legal framework. Third, in addition to the four countries above, several other developed countries would participate. (Such countries might include Japan, Belgium, Italy, and Norway.) Finally, a reciprocal agreement with United States ocean mining regulations forming the foundation of a legal framework would be created.

The second scenario shall be called a reciprocal arrangement. It has three variations. The first is dependent upon future LOS negotiations. The Conference could conclude and a Treaty enter into force over the objections of the United States; the United States could consent and sign the Treaty but fail to ratify it (a definite possibility); or the Conference could separate deep seabed mining issues from the rest of the Treaty (less likely). The second variation (which is similar to the fourth variable of the above scenario) involves the extent of participation in a reciprocal regime. The United States, West Germany, Great Britain, and France alone could participate; or Japan, Italy, Holland, and Belgium might commit themselves. (This is not likely to happen if there is sharp negative reaction to the reciprocating arrangement by other nations.) Alternatively, the Soviet Union and its satellites might become involved; or all the above states, and in addition, Canada and some developing countries, could become parties to the arrangement. The third variant concerns Third World reaction to a reciprocating state arrangement. The Group of 77 could react with outrage, the committed (knowledgeable) leadership of those countries could be opposed; Third World governments might take retaliatory action (resource boycott?); or finally, they could issue competing claims against mine sites.

The third scenario is a Law of the Sea Treaty. There are two variants to this scenario. The first is that there are no guarantees for prior investment protection for ocean mining companies. (It is unlikely that there will be substantial improvements in Part 11 of the Treaty, though minimum improvements are probable.) The second variant concerns grandfather rights (investment) protection. The protection guarantees could be site specific with Authority regulations (which is clearly negotiable), or could follow the State Department's Preparatory Investment Proposal (PIP) plans—which is much less likely as neither the Group of 77 nor the companies are totally satisfied with this proposal.

Whatever alternative is considered, it would be a mistake to assume that it would alleviate the need for international agreement. For example, there may be confrontations between the industrialized countries authorizing mining and the many developing countries that oppose national systems until such an agreement is reached and enters into force. Some developing states have indicated that they might "claim jump" and themselves make or authorize deep sea claims on the various areas covered by national licenses.

The earliest commercial mining will probably begin in the late 1980s or early 1990s, and will most likely be under one or more national regimes.[24] The political forces that exist and the longer-term benefits that would come from a comprehensive approach should ultimately lead to ratification of a treaty before or near that time. Even if a final agreement is reached at UNCLOS III, it will still take one to three years before the required sixty nations ratify it for it to enter into force. Each of the national systems proposed thus far are interim in the sense that they contemplate the eventual adoption of a Treaty. When, or if, the Treaty does enter into force several latent functional problems surrounding the governing structure of the Authority shall have to be faced. These problems will ceate legal, political, and bureaucratic difficulties which will create obstacles to a smooth running Authority.

The character of contemporary international negotiations suggests that the final result of a comprehensive Treaty will fall closer to the aspirations of the LDCs and their preferred New International Economic Order than many industrialized nations of the North would find acceptable. Even so, a joint-venture form of mining operation involving the Enterprise and countries or private companies would be the best arrangement. A format of this nature is preferable because a parallel system will pit the Enterprise and private or states' parties against one another. A joint-venture on the other hand would be more of a partnership with both working to achieve efficiency and equity. But it would be wrong to think that a joint-venture is a panacea for resolving all issues in international resource management.[25]

Whatever the practical results attained by the Treaty, the international community has demonstrated a new understanding of worldwide economic relationships. The successful implementation of the Treaty, should it be ratified by the United States, is more easily planned in policy papers than it is at the negotiating table. Consequently, compromises will have to be made at times which transcend the logic of pure economics and captures the goals and objectives of the NIEO.[26] The need for compromise has been realized by the international community at UNCLOS III. The negotiators have attempted to establish an interim period of twenty to twenty-five years followed by a review period. The review process will enable negotiators to formulate optimum courses of future action. In establishing a resource policy for the exploitation of seabed minerals, it is much more relevant to reach agreement on the overall principles of such a policy than to attempt to work out precisely the possible rates of growth or the exact numbers of mine sites or quantities of metals to be produced. The proposed governing structure of the Authority will eventually decide these specific points. The number of details worked out in the negotiations, however, is quite remarkable.

In sum, what is needed is a political agreement on a new type of international economic relationship to be applied to what is considered as a common resource in an international area. The ultimate result of such a political agreement would be to place the scientific and technological advances of some industrialized countries at the service of the whole international community. The goal of the more moderate negotiators at UNCLOS III has been to accomplish this through the adoption of a truly effective international regime that is acceptable to both the developed and developing nations.

Policy planners should be asking two related questions at this point: is it possible or feasible for a comprehensive international agreement to function efficiently; and, given the increasing importance of resource ownership in the future, is such a Treaty really what the United States needs if it limits our access to deep seabed minerals? If the Treaty is adopted it would translate for the first time into practical terms--through an international seabed mining regime--the fundamental concepts underlying the establishment of a new international economic order.[27] Both the developed and developing nations should be cautious not to become overly entangled in the processes of the redistribution of global wealth at the expense of its creation.

The advanced nations, however, clearly cannot afford years of negotiations if it substantially hinders research and development for a new high-technology resource industry. This is a particularly important point for the United States government to keep in mind-- especially those agencies concerned with the availability of crucial resources over the next several decades. Negotiators from all nations at UNCLOS III have become so involved with the dynamics of conference diplomacy and posturing for national goals, that the larger and more specific interest of obtaining resources from the ocean in an engineering and practical sense is lost at times. Fortunately for the United States the need to have access to the minerals in manganese nodules has not become extremely critical thus far. As a result the economic costs of the UNCLOS III conference have not been that great yet. Given the lead time of the ocean mining industry to begin full-scale production and the need for those minerals in the next fifteen to twenty years, however, the Treaty should be ratified or altered within the next few years. Sufficient concessions have been made by the American LOS delegation. The United States should now take further initiatives in obtaining access to the nodules. Domestic legislation and a reciprocating state arrangement were the first steps in this direction.

CONCLUDING REMARKS

There are numerous difficulties with the various alternative regime structures that have been discussed here. A basic problem with an "open access and free use" regime (favored by several American alternatives to a comprehensive Law of the Sea Treaty), is its assumption that interference by users with one another will be an exceptional rather than a normal occurrence. There is little assurance that the resolution of conflicts of interests under this type of regime would be efficient, equitable, or ecologically sound. It is also doubtful that the objections of assuming responsibility for the care of the ocean and creating juridicial stability conducive to its efficient exploitation can be attained through a national management approach alone.[28] A viable alternative are the agreements between reciprocating ocean mining nations that are now being made.

The difficulties with an international management approach to an ocean regime are primarily political. Most of today's nation states have attained their independence from one or another of the European empires only since

the Second World War. Many developing states are struggling to maintain internal cohesion against ethnic or
religious groups insisting on greater local autonomy.
The leaders of most of these states tend to be very suspi-
cious of attempts to restrict their national sovereignty
and are particularly resistant to international limitations on their freedom of action. Consequently, both
developed and developing countries support the expansion
of territorial limits out to 12 miles and exclusive
economic zones of 200 miles. Because individual LDCs lack
the capability of mining the deep seabed, they have been
anxious to support international control of that area.
At the same time, however, they want to maintain as much
national control as possible over areas of the ocean that
they do have the ability to exploit.

An analysis of developing country positions at
UNCLOS III indicates that coastal developing states tend
to be highly nationalistic about control of offshore
resources. It is not surprising that they are anxious to
maintain their political autonomy against foreign
encroachment and also to keep for themselves the potentially large income from exploitation of the resources of
the continental margin. In many ways the acceptance of
200-mile EEZs will be detrimental to the several LDCs that
are not major coastal states or are landlocked. Leaders
of the Group of 77, such as Mexico, Brazil, India, and
Indonesia have benefited greatly by 200-mile EEZs because
they have large coasts. This small group of nations has
led other LDCs to follow their demands for increased
economic jurisdiction into international waters. Many
geographically disadvantaged developing and developed
countries have therefore not benefited by the 200-mile
extension into the oceans (because of narrow or non-
existent coastlines). The leadership of key committees
and negotiating groups at UNCLOS III are held by Third
World delegates from nations which had much to gain from
extending national economic jurisdiction into the free
seas. This indicates the importance of personalities at
international resource conferences and their role in
influencing conference diplomacy and outcomes.[29] The
nature of the negotiating structure at UNCLOS III has
permitted the leaders of the Group of 77 a great deal of
influence in the wording and direction of the entire
Treaty. Policy planners in the United States would do
well to use this fact to their benefit for mapping out
future conference strategies.

The political difficulties discussed throughout
this study are substantial but need not be regarded as
insurmountable obstacles to international ocean resource
management. It is necessary for any durable ocean regime
to require considerable international accountability and
coordination because of the large number of interdependencies of ocean waters. A Brookings Institution study found

that the task of diplomacy, therefore, is to create
substantive and institutional bargains between countries,
taking into account both technical characteristics of
different uses, and variations in the number, location,
and economic and political power of the relevant nations
and affected populations.[30] This is a difficult task.
Given the significance of developing an acceptable regime
for the management of the deep seabed as a common heritage
of mankind it is all the more important and necessary.

FOOTNOTES

Chapter 5

1. Robert O. Keohane and Joseph S. Nye, Power and Interdependence: World Politics in Transition, (Boston, Little, Brown and Co., 1977).

2. Ibid., p. 99.

3. Ann Hollick, "Seabeds Make Strange Politics," Foreign Policy 9, (Winter 1972/73): 148-170; and H. Gary Knight, "Special Domestic Interests and United States Oceans Policy," in Robert G. Wirsing, ed., International Relations and the Future of Oceans Space, (Columbia: University of South Carolina Press, 1974). See also Ann Hollick, U.S. Foreign Policy and the Law of the Sea, (Princeton, Princeton University Press, 1981).

4. From an overview of ocean related legislation by Thomas R. Kitsos, Legislative Analyst, Committee on Merchant Marine and Fisheries, U.S. House of Representatives. A paper entitled: "The Implementation of Ocean Legislation in the Eighties: A Legislative Perspective," prepared for presentation at a seminar entitled, Future Directions in U.S. Marine Policies in the 1980s. University of California, Santa Barbara, June 4-6, 1981.

5. Keohane and Nye, Power and Interdependence, p. 105 and p. 110. Also see, John V. Granger, Technology and International Relations, (San Francisco: W.H. Freeman and Co., 1979).

6. Edward L. Miles, "Transnationalism in Space: Inner and Outer," in Robert O. Keohane and Joseph S. Nye, eds., Transnational Relations and World Politics, (Cambridge, Mass.: Harvard University Press, 1972). Also see, Warren Wooster, "Interaction in Marine Affairs," International Organization 27, (Winter 1973): 252-275.

7. Keohane and Nye, Power and Interdependence, p. 126.

8. Ibid., p. 149.

9. The following discussion is based on Roger D. Hansen's chapter, "Prominent Perspectives on the North-South Split," in his book, Beyond the North-South

Stalemate, (New York: McGraw Hill Book Co., 1979). The book is part of the 1980s Project of the Council on Foreign Relations.

10. Ibid.

11. These points are raised by H. Gary Knight, "Alternatives to a Law of the Sea Treaty," in The Law of the Sea: U.S. Interests and Alternatives, Ryan C. Amacher and Richard Sweeney, eds., (Washington D.C.: American Enterprise Institute for Public Policy Research, 1976), pp. 133-148.

12. For a discussion of the types of jurisdictional claims that can be expected from certain nations in specific instances, see H. Gary Knight, "Alternatives," pp. 133-148.

13. Ibid., p. 143.

14. Some analysts have urged that UN Resolution 2749, because it declares that the resources of the deep seabed are to be exploited only pursuant to an international agreement to be reached, constitutes a de facto moratorium on all seabed mining activities. Most American analysts, however, argue that this position is unsound for two reasons: (1) General Assembly resolutions are not binding legal obligations but constitute only indications of nations' general expectations, and (2) Resolution 2749 was a compromise agreed to by nations only to facilitate the progress of the Law of the Sea negotiations. See Ted Kronmiller, The Lawfulness of Deep Seabed Mining, (Department of Commerce, 1979). Kronmiller argues in great length and detail that there are no national or international legal reasons why the United States could not mine the deep seabed. Gonzalo Biggs, a member of the Executive Council and the Executive Committee of the American Society of International Law, offers a different legal viewpoint on the legality of American unilateral ocean mining legislation. Biggs points out that UN Resolution 176 (XVIII) which was adopted by the Trade and Development Board of the United Nations Conference on Trade and Development (UNCTAD) on September 17, 1978, declares that any unilateral actions designed to carry on the exploitation of the seabed and ocean floor, and the subsoil thereof, beyond the limits of national jurisdiction, as well as the resources of that area, before a Convention of the Law of the Sea is adopted, would not be recognized by the international community and would be invalid in accordance with international law. His argument is well taken; but the United States voted against both the 1970 Declaration of Principles (Resolution 2749) and Resolution 176 (XVIII). Biggs believes that U.S.

ocean mining legislation is contrary to the common heritage of mankind concept (which he argues is now a rule of customary international law), and may create serious conflicts of jurisdiction, and are not considered to be in conformity with accepted principles of international law. See, Gonzalo Biggs, "Deep Seabed Mining and Unilateral Legislation," Ocean Development and International Law 8: 223-257. Kronmiller's view on the legality of unilateral legislation is the one obviously preferred and used by the United States government. Whether or not there will be serious international conflicts between the Group of 77 and the United States and its Northern allies if the industrially advanced nations proceed with ocean mining activities on a commercial basis without a Law of the Sea Treaty is not known. After the passage of U.S. legislation in 1980, most Third World nations at UNCLOS III made official statements deploring the action. It is unlikely that they will be in a position to significantly apply pressure on the U.S. to alter its position should commercial mining take place after January 1, 1988 without an international LOS agreement.

15. West Germany passed similar legislation immediately following the U.S. action. Great Britain, France, and Japan may do so as well.

16. Michael Hardy, "The Implications of alternative solutions for regulating the exploitation of seabed minerals," International Organization 31 (Spring 1977): 313-342.

17. Ibid.

18. See, Lawrence Juda, "UNCLOS III and the New International Economic Order," Ocean Development and International Law Journal 7 (1979): 221-256; and A.O. Adede, "The Group of 77 and the Establishment of the International Seabed Authority," Ocean Development and International Law Journal 7 (1979): 31-64.

19. Jack N. Barkenbus, "How to Make Peace on the Seabed," Foreign Policy 25 (Winter 1976/77): 211-220.

20. A good example of this is Jack Flipse, formerly of Deepsea Ventures, who has done research and consulting work for French and Mexican concerns.

21. The UN has singled out the "least developed countries" for special attention. They are defined as: "countries with severe long-term constraints on development assessed on three basic criteria: viz--per captia GDP of $100 or less at 1970 prices, share of manufacturing of 10 percent or less of GDP, and 20 percent or

less literate persons aged 15 or more." They have a
population of 58 million (1977 estimate) or 13 percent of
the population of all the developing countries. Most of
the least developed countries--the present UN list
includes 29 of them--are found contiguously in two areas
which have been called "poverty belts." One extends
across the middle of Africa, from the Sahara in the North
to Lake Nyara in the South. The other, beginning with
the two Yemens and Afganistan, stretches eastwards across
South Asia and some East Asian countries. These belts
extend into other regions and parts of countries, for
example parts of Kenya in Africa and, in Asia, Burma,
Cambodia, Vietnam and parts of India. See, North-South,
A Program for Survival, The Report of the Independent
Commission on International Development Issues, under the
Chairmanship of Willy Brandt, (Cambridge: The MIT Press,
1980). See especially chapter 4 of the Report.

22. See, Richard Darman, "United States Deepsea
Mining Policy: The Pattern and the Prospects," a paper
prepared for presentation at the M.I.T. seminar series on
Deepsea Mining and U.S. Materials/Resource Policies,
January 12, 1979. Darman conceeds that the pursuit of
this course would require a greater preference for decentralized institutions than now exists, or a greater
relative weighting of U.S. seabed interests, or a lower
assessment of the probability of success within the
Conference framework than has been characteristic among
U.S. negotiatiors up to this time. He also feels that
pursuit of such a course might be based on "reasonable
judgement that the current international climate is not
propitious for the negotiations of universal norms by all
the nations of the world...."

23. Ibid.

24. Robert B. Krueger, "Current View of Deepsea
Mining Issues," in Alternatives in Deepsea Mining, Law of
the Sea Institute Workshop, December 11-14, 1978,
(Honolulu: University of Hawaii, 1979). Krueger is a
partner in the law firm of Nossaman, Krueger, and Marsh,
Los Angeles, California, which has been involved in
several natural resource policy studies.

25. With reference to a joint venture form of
operation for the mining of manganese nodules, Robert
Krueger accurately notes that: "A decision still must be
made as to the extent of the respective interests of the
resource owner and the co-venturers and the method of
payment of their shares of the costs of mineral development with the most frequently used contemporary method
involving some form of 'carry' [payments] to the resource
owner [in this case, the Authority representing all

mankind]." Robert Krueger, <u>Alternative in Deepsea Mining</u>.

26. See, Dr. Jean-Pierre Levy, "The Evolution of a Resource Policy for the Exploitation of Deep Sea-Bed Minerals," <u>Ocean Management</u> 5 (April 1979): 49-73. Dr. Levy is head of the Ocean Economics and Technology Office of the United Nations Secretariat.

27. Ibid., p. 73.

28. Seyom Brown, Nina W. Cornell, Larry L. Fabian and Edith Brown Weiss, <u>Regimes for the Ocean, Outer Space, and Weather</u>, (Washington D.C.: The Brookings Institution, 1977). See pp. 109-112. Brown et al. concluded that an ocean regime modeled on the nation-state system that is traditional on land: "will be ill-equipped to arbitrate volatile jurisdictional conflicts or to accomodate overlapping uses on the basis of what is best for ocean ecology or for general welfare, and it portents increasing international conflict and bitterness of the part of those who cannot prevail."

29. Based on interviews with Dr. Arvid Pardo, Senior Fellow at the Institute of Marine and Coastal Studies, University of Southern California, March 1980. Interviews with Dr. Pardo were also held in August, October and November 1979, as well as in June 1980. Several of the influential posts with the Group of 77 have been held by delegates from the Asian group. These include: H. Shirely Amerasinghe of Sri Lanka who was President of the Conference until his death in 1980, Jogota of India, Chao and T.B. Koh of Singapore, Dajalla of Indonesia, and Yango of the Philippines.

30. Brown et al., <u>Regimes</u>, p. 113. See pp. 113-120 for their strategy for implementing the International Management Concept-something perceived as a two-stage strategy encompassing "(1) functional pluralism overlaid by (2) more integrated multinational and multisectoral accountability, including machinery for the resolution of disputes and, if possible, a comprehensive authority for management of the area."

6
Precedents for
Other Global Commons

INTRODUCTION
     A political analysis of international resource
management, and of deep seabed mining in particular,
indicates that access to resource commons will be of
growing political and economic concern for all nations.
International resource management conflicts will therefore
strain the political and economic structures of both
national and international institutions. The precedents
set by an international deep seabed mining regime will
thus have significant implications for the economic,
political and strategic interests of the United States
and other industrially advanced states. The deep seabed
is just one of several areas of common space and resource
use. Other areas include the high seas, international
airspace, the electromagnetic spectrum, outer space, geo-
stationary orbits, and Antarctica.
     Three conclusions can be drawn from a closer
analysis of increased interest in obtaining access to the
various types of resources considered the global commons.
The first is that ocean resources beyond the 200-mile EEZ
are now, almost exclusively, regarded as the common
heritage of mankind. And although the thirteen member
nations of the Antarctic Treaty do not consider Antarctica
a resource commons to be equally shared by all countries,
a growing number of Third World states believe it should
be. The second is that resource management precedents
set by the regime framework for the International Seabed
Authority may be used by the Group of 77 to gain benefits
from the resource exploitation of Antarctica and outer
space. The third is that there is increasing pressure in
the United States to retain as much national control over,
and free access to, resource commons as possible. The
pressure is occurring in large part due to growing Third
World demands for the sharing of technology and revenues
associated with resource commons exploitation. In essence,
Third World demands are for a redistribution of the
world's wealth. But redistributive policies are the most
difficult and politically volatile to enact. This is

especially true of new international economic orders and institutions that demand economic advances for the poor nations at the apparent expense of the rich.

Will there be a redistribution of the world's wealth over the next twenty years derived from the exploitation of the deep seabed, outer space, and Antarctica? Or will concern for access to these resources prompt the governments of the United States and other industrially advanced states to be less concerned with Third World demands for a New International Economic Order (NIEO) and a sharing of revenues and technology associated with resource commons exploitation?

DEEP SEABED MINING AND OTHER RESOURCE COMMONS:
SIMILARITIES AND DIFFERENCES

Of the many provisions in the Law of the Sea Treaty, the nature and scope of the International Seabed Authority will be a decisive factor in consideration of the Treaty for ratification by the United States Senate. This is so, not only because the long-term national interest requires assured access to the minerals of the deep seabed, but also because institutional and economic aspects of the deep seabed regime could create significant precedents for future international regime arrangements of other global commons.

Over the last two decades, technological advances have increased the use and potential benefits of the oceans, Antarctica, and outer space. The position of the technologically advanced states on the issue of access to these areas is based on theories of international equity and political expediency. There is a growing feeling both in industry and the government that if American companies do not exploit the resources then foreign competitors will. In terms of national security and economic strength, the United States government obviously prefers to have assurances that American companies will enjoy access to resource commons. The United States would also like to minimize conflicts that occur during international negotiations for resource management from spreading to other international problems. Conflict can be reduced by endorsing a management framework that enables less developed countries (LDCs) to share in the benefits of resource commons exploitation. The posture of the developing countries, however, is primarily based on the concept of a fundamental redistribution of global wealth.[1]

The 1970 United Nations "Declaration of Principles" on the deep seabed and the Law of the Sea Treaty currently under consideration, have already begun to affect other areas of international life. For instance, the Moon Treaty, which is open for signature by all states, declares that the resources of outer space are the common heritage of mankind and obligates states' parties to establish an exploitation regime based on that principle. At the heart of the proposed agreements on the oceans and outer space is the Third World demand for the establishment of a New International Economic Order which would entail a fundamental redistribution of global wealth. The declared goal is for greater Third World control of international resources and of global political and economic institutions.

A comparison of the Moon Treaty text with the 1970 deep seabed resolution and the Law of the Sea text shows several basic similarities. For example, paragraph 1 of the resolution states:

> The seabed and the ocean floor, and the subsoil thereof, beyond the limits of national jurisdiction ...as well as the resources of the area are the common heritage of mankind.

And article 136 of the proposed Law of the Sea Treaty states:

> The Area [international deep seabed] and its resources are the common heritage of mankind.

Article XI, paragraph 1 of the Moon Treaty provides that:

> The Moon and its natural resources are the common heritage of mankind which finds its expression in the provisions of this agreement and in particular paragraph 5 of this article.

Paragraph 9 of the 1970 resolution on the deep seabed states that:

> On the basis of the principles of this Declaration and international regime applied to the area and its resources and including appropriate international machinery to give effect to its provisions shall be established by an inter- national treaty of universal character, generally agreed upon. The regime shall, inter alia, provide for the orderly and safe development and rational management of the area and its resources and for expanding opportunities and the use thereof and insure the equitable sharing by States in the particular consideration of the interests and needs of the developing countries, whether landlocked or coastal.

Article 150 of the LOS Treaty text provides that the policies for deep ocean mineral development include among others, "orderly and safe development and rational management of the resources of the area...and the expanding of opportunities for participation in such activities." Article 140 of the text provides that the envisioned International Seabed Authority "shall provide for the equitable sharing of benefits derived from the area...." Article XI, paragraph 5 of the Moon Treaty provides:

> States' Parties to this Agreement hereby undertake to establish an international regime, including appropriate procedures, to govern the exploitation of the natural resources of the moon as such exploitation is about to become feasible.

Paragraph 7 of Article XI of the Moon Treaty states:

> The main purposes of the international regime to be established shall include:...the orderly and safe development of the natural resources of the moon...the rational management of those resources ...the expansion of the opportunities in the use of those resources...and an equitable sharing by all States Parties in the benefits derived from those resources, whereby the interests and needs of the developing countries as well as the efforts of those countries which have contributed either directly or indirectly to the exploration of the moon shall be given special consideration.

Because of the similarities between the Law of the Sea text and the Moon Treaty, Senators Frank Church and Jacob Javits requested, in 1980, that the Secretary of State seek a return of the space agreement to the United Nations Committee on the Peaceful Uses of Outer Space. They advised against signature of the treaty unless revisions were achieved to protect the national interest. The Department of State, however, denied their request for renegotiation. The issue of whether the United States will sign the Moon Treaty or ratify the LOS Treaty remains unresolved at this time (1981).

One of the key aspects of an International Seabed Authority for the sharing of the seabed commons is revenue sharing. In terms of precedents, revenue sharing, however structured, would constitute a model for other international arrangements relating to development of common resources. Antarctica, for example, has already been identified by some Third World countries as an area in which resource development should provide revenues to the developing countries. The argument is that Antarctica, like the deep seabed, should be considered the common heritage of all mankind and not just for the use of a handful of nations currently comprising the Antarctic Treaty. At a seminar on Antarctic resources in September 1979, Ambassador Alvero de Soto, a leading spokesman for

the Group of 77 at the Law of the Sea Conference, summarized the position of many Third World governments:

> The temptation to apply to Antarctica the prin-
> ciples which are the basis for the regime of the
> seabed is very great, and some have not been able
> to resist it. This temptation should increase now
> that the United Nations Committee on the Peaceful
> Uses of Outer Space has decided to recommend to
> the General Assembly a draft treaty that would
> declare that the Moon also constitutes the common
> heritage of mankind.[2]

Indeed, it would appear very natural to apply
revenue sharing for communications, energy development
and transmission, or other purposes in outer space. The
political consequences of such action, though, are
potentially volatile. The less developed countries would
like to have the advanced states provide aid to them from
revenues generated by the utilization of geo-stationary
orbits as well. The revenue could be collected in the
form of user taxes or fees by the governments of the user
nations. The money could then be channeled through the
United Nations or a special international resource agency
specifically concerned with the management of geo-
stationary orbits.

Revenue sharing, however, would minimize the return
on investments made in outer space. This in turn, acts
as a disincentive for private business to become aggressively involved in high technology research for outer
space applications. Nations such as Japan and West
Germany which are developing their own space technologies
are benefiting from an increase in closer ties between
government and private industry. By working more closely
with their high technology companies, the governments of
these nations hope to develop large enough enterprises to
compete with American private business in industrial space
applications. They would also be in a better financial
and a bargaining position vis-a-vis international revenue
sharing costs that may have to be paid to an international
fund. The underlying question of whether there should
even be a sharing of the benefits and wealth to be derived
from resource commons remains open. Political maneuvering
on many fronts, however, has made it likely that most
resource commons will legally be considered the common
heritage of mankind, and as such, their exploitation will
be taxed for revenue sharing with the developing
countries. It follows, therefore, that the American
government and certain high technology industries may have
to make some radical changes in their traditional roles
vis-a-vis each other and the nature of international
resource exploitation in the future. In other words,
there is a need for closer ties and cooperation in order

to meet foreign competition from countries where governments already heavily support high technology industries.
The age of outer space resource exploitation of
various types has already begun; this can be seen in the
use of air waves and geo-stationary orbits used for remote
sensing of the earth. Additional uses of other space
related resources will occur rapidly. Policy planners in
the technologically advanced nations, as well as the less
developed countries who are concerned about long-term
political stability, have seen the need to develop
international management of those resources. The advanced
states favor an orderly development of the resources,
while the LDCs favor protection of their rights to exploit
at a later date and to enjoy revenue sharing in the short
term. Because their goals are somewhat different, the
process for determining management structures has been
very difficult. Eventually there will be international
management of one type or another of the deep seabed and
outer space. Because this will most likely entail some
form of revenue sharing, independent free market corporations may not be able to realize typically high rates of
return on investment (i.e. 20-30 percent).
If the United States is to enjoy the maximum
benefits from these resources it is apparent that the
government will have to step in and assist those companies
in some manner. The assistance could take many forms.
These might include tax breaks, government guaranteed
loans for research and development, the paying of an
international tax to an International Seabed Authority
type organization, outright government-industry joint
operations, or combinations of all of the above. One of
the major problems of the ocean mining industry is how to
make a sufficient return on investments to attract capital
while paying a revenue sharing tax to an International
Authority. If the United States government provided funds
to help ocean miners pay those taxes until operations were
profitable enough for the industry to bear full responsibility, then the American ocean mining industry would
be greatly helped in its efforts to mine the seabed for
minerals very important to the nation's long-term security
and economic interests. Assistance of this type could be
repeated, with changes if needed, to ensure American
access to the resources of Antarctica and outer space
while maintaining friendly relations with the Group of 77.
In sum, a revenue sharing plan premised on minimum
return on investment (due to paying user taxes or fees to
an international authority), would seriously risk the
development and use of common resources by United States
private enterprises.[3] The suggested regime frameworks
for most global commons, though basically legitimate,
indicate that this fear is often exaggerated. The
direction of American policy will depend on whether or
not the United States is willing to accept the underlying

principle of common heritage, and the idea that resource commons should be shared with all nations. This debate, of course, centers on exactly how that should be accomplished. For example, should it entail transfer of technology; and if so, by what method and degree? Another question is how much revenue should be collected to share with other nations? A broader question is whether the United States, one of the few industrially advanced nations with the economic and technological power necessary to exploit the deep seabed, Antarctica and outer space, should make political or economic concessions to developing countries in its attempts to secure access to needed resources. Even if the United States government answers this question affirmatively, the formation and implementation of a resource commons policy to maintain national economic efficiency and help provide for an equitable international distribution of the global commons will prove very difficult.

There are two basic reasons why the global commons have remained mostly unappropriated by states or private parties. The first is that their very nature--beyond national jurisdiction, intangible, and sometimes non-terrestrial--has made them less susceptible than land areas to being divided into exact political jurisdictions. The second reason is that their vastness or presumed abundance has encouraged general acceptance of regimes allowing open access and free use. It is only in the last decade or so that this "abundance" has been questioned and no longer taken for granted. In the absence of substantial regulation, previously plentiful resources have at times become "scarce" or subject to depletion and major ecological abuse.[4] Those resources which have remained plentiful have become more valuable and in turn more likely to generate conflict among potential exploiters. At the same time, changing norms in international politics (the North-South split, the demands of the Group of 77), have made it diplomatically costly for the technologically advanced nations to use the global commons without the consent of other countries.[5]

In response to these developments, efforts have been made to shape the means by which resource commons will be exploited in either of two ways. One is a substantially greater assumption of management authority, and sovereign control where possible, by various nation states. A second way involves marginal increases, on a eclectic basis, of limited management authority at various levels of the international system--national, regional, and global--resulting in a mix of specialized functional institutions allowing for very little open access and free use. Seyom Brown and Larry Fabian, in an article on mutual accountability in the nonterrestrial realms, found that both of these responses to the "obsolescence" of the open access and free use regimes for the global commons were inadequate on grounds of practicality and legitimacy. They do, however, suggest an alternative which despite its problems appears to offer the basis for a sound management approach to resource commons.

According to Brown and Fabian this approach would be based on the twin assumptions of the essential non-divisibility of the global commons and the scarcity or high values of many of their important resources. Even more importantly, it would incorporate the normative judgement that global commons should belong to all human beings equally. This, they say, means that no segment of the human community, be it a corporation or a nation state, should derive from the realms disproportionate gain at the expense of others.[7] This is a legitimate goal to strive for, but is is not a likelihood in a world of realpolitik. Furthermore, the question of just how much is disproportionate remains both a political and economic issue. Their approach does not rule out the need, in advance of legitimate collective arrangements, to vest temporary authority over resource commons by groups acting only as custodians for the entire community, and ultimately accountable to it.

Thus the favored approach would accept short term national and limited member multinational arrangements for managing resource commons--but would eventually prefer management by the whole international community.[8] If this approach worked well it would stimulate political accountability among developing and developed states by reflecting the interests of the widest possible number of nations. It would not, however, impose a unified management framework on the inherently diverse plurality of international arrangements presently in effect. It would on the other hand promote an effective international overview of such arrangements for the efficient exploitation of the commons and for the sharing of benefits derived from them. It would also actively promote the cooperation of highly interdependent functions under umbrella institutions.[9]

Current international politics and law are such that nations have been able to avoid rather than be responsive to normative precepts of international accountability.[10] An example of the historical pattern of narrow nationalist-based accountability is ocean pollution. If one nation does not care whether it pollutes the ocean or not, it will be under no international obligation to cease polluting. Another example is the over-exploitation of various ocean resources such as whales, seals, and different species of fish. In Antarctica, with its special pristine quality, there is a great need to protect both living and non-living resources from traditional parochial interests of states to exploit resources with limited regard for the environment. Air waves and geo-stationary orbits must be protected as well if they are to be used and developed in an efficient manner. Table 1 provides a summary of the major similarities and differences involved in resource commons issues surrounding the oceans, Antarctica and outer space exploitation.

The United States is increasingly aware of the importance of access to resource commons. Consequently, there is pressure from industry and the Congress for international management structures that guarantee free access with minimal technology transfer and revenue sharing restrictions. The less developed countries have made several political and ideological demands to share in the benefits of resource commons exploitation. To deal with these demands the State Department has been at the forefront of United States efforts to establish new management structures for the oceans and outer space that would minimize international conflict and maximize American access to those resources.

The world community is at a crossroad down which lie international control of resource commons or continued, but increasingly politicized, national exploitation of those resources. Under the Reagan Administration it is unlikely that the United States will promote or actively participate in an international management framework for the exploitation of common resources that significantly limits American corporate access to them. If an international management approach fails to provide mechanisms for the orderly, efficient, and equitable exploitation of resource commons for the United States, then the system will break apart. If it succeeds, it could usher in a period of increased international cooperation and mutual control in areas traditionally held by individual nation states. These areas include energy, food, medicine, economics, and technology. Such control has been discussed in the "futurist" literature for over a decade, and called for on a more regional basis by the European Economic Community and the Trilateral Commission. It is readily apparent, however, that the first steps toward greater international control and management have been taken. These include the United Nations organization, multilateral military and economic unions and, of course, the call for international control over the resource use of the oceans and outer space. The success or failure of these early resource management attempts will determine the likelihood and progress of later international management regimes for broader political, military, and economic purposes. A description and analysis of the nature of each specific resource commons currently under consideration will be made in the next two parts of this chapter.

TABLE 1

RESOURCE COMMONS: SIMILARITIES & DIFFERENCES

FACTOR:	OCEANS (Law of the Sea)	ANTARCTICA (Antarctic Treaty)	OUTER SPACE (Moon Treaty)
Common Heritage	YES U.N. Declaration 1970	NO (But increasing pressure for it)	YES
Potentially vast Resource Base	YES Living and Non-living	YES Living and Non-living	YES
Third World attempts to secure access or benefits	YES	YES	YES
Resources available to all nations	YES Beyond 200-mile EEZ or by agreement	NO Only Treaty states and by special agreement	YES
Current working treaty	May be signed in 1982, but still must be ratified by 60 nations,	YES 1959	YES (The treaty has been signed by sufficient nations (5) though U.S. has not signed).
Perceived U.S. need for Intl. management	YES	YES (Among Treaty members only)	YES (Though the U.S. has not yet signed).

ANTARCTICA

There are certain similarities between the oceans and Antarctica as regions of the global commons. But what makes Antarctica different from the oceans or outer space as a region of resource commons is that from 1959 on there has been an Antarctic Treaty among a handful of nations who have been successful, thus far, in keeping whatever problems arise over resource management to themselves. There are, however, increasing pressures within the Treaty framework, and from nations left out of it, which indicate that a major change in the resource management of this region will occur over the next fifteen to twenty years.

The continent of Antarctica, long maintained as a scientific preserve, suddenly is coming under scrutiny for commercial development as the world's known reserves of natural resources continue to diminish. To date the search for development has concentrated on Antarctica's marine life, notably on an abundant crustacean known as krill. By the end of the century, Antarctica's petroleum and other mineral resources may also be opened to exploitation. The search for natural resources in Antarctica represents a major change in mankind's approach to the earth's coldest, least accessible and most pristine continent. Already the signs of impending development have caused unease among nations with competing interests in Antarctica. In addition, the possibility of environmental harm threatens to lead to bitter resistance by conservation organizations in the United States and other industrialized countries.

The political issues of resource commons ownership and management are becoming more complex as technological advances extend the limits of our abilities to exploit new resources. At the same time the need for natural resources continues to grow--which makes the access problem all the more severe. Therefore, the examples learned at UNCLOS III about international resource management may help shape a better management regime for Antarctica. United States policy experts will be in a position to avoid the mistakes of UNCLOS III and build upon its successes in negotiating ways of exploiting the living and non-living resources of Antarctica. (A brief description of Antarctica and its major resource and environmental problems can be found in Appendix 12.) An entirely different set of problems concerning the resource potential of Antarctica looms on the horizon: the complex political questions involving resource access and ownership. These issues need to be sorted out before suggestions for a resource management regime in Antarctica can be made.

The Antarctic Treaty

All lands south of 60° South are controlled by the Antarctic Treaty, which became effective in 1961. (See Appendix 13.) The antecedents of this Treaty lie in the cooperative scientific programs which took place in Antarctica during the International Geophysical Year (IGY) of 1957-58. The Treaty emerged shortly after the IGY because the twelve nations that conducted extensive research there desired to continue their activities under the same conditions of cooperation and freedom of access that prevailed in 1957-58. Of the twelve nations, seven--Argentina, Australia, Chile, France, New Zealand, Norway, and the United Kingdom--claim sovereignty over parts of Antarctica. The United States, along with Belgium, Japan, South Africa, and the Soviet Union, neither assert nor do they recognize such claims. The key to maintaining the political status quo of the IGY was the agreement among the twelve contracting parties to suspend all further territorial claims and to hold in abeyance all existing claims. Three of the claimant nations--Argentina, Chile, and Great Britain--have overlapping claims. Poland acceded to the Treaty in 1961 but did not become a full participant until 1977.

Following the IGY of 1957-58, the United States took the initiative to conclude a treaty providing for lasting international cooperation in scientific research in Antarctica. It was also hoped that the treaty would prevent Antarctica from becoming the object of international competition and conflict. The Antarctic Treaty was signed in 1959 and entered into force in 1961. One of the key provisions of the Treaty is section 2 of Article IV, in which the Parties agree to disagree over the issue of territorial sovereignty. This provision has done a lot to ensure the basis of international cooperation that has thus far prevailed in Antarctica. It is also at the heart of several problems regarding the resource management of Antarctica. These problems will become more acute as the technology to exploit Antarctic resources increases--spurred on by the higher price of natural resources.

Some of the major provisions of the Treaty are especially worth noting. It sets aside Antarctica and the water below 60° South latitude for peaceful purposes only and prohibits nuclear explosions or the disposal of nuclear waste there. The Treaty prohibits any measures of a military nature such as the establishment of military bases and fortifications, the carrying out of military maneuvers, or the testing of military weapons. It also states that employment of military personnel or equipment is permitted only in support of scientific research in Antarctica. In order to promote these objectives and ensure the observance of the Treaty provisions, each contracting party has the right to designate observers to carry out inspection activities.

The Treaty also provides for regular Consultative Meetings of representatives of the twelve original signatories and other parties which demonstrate their interest in Antarctica by the conduct of substantial scientific research there. As of 1982, eleven such meetings had been held since the Treaty formally came into effect. The twelfth meeting should be held in Canberra, Australia in 1983.

In broad terms the Treaty has been both an unusual and successful example of international political cooperation among states with various political systems as well as different legal and political views regarding Antarctica itself. One of the main reasons for its apparent success thus far is that it is a limited purpose agreement only. The Treaty defines specific objectives and establishes a legal and political framework to allow attainment of those objectives. The Treaty does not apply to activities in Antarctica other than those specifically enumerated in it. Areas not dealt with include the questions of resource development. At the time of the conclusion of the Treaty, the prospect of these activities seemed too remote, and the issues that they posed too difficult for final consideration.[11]

Current and Future Problems

Living Resources. Important changes in perceptions regarding the possibilities of resource development in the Antarctic area have occurred in the twenty years since the Treaty entered into force. Questions relating both to Antarctic marine living resources and Antarctic mineral resources were addressed by the Eighth Consultative Meeting in 1975. By 1977, the Parties had agreed that conclusion of a regime to provide for the conservation of Antarctic marine living resources was their first priority.[12] They agreed that a conservation regime should be in place prior to the initiation of any large-scale harvesting activities. The Consultative Parties also agreed that the difficult legal and political issues inherent in negotiating a regime should be approached on the basis of the same principles which underlie the accommodation on the sovereignty issue in the Treaty itself. The resulting Draft Convention on Marine Living Resources was originally to be signed by 1978, but was not signed until May 1980. The Convention will enter into force once eight of the Consultative parties ratify it. As of January 1982, six nations had done so—with high expectations by the United States Department of State that by the end of 1982 the remaining ratifications would be made. The United States Senate gave its "advice and consent" to the Convention in December 1981; the United

States is expected to formally ratify the Treaty in 1982.

The Convention has greater jurisdiction than the Treaty area itself. It applies to all living marine resources south of the Antarctic Convergence. Nothing in the Convention can prejudice rights or claims "to exercise coastal state jurisdiction under international law" in the Convention area. It is designed to permit common management of the entire Convention area (including any 200-mile EEZs), without that management having any legal effect on the validity of territorial claims or on any party's recognition or non-recognition of those

Claimant states have a desire to protect territorial claims while non-claimant states wish to protect the principle of freedom of access. Both wanted the negotiations to finish quickly and on friendly terms so that the issue did not go beyond the effective control of the Treaty powers. Indications that control might eventually become more broad is evidenced by the fact that at the Tenth Consultative Meeting in Canberra, Australia in 1980, the European Economic Community obtained observer status. Throughout the negotiations on the Marine Living Resources Convention, all Parties to the Treaty were well aware that acceptance of such a convention by the international community would smooth the way for the development of a minerals agreement to be worked out at a later date by the Treaty Parties.

The main strength of the Living Resources Convention is that it represents an international attempt (though limited to the Treaty powers), to manage a marine living resource based on a strong ecosystem approach to conservation and prevention of adverse effects on other life forms. Despite its strengths there are several aspects of the Convention which will make it necessary for additional living and non-living resource agreements to be made. For example, there will be strong incentives for both claimants and non-claimants to maintain their opposing points of view. These incentives will become more intense as the fishery develops, and as negotiations start on a regime to control oil and other Antarctic minerals. Also, the United States and some other Treaty states would have liked the negotiations to have been open to all interested states. In addition, there is no clear recognition in the Convention of the interests of a wider international community beyond the Treaty states or states which already possess the technology to exploit krill and Antarctic fish. This is in marked contrast to the agreement reached by the Treaty powers in 1977, which stated that the interests of mankind were not to be prejudiced in the establishment of an Antarctic minerals regime.[14]

Mineral Resources. Until 1972, the question of mineral resources never surfaced officially. At the

Consultative Meeting in 1975, the United States sought endorsement of a recommendation calling for development of an international agreement to govern possible mineral resource activities in Antarctica. A majority of other Consultative Parties preferred to push for a moratorium on such activities pending study of their possible effects. The Meeting concluded with a recommendation for Treaty States to voluntarily refrain from exploration and exploitation activities while making progress toward solution of the problem.

It was not until 1977 that the Treaty nations agreed to face the difficult legal and political aspects of the mineral resource issue. The delay is understandable considering that these nations are dealing with international problems that have not been faced before. The need to proceed slowly in resolving these complex issues is appreciated. Antarctica is, after all, an entire continent where land ownership does not exist, where no government or private party can issue licenses, lease or sell mineral rights, or receive royalty payments.[15] Because of uncertainties about the world energy situation over the past five years, a great deal of emphasis has been placed on determining the feasibility of exploiting oil and natural gas from areas just off the Antarctic continent. The increased activity and likelihood of expanded programs for exploratory drilling has put pressure on the Treaty Parties to set legal and ecological guidelines for mineral exploration and exploitation.

At the Ninth Consultative Meeting in 1977 the Treaty nations called for intensified consultation on minerals, and recommended the following principles in Recommendations IX-1 Antarctic Mineral Resources:

Parties should continue to play an active and responsible role on mineral resources.

The Antarctic Treaty must be maintained in its entirety.

Protection of the unique Antarctic environment and of its dependent ecosystems should be a basic consideration.

The Consultative Parties, in dealing with the question of mineral resources in Antarctica, should not prejudice the interests of all mankind in Antarctica.

At this meeting it was also recommended that the provisions of Article IV of the Treaty (the freezing of the territorial status quo) should not be affected by any minerals regime. The Treaty powers agreed that their

governments ought to urge their nationals and other states
to "refrain from all exploration and exploitation of
Antarctic mineral resources while making progress towards
the final adoption of an agreed regime concerning
Antarctic mineral resource activities...." Since that
time exploration by several nations, including the United
States, has continued. At the Tenth Consultative Meeting
in 1980, it was hoped that a meeting on minerals issues
would be held before the Eleventh Consultative Meeting of
June, 1981. Also at the 1980 Meeting, the West Germans
pushed for Consultative status before the Eleventh Meeting
took place. The West Germans are very dependent on
mineral imports to maintain their economy, and as such
are aware of the need to diversify and expand their
sources of supply.

The major underlying issue is whether the Antarctic
Treaty can be extended to cover minerals exploitation.
Non-claimants maintain that the freedom of access provisions in the Treaty should also prevail for minerals.
Claimants, however, maintain that they only agreed to free
access in 1959 for the conduct of scientific research.
Because the minerals in question are found under the land
or the seabed--areas within the Treaty jurisdiction--it
is hard to separate the minerals issue from the Treaty as
a whole. The existing provisions of the Treaty cannot
easily be stretched to cover minerals. Any amendments to
do so, would threaten the crucial sovereignty compromise
between claimants and non-claimants. At the same time,
those Treaty powers most in favor of mineral activity,
such as the United States, are continually pushing the
issue. Recommendations were made at the Eleventh
Consultative Meeting to begin negotiations to develop a
new legal framework for the exploration and exploitation
of non-living resources in Antarctica. These negotiations
will no doubt raise many of the jurisdictional issues that
the States Parties have for two decades been able to avoid
settling. At the 1981 Meeting the government of New
Zealand offered to formally hold detailed negotiations on
a Mineral Resource Convention for Antarctica in mid-1982.

The 200-Mile EEZ. Another key issue which connects
the resources of the marine living environment with those
of the continental shelf and those on the continent
itself, concerns islands and resources within the 200-mile
exclusive economic zone. The LOS Treaty declares
200-mile EEZs part of international ocean law. The
claimant States in Antarctica, therefore, also claim
200-mile economic jurisdiction out into the Southern
Ocean. Non-claimants, because they do not accept the land
claims, reject the 200-mile economic zones claimed.

The Convention on Marine Living Resources covers a
wider area than the Antarctica Treaty, and includes some
sub-Antarctic islands. The Convention refers to high

seas and coastal states rights. The mainland claimants understand this to refer to coastal rights off the Antarctic mainland. The non-claimants understand the same language to refer only to coastal rights off the islands.[16] In other words, the claimant states have used the existence of islands within the Convention area, but beyond the Treaty's jurisdiction, as an excuse to refer to "coastal state jurisdiction." Claimant states can interpret this language (found in Article IV of the Convention) as referring to both subantarctic islands and mainland claims. Non-claimant states can interpret it as referring solely to islands.

The language of the Convention, therefore, means different things to different states. This tenuous compromise has been called the bi-focal approach. It has attempted to meet the needs of both claimant and non-claimant demands; but will remain a major political issue as increased resource exploitation occurs.

International Problems. There are three competing interests involved in the resource politics of Antarctica. These have been expressed by the claimant Consultative Parties, the non-claimant Consultative Parties, and the non-Treaty states. Each group has its own diverse interests, making it difficult to devise a successful resource management regime. It is an especially arduous task given that agreement must be reached between the Consultative Party nations and the more than one hundred other states of the international community.

Even if some sort of compromise can be worked out among the Antarctic Treaty states, there will be increasing pressure from nations outside the Treaty, particularly Third World countries, to benefit from the potentially safe exploitation of certain resources in Antarctica. The negotiations at UNCLOS III have inspired many representatives of the Third World to demand that Antarctic resources be shared for the benefit of all mankind. In many ways UNCLOS III has served as a major learning device for the Third World countries. Since its beginning, LDCs have become more vocal in expressing their misgivings about the Antarctic Treaty regime. For example, in 1975, LOS President Shirley Amerasinghe of Sri Lanka made the following statement:

There are still areas of this planet where opportunities remain for constructive and peaceful cooperation on the part of the international community for the common good of all rather than the benefit of a few. Such an area is the Antarctic continent.... There can be no doubt that there are vast possibilities for a new initiative that would redound to the benefit of all mankind. Antarctica is an area where the now widely accepted ideas and concepts relating to international economic cooperation with their special stress on the principle of equitable sharing of the world's resources, can find ample scope for application.[17]

Antarctica is one of the few areas of the planet where peaceful cooperation by the international community could benefit the majority rather than a few. Thus far, the Antarctic Treaty powers have successfully rebuffed various initiatives in the United Nations to allow "outsiders" a say in the management of Antarctica. These pressures have inspired the Treaty nations to work more swiftly and amiably on resource policy issues in the Antarctic.

Possible Solutions

Several solutions to the Antarctic resource problem have been offered over the years. These have included the following suggestions: (1) An international approach that would include the entire world community in a single management framework. The Consultative Parties do not favor such an approach. (2) Recognition of the assertions of sovereignty by the claimant Consultative Parties. This approach is favored most highly by those nations, but not by most other countries. (3) Resolution of the conflicting and disputed sovereignty claims by the International Court of Justice. This approach raises as many questions of sovereignty as it would hope to settle. In addition, it is improbable that Chile and Argentina would submit to the jurisdiction of the Court. (4) A "pooling" of the claims of the Consultative Parties and a declaration of Joint Antarctic Sovereignty to establish an exclusive but community-oriented jurisdiction over the entire Antarctic region. That is, the region would still remain in the jurisdictional control of the Treaty states, but with the recognition that other states should benefit from, or have access to, the resources of the Antarctic on a controlled basis. (5) A Trusteeship solution whereby the Consultative Party states would act as trustees for the entire international community in Antarctica regarding resource, ecological, and scientific projects. (6) A Joint Antarctic Resource Jurisdiction approach similar to (4) above.[18]

The fourth proposal, dealing with joint sovereignty, poses several questions which indicate the difficulties involved in formulating a new resource regime structure for Antarctica. For instance, would the new legal entity have to be declared a separate and independent state; and would it therefore pass its own laws and have its own legislature? In addition, a declaration of joint sovereignty would probably be construed as a new claim, and thus be in derogation of the Antarctic Treaty. Article IV of the Treaty provides in part that: "No new claim, or enlargement of an existing claim, to territorial sovereignty in Antarctica shall be asserted while the present Treaty is in force." Furthermore, claimant Parties would feel uncertain about their jurisdiction and be unlikely to submit to this solution. Finally, this approach might appear to non-Treaty members as a blatant attempt by the Treaty Parties to appropriate Antarctica for their exclusive domain without regard to other interests.

If pressure from nations outside the Antarctic club continues, then the Treaty powers may opt for a Trusteeship solution that would satisfy the complaints of the larger world community while leaving a large degree of effective management of the area to the Antarctic Treaty Parties.[19] A brief description of the Trusteeship solution and a Joint Antarctic Resource Jurisdiction can be found in Appendix 14.

The various management proposals put forward in the past few years, in addition to the rapid development of drilling technology and the changing overall international political environment (which will be influenced by the outcome of UNCLOS III), will do much to determine the Treaty future in 1991. In that year, any of the Treaty nations may call for a general conference of the signatory nations to review the operation of the Treaty. If amendments agreed to by a majority of the Parties are not ratified by one or more of the participating nations within two years of the conference date, those nations are free to withdraw from the Treaty and will no longer be obliged to abide by it. It is likely, however, that the Treaty Parties will come to some sort of agreement over territorial claims, if for no other reason than to keep the Treaty together and ensure the continuity and privileged position of the present "club" of Treaty nations. Pressure from the Third World to obtain access to the resources of Antarctica for the "benefit of all mankind" will increase if the International Seabed Authority enters into force.[20]

OUTER SPACE

Another resource commons that is undergoing pressure for regime change, and which may be affected by the underlying precedents of an International Seabed Authority, is outer space.

The management problems found in each field of outer space activity are usually specific to that field, even though in some cases there are similarities among the fields. Consequently, outer space differs from the oceans, where the central issues often involve a good deal of interference between different ocean uses and the need to make exchanges between them. In the oceans, for example, there are often competing interests for fishing, navigation, recreational or commercial use, and scientific research. In outer space this type of resource use conflict has not yet occurred to any significant extent. The similarities between outer space resource activities and those of the ocean are found in the need to devise an acceptable international agreement for the management of these common resource realms. They are similar in two important aspects: they contain resources of various sorts, and they are found beyond the traditional lines of territorial sovereignty. The common heritage principle, demands for the sharing of benefits to all nations, and Third World claims for future access to space related resources have, therefore, often been found in international negotiations for treaties of these resources.

In addition to the common heritage principle, a plea to share in resources development creates another link between the Law of the Sea Treaty and the Moon Treaty. Those opposing the Moon Treaty (which covers a wide range of outer space use), claim it will destroy incentives to use outer space resource potential. The Treaty does not, however, ban use of resources. It aims to make it easier by calling for an eventual system to guide development. The regime, like the Law of the Sea, would be a means to carry out development in a spirit of cooperation necessary in areas not subject to national claims. The LOS Treaty is much more specific than the Moon Treaty, and may provide a rough blueprint for later outer space resource regime frameworks.

Activities in outer space are becoming increasingly politicized for four principal reasons. One of these is the growing emphasis on earth-oriented uses of satellites. This includes both the traditional use for military purposes and, especially since 1965, the use of satellites for surveying earth resources for minerals, agriculture, navigation, and communications. A second reason is that there has been a large increase in the number of countries or special interests relying on space-technology services. This widening circle of actors increases rapidly as the technology needed for utilizing data and actively participating in satellite development become more widespread. The net result is that more areas for resource use conflict arise as the number of actors involved, and uses of the resources, increases. The third major reason for the politicized nature of outer space activity has been the warming of Cold War bipolarity over the last decade. The 1967 Outer Space Treaty and the 1963 Nuclear Test Ban Treaty have added a new emphasis on civilian space uses. The United States and Soviet Union are increasingly played off against each other by numerous other countries to advance their own interests. Both

superpowers, however, have lost much of their previous
ability to rally support for preferred space policies from
allies by appeals to bloc or ideological loyalties.[21]
A fourth reason is the increasing use of outer space for
military purposes by the United States and Soviet Union.
A growing percentage of United States funds spent on outer
space activities is related to the Defense Department.
Most current and planned research and development space
programs are also Defense oriented. At present outer
space is primarily used for military communications and
surveillance satellites. Within ten years both superpowers will have numerous "killer satellites" in space
designed to destroy other satellites. There is some
speculation that the Soviets have already tested and
deployed such satellites capable of destroying American
surveillance satellites. It is also possible that within
fifteen years satellites equipped with laser and high-
energy particle beam weapons will be placed in orbit to
destroy Intercontinental Ballistic Missiles and other
satellites. The first steps of using outer space as a
new theatre of war have already been taken. Despite
international attempts to stop this, the United States
and Soviet Union are unlikely to slow the pace of development for outer space warfare for fear the other side
will gain the upper hand.

An indicator of the changes occurring in outer
space resource activity is the transformation of the 1964
International Telecommunications Satellite Consortium
(INTELSAT). When formed it was an almost exclusively
American dominated organization reflecting both a Cold
War split with the Soviets and the monopoly of high
communications technology held by the United States. When
some of the West European nations and Japan developed the
necessary technology, and the American predominance in
the world as a superpower and monopolizer of technology
declined somewhat, INTELSAT took on a more international
structure. For these reasons, the interim arrangements
were renegotiated between 1969 and 1971. By 1974, the
Soviets had an earth station in orbit to permit a tie-in
with the INTELSAT communications network. China also had
a similar operating ability.

Are both open access/free use and national management regime alternatives for managing the resources of
outer space adequate to meet the political demands of the
new era of space utilization? The rationale for
international management of the uses of outer space is
based on the premise that this realm belongs to all
mankind. Therefore, all users are accountable to the
international community for any problem arising from
resource use of the area. There is also increasing
pressure to ensure that any benefits from space resources
must be shared. The connections between these premises
and the International Seabed Authority proposed in the

Law of the Sea are evident.

International management is currently being considered for different kinds of space satellite functions. These include the distribution and analysis of data acquired from remote sensing activities; international broadcasting via satellite; maritime communications resources; and frequency and orbital use. Because some groups of nations feel at a disadvantage with the present open access and free use regimes in these fields, they are attempting to get multilateral oversight of the activities of the major space powers.[22]

In each of these areas the LDCs have feared that their economic or political interests might be undermined by an open access regime. They have thus tried to gain some leverage on the activities of the more technologically advanced nations for using the space environment. Except for air frequency use and orbital satellite flight paths, the pressures have not been toward national claims to resources, as has occurred in the oceans. Even in these two areas, only a few countries have made claims of exclusive rights for their use. Generally, these claims are limited to a small part of the total resource: for instance, the air and space area directly above a nation's territory. For the most part, demands in the resource allocation and management of outer space have been for increased accountability of the space powers to the international community. An overview of the major issues involved in current activities in outer space can be found in Appendix 15.

The split between the developed and developing countries over these resources is similar to that over the deep seabed. Like the disputes over access to deep seabed resources, ownership, technology transfer and the sharing of benefits to less developed countries, similar conflicts are becoming central issues at international management forums for the utilization of air waves and orbital paths. The Third World countries have learned from UNCLOS III that they must join forces over resource commons issues in order to secure access to resources they presently lack the technology to exploit. In addition they are eager to have the benefits derived from the current exploitation of those resources shared immediately. This has resulted in increasingly politicized World Administrative Radio Conference (WARC) meetings. And, like the ocean mining issue, there are certain differences within the highly industrial nations. For example, Canada and the United States have differences over production control of ocean mining, and are at odds over what portion of the spectrum should be devoted to satellite services. Evidence from oil, seabed, and other critical resources, clearly indicates that access to resources will also be a growing political problem among the industrially advanced nations. The need for international resource planning is

readily apparent. The political and economic pressures
within each individual state to secure access on a purely
nationalistic basis, however, does not portend for easy
agreement.

For the most part, conflicts over air waves and
geo-stationary orbits are between North and South. A
major problem involves a fight over the air space directly
over the equator where a communications satellite can
exactly match the earth's rotational speed and therefore
remain "stationary." The LDCs want to block out portions
of the orbit for later use even though they now lack the
means to launch and operate satellites. India now has
launch capability, and is particularly concerned that
access to geo-stationary orbits remains possible for it
and other Third World nations.[23]

Another potential area of orbit use conflict
concerns the possible placement of Solar Powered
Satellites (SPS) in orbit. Satellites in strategically
placed orbits would collect solar energy twenty-four hours
a day; turn that radiation into electricity by using solar
cells; convert that energy into microwaves; and then beam
it down to specific locations on earth using high energy
microwave beams to be transformed back into electricity.
There is great potential for international cooperation in
this project--which is still in the early stages of
development in the United States and a handful of other
technologically advanced nations. But there will be
conflict if agreement cannot be worked out on orbit
access.

The management of resource decisions in these
fields has become more politicized over the past decade
as the major issues are being seen as involving another
North-South confrontation over common resources.
International resource management decisions will therefore
be increasingly affected by, and will in turn affect,
overall political relations among the developed and
developing countries.

One study found that user fees would be the best
way of bringing the costs of using these resources into
line with their value (as determined by availability).[24]
This would, for example, free some portions of the
spectrum that are now under-utilized for use by others.
While such a system would constitute de facto recognition
that the spectrum and orbits are internationally owned
resources--like, the seabed beyond national jurisdiction--
it does have problems. For instance, it will most likely
be the developed nations that can best afford the fees,
leaving the developing countries in the same position of
not having access to the resources. The user fees would,
however, provide revenue to the international community
to be applied to increase the communications capabilities
among the developing countries. The tax on seabed mining
by the International Seabed Authority sets a precedent

for such a fund.

The Moon Treaty

The United Nations draft treaty agreement on the Moon is officially known as "The Agreement Governing the Activities of States on the Moon and Other Celestial Bodies." On July 3, 1979, the United Nations Committee on the Peaceful Uses of Outer Space completed negotiation of the treaty. The United Nations General Assembly approved the Treaty December 5, 1979. Since that date it has been submitted to governments throughout the world for ratification. In order to bring the treaty into force only five nations need ratify it. By the end of 1980, France, Chile, Romania, the Philippines, and Canada had done so. The treaty is now international law for all nations that sign it.

There are many significant resource issues surrounding the Moon Treaty. Two of the most central are discussed here. The first concerns the special nature of the resources involved. They are vast, would require great technological sophistication to exploit, and have been declared the common heritage of mankind. The Moon Treaty is concerned with resource use and ownership of both the moon and other celestial bodies in outer space. It is a treaty framework for dealing with potentially vast and incredibly rich resources that will not become fully exploitable until the twenty-first century. A second central issue of the treaty concerns the politics of North-South economic relations. As with UNCLOS III (particularly the framework for an International Seabed Authority), negotiations for a potential resource management regime have come down to economic and ideological issues pitting the developed against the developing nations; that is, between a free enterprise system and a more socialist or collective framework for exploiting the moon and other celestial bodies in outer space. Indeed, Article 1 of the Moon Treaty states this very clearly.

Opposition to the Moon Treaty. The Moon Treaty is an elaboration of international law on outer space, following the initial 1967 Treaty on Peaceful Uses of Outer Space, which was ratified by the United States in 1967. Shortly after the completion of the Moon Treaty in 1979, opposition to it arose within the United States. Although the United States Department of State favored ratification of the Treaty, the small but intense and growing opposition to it has succeeded in delaying United States signature of the agreement. The attacks on the Treaty came originally from an organization called the L-5 Society.[25] Its board of directors includes scientists, authors, engineers, and legislators.

The L-5 Society has hired Washington lobbyist Leigh Ratiner, who was a key United States representative to UNCLOS III (up to 1979), and later lobbied for Kennecott Copper Corporation in the Congress for United States unilateral deep seabed mining legislation. Ratiner has presented his case against the Moon Treaty in a manner similar to the way he lobbied against United States ratification of the Law of the Sea and for unilateral legislation. (Ratiner also played a key role in review of the United States position vis-a-vis the LOS Treaty that was conducted by the Reagan Administration in 1981.)

A central thesis of his argument is that the Moon Treaty would "doom free enterprise initiative in outer space" and subjugate American interests to those of developing Third World nations.[26] State Department spokesmen, on the other hand, defend the Treaty as an improvement on existing international rules. They contend that it simply establishes fair-play rules for resource exploitation, including "orderly and safe development... rational management...and equitable sharing by all nations in the benefits derived from these parties." (Article XI of the Moon Treaty). Skepticism about the treaty had been voiced by former Senators Jacob K. Javits and Frank Church. In the House, Congressman John Breaux has been a leading spokesman against United States ratification of the Moon Treaty, as well as a leading proponent of unilateral deep seabed mining legislation. The L-5 Society has drummed up support against the Treaty by misleadingly portraying it as a Soviet backed socialist arrangement for the exploitation of resources in space. Actually, the Soviet Union has long been opposed to the inclusion of the "common heritage" principle in the Treaty. The Soviets eventually agreed to its inclusion for political reasons. They hoped to gain political points with the Group of 77 by supporting Third World demands for "common heritage" being a part of the Treaty language.[27]

Opponents of the Treaty argue that the inclusion of the common heritage principle in the text will have the effect of blocking the assurance of adequate return on investment that is necessary to interest private industry in spending the huge sums of money required to get outer space resource activities underway. Industrial opponents also argue that the draft agreement would have the effect of imposing an indefinite delay on commercial development of space at a time when the United States is a world leader in space technology. It is felt that if the treaty stands up in Congress, American inventiveness and enterprise would be shut off from the industrialization of space.[28] This argument is very similar to that given by American ocean mining companies who lobbied successfully for unilateral legislation to provide economic and legal assurances for their ventures. If the effect of the Moon Treaty is to curtail investment in space resource-related activities then there are obviously many arguments against the United States ratifying it.

The treaty's supporters maintain, however, that no such inhibition is either stated or implied in the Treaty. State Department spokesmen have pointed out that nothing in the Moon Treaty calls for a moratorium while such an international regime is being set up.[29] The Treaty requires only that the signatories work toward defining the regime and getting it established. Furthermore, the ban on unilateral claims implied by the "common heritage" phrase is already covered by the 1967 Treaty on the Peaceful Uses of Outer Space--which the United States has signed. The principles on non-appropriation, access by all, and use for the benefit and interest of all nations have been embodied in the 1967 Treaty for well over a decade.

Opponents of the Moon Treaty claim that its call for the ultimate negotiation of an internatinal regime for resources development, is in effect a moratorium on any exploitation activities prior to that time. They argue that any regime negotiated under the common heritage principle would be completely contrary to United States national interests given the emerging regime for the exploitation of deep seabed resources in the Law of the Sea talks. Indeed, it would appear that in an era when resource access and ownership is taking on increasing, if not predominant, importance it would be in the nation's best interest to ensure access to as many alternative resources as possible. This is especially so for the United States, which uses more resources than any other nation, and currently has enough of a technological lead to maximize its interests in the oceans and outer space.

American delegates have specifically stated throughout the negotiation and adoption process of the Moon Treaty that they do not consider the provisions of the Treaty to invoke a moratorium on any prior natural resources development activities, pending establishment of an international regime. Ratiner and other opponents point out that the United States did not agree to the seabed development moratorium, but that other nations are in effect claiming that no seabed development may take place before a LOS Treaty regime is complete as this would violate the rule of good faith in the negotiations. If seabed mining is to serve as a precedent in this area, then it is important to remember that the United States enacted domestic seabed mining legislation that seeks to protect national interests in obtaining seabed minerals and to keep the door open for eventual United States ratification of an acceptable LOS Treaty. Unlike the 1970 Declaration of Principles, which underlies the deep seabed negotiations at UNCLOS III, the Moon Treaty grants "special consideration" to those countries "which have contributed either directly or indirectly to the exploration of the moon" (which would include the United States) as well as to the interests and needs of the developing countries, with regard to equitable benefit sharing under the international resources regime that the Treaty seeks to establish.

In sum, the Moon Treaty should not inhibit commercial investment by American interests. If it can be shown at a later date that the Treaty does act as a restraint on American space activities then support will have to be reevaluated. Article XI makes clear that all states' parties to the treaty must have a sufficient interest in the possible future exploitation of the natural resources of the Moon and other celestial bodies and that their views are to be given serious consideration at any future international conference. Any such negotiated regime would have to give special consideration to the "efforts of those countries which have contributed either directly or indirectly to the exploration of the Moon" as well as to the "interests and needs of the developing countries."[30]

Even if the United States were to ratify the Moon Treaty, its only obligation would be to participate in a future international conference on outer space. The main purposes of such an international regime would be those described in Article XI, paragraph 7 of the Moon Treaty. States parties to the treaty would not be obligated to accept the results of such a negotiation if they deemed the results to be contrary to their national interests. Finally, refusal by a state to accept any such international regime would not preclude a state or its nationals from exploiting the natural resources of the moon or other celestial bodies.[31]

The debate on whether or not the United States should sign the Moon Treaty has raised several common resource issues. The underlying differences between free access and international institutional management regimes are fundamentally similar to those raised about an International Seabed Authority. These differences will undoubtedly be argued over until attempts to devise international frameworks for the management of other outer space resource uses, the seabed, and aspects of a resource regime for Antarctica, meet with success. Total agreement on all the issues is likely to remain elusive. The basic theoretical and practical questions which are at the center of this debate concern the purported need to have international institutional mechanisms for the management of resource commons in order to maintain world harmony and insure an equitable distribution of the world's wealth.

CONCLUDING REMARKS

This chapter has discussed the differences and similarities between the major resource issues of the oceans (Law of the Sea), Antarctica, the Moon Treaty, and outer space use. In each of these areas, the exploitation of potentially vast resources is already a reality. With advances in technology for exploiting these realms even more resources will become available. Although there are many differences in the nature of the resources and the type of management structure governing them, there are important similarities.

The major similarities of the resource regimes offered by the Law of the Sea and the Moon Treaty center on the fact that both have the common heritage principle as an underlying foundation for management. In both cases, the Third World nations have made demands for revenue sharing, technology transfer, or guaranteed future access to the resources. In the case of Antarctica, increased Third World pressure on the Thirteen Antarctic Treaty countries may result in a new resource regime framework for that continent by the end of the century.

Particularly for the oceans and the various uses of outer space, new, more specific, and powerful management frameworks can provide coordination for scientific and political issues. On the other hand, international management structures that are too constricting for nations with the ability to exploit these areas, will either not get off the ground or fail to function as originally designed. Either way, they will fail in their attempts to assist in the economically efficient exploitation of these resources and provide an equitable distribution of the benefits derived from them. The success or failure of the Law of the Sea, and especially the International Seabed Authority, will do much to determine future regime frameworks for outer space use. It may also influence the future of resource exploitation in Antarctica once the Antarctic Treaty expires in 1991.[32]

FOOTNOTES

Chapter 6

1. John Breaux, "The Diminishing Prospects for an Acceptable Law of the Sea Treaty," Virginia Journal of International Law 19 (Winter 1979): 257-297. Also see, U.S. Congress, House Committee on Merchant Marine and Fisheries, Oceanography Miscellaneous Pt. 2, Hearings before a subcommittee of the House Committee on Merchant Marine and Fisheries, 95th Cong., 2nd sess., 1977-1978. See especially pages 71-72, 109, 124, 131-150.

2. Statement by Deputy Permanent Representative of Peru, Alvero de Soto, to the United Nations Office in Geneva. Quoted in proceedings of the Seminar on Antarctic Resources and the Environment, held in Washington, D.C., September 14, 1979.

3. John Breaux, "Diminishing Prospects," p. 277.

4. See Garrett Hardin, "The Tragedy of the Commons," in Garrett Hardin and John Baden, eds., Managing the Commons, (San Francisco: W.H. Freeman and Co., 1977), pp. 16-30.

5. Seyom Brown and Larry L. Fabian, "Toward mutual accountability in the nonterrestrial realms," International Organization 29 (Summer 1975): 877-892.

6. Ibid, p. 878.

7. Ibid, p. 881.

8. Ibid.

9. Ibid.

10. Brown and Fabian summarize this deficiency as follows: "The protective shield of asserted sovereign rights has traditionally diminished rather than increased accountability, and overwhelmingly parochial defenses of national interests have traditionally narrowed rather than widened the scope of accountability."

11. Statement by John D. Negroponte, Deputy Assistant Secretary of State for Oceans and Fisheries Affairs, U.S. Congress, House Committee on Science and Technology, Hearings on Antarctic Issues before a subcommittee of the

House Committee on Science and Technology, 96th. Cong., 1st sess., 1979.

12. This development had several antecedents which are important for understanding this aspect of resource management in Antarctica. They are, however, beyond the scope of this chapter. Therefore, see the Statement by John D. Negroponte, Hearings on Antarctic Issues; "Antarctica and its Resources," Earthscan Press Briefing 21, pp. 57-60; and G.M. Auburn, "United States Antarctic Policy," in Marine Technology Society Journal 12 (February-March 1978): 31-36.

13. See, Earthscan 21, pp. 57-59. The authors of this study point out that the Antarctic Treaty powers had various motivating factors in these negotiations--some of which are contradictory. These include: A desire (by the claimants) to protect territorial claims, both on land and at sea, and both in relation to island and to the Antarctic mainland. A desire (by the non-claimants) to protect the principle of freedom of access to claimed areas. A desire to conserve the Antarctic ecosystem. And a desire to conclude negotiations as quickly and in as friendly an atmosphere as possible, so that the issue does not escape from the effective control of the Treaty powers.

14. Ibid., p. 65-76.

15. James Zumberge, "Mineral Resources and Geopolitics in Antarctica," American Scientist 67 (January-February, 1979): 68-77.

16. The bi-focal solution is very unstable. If it fails it would seriously threaten the Antarctic Treaty itself. The Treaty specifically states that no new claims, or enlargements of existing claims, to sovereignty in Antarctica, will be asserted while the Treaty is in force. Any declaration of Antarctic mainland EEZs by a claimant state could be held in breach of this claim. See, Earthscan 21, pp. 72-73. See also Christopher C. Joyner, "The Exclusive Economic Zone and Antarctica," Virginia Journal of International Law 21 (Summer 1981): 691-725.

17. In Barbara Mitchell and Richard Sandbrook, The Management of the Southern Ocean, International Institute for Environment and Development, (London: IIED, 1980), p. 25.

18. See, Frank C. Alexander, Jr., "A Recommended Approach to the Antarctic Resource Problem," University of Miami Law Review 33 (December 1978): 371-425. See

also, Ralph L. Harry, "The Antarctic Regime and the Law of the Sea Convention: An Australian View," Virginia Journal of International Law 21, (Summer 1981): 727-744.

19. The Trusteeship solution as discussed here is from James N. Barnes, "The Emerging Antarctic Living Resources Convention," Paper for the Center for Law and Social Policy, Washington D.C., 1979. See also, P. Jessup and H. Taubenfeld, Controls For Outer Space and the Antarctic Analogy, (New York: Columbia University Press, 1959). In addition, see, "International Trusteeship System," The United Nations, Articles 75-85 of the United Nations Charter.

20. See Barbara Mitchell and Lee Kimball, "Conflict over the Cold Continent," Foreign Policy 35 (Summer 1979): 124-141.

21. This has resulted in a space diplomacy framework that features the superpowers in a mixed pattern of agreement and contention with each other. See Seyom Brown, et al., Regimes for the Ocean, Outer Space, and Weather, (Washington, D.C.: The Brookings Institution, 1977), see especially pp. 125-126. See also, Ernst B. Haas, "Why Collaborate? Issue-Linkage and International Regimes," World Politics 32 (April 1980): 357-405.

22. Brown et al., Regimes, pp. 131-132.

23. See, "Into the Space Club," The Economist, July 26, 1980, p. 40, and "Europe's Battle for the Sky," The Economist, July 19, 1980, pp. 93-94. The satellite issue is an important one for American and European business. It will have a direct impact on large new data networks being developed by SBS (Satellite Business Systems), a consortium of IBM, COMSAT, and Aetna Life Insurance. It will also affect a data transmission system proposed by Xerox and COMSAT's plan for a direct broadcast service; a non-cable television system in which signals would bounce from a satellite directly into a viewer's home.

24. Brown et al., Regimes, pp. 182-196.

25. The "L" is for liberation, a point at which the gravitational pulls of the Earth, moon and sun are equalized. L-5 is the fifth liberation point. See, Science 206, (November 23, 1979) pp. 915-916.

26. Quoted in The Washington Post, Tuesday, October 30, 1979, p. A-3.

27. In brief, Treaty opponents argue that no entity would be permitted to use the moon's resources in a

commercial operation without obtaining authorization from
an international organ whose policies and decisions would
be made by a United Nations General Assembly-type body.
They fear that in order to obtain that authorization, the
entity would have to agree to submit a large share of any
profits it makes to the international organization and to
transfer to other countries on a subsidized basis any
technology it uses. Opponents also argue that authorization would probably be withheld, if the entity was from a
country that was already exploiting moon resources.
Ultimately, they say, no national entity would be permitted to exploit the moon's resources; instead an international monopoly would be created. A close look at the
treaty's provisions will show that many of these fears
are somewhat exaggerated. The above points were made in
a letter to the L-5 Society by Leigh Ratiner, dated August
15, 1979.

28. On February 14, 1980, United Technologies placed
a large advertisement in The Washington Post making these
points.

29. Especially Stephen R. Bond, Assistant Legal
Administrator for UN Affairs, Department of State, under
the Carter administration.

30. These points are from a letter to Senator Alan
Cranston (D. California), by J. Bruce Atwood, Assistant
Secretary for Congressional Relations, Department of
State, dated October 15, 1979. The Moon Treaty does not
place limitations beyond those in the 1967 Outer Space
Treaty on the exploitation of natural resources by any
government or private entity except that the activities
with respect to the natural resources of the moon shall
be carried out in a manner compatible with the purposes
specified in paragraph 7 of Article XI, and the environmental protections contained in Article VII. Efforts by
some developing countries to have the treaty provide for
a moratorium on the exploitation of the natural resources
of celestial bodies other than earth, pending the establishment of an international regime, were rejected by the
United States. The non-ownership of natural resources
provision (Article XI, para. 3), applies only to resources
still "in place" and thus does not apply to the exploitations of natural resources once they are physically
separated from the surface or sub-surface of the moon for
use on the moon or elsewhere in space or for return to
earth.

31. For similarities between the Moon Treaty and
the 1970 resolution on the deep seabeds, see Statement
of Honorable John Breaux, Chairman, Subcommittee on
Fisheries and Wildlife Conservation and the Environment,

and Statement by Leigh S. Ratiner on behalf of the L-5 Society, U.S., House, Committee on Science and Technology, Hearings before a subcommittee of the House Committee on Science and Technology, 96th Cong. 2nd sess. 1979.

    32. For an excellent article which examines the outcome of and the process of agreement on the deep sea-bed mining regime in the Law of the Sea negotiations and their implications for resource exploitation in other international "commons" areas, see Lee Kimball, "Implications of the Arrangements Made for Deep Seabed Mining for Other Joint Exploitations," The Columbia Journal of World Business 15, no. 4., (Winter 1980): 52-61. Kimball, who is consultant to the United Methodist Law of the Sea Project, the International Institute for Environment and Development, and to Citizens for Ocean Law, emphasizes the importance of certain procedural aspects as precedent.

7
The Current Status
of U.S. Ocean Mining Policy

OVERVIEW

Several aspects of United States ocean mining policy merit final comment. Events pertaining to ocean mining on both the national and international levels have changed over the past year, so that various parts of this study have been revised more than once. The following discussion brings together significant developments as of January 1982.

The United States deep seabed mining policy that has emerged over the past decade has only in the last two years (1980-1982) shown signs of coordination and purpose. It has been difficult for policy makers to design a seabed mining program because of the complexities of negotiating a comprehensive Law of the Sea Treaty with 150 other nations while attempting to pass and now implement domestic ocean mining rules and regulations.

Some success on both international and domestic fronts was achieved in 1980 and 1981. Internationally, UNCLOS III came close to concluding a draft Treaty in early 1981. In March 1981, however, President Reagan changed the leadership of the United States delegation to UNCLOS III and began the Administration's review process, which generated uncertainty throughout 1981. Ambassador James Malone listed several problem areas within the Treaty text that the Administration wanted to renegotiate. Domestically, the National Oceanic and Atmospheric Administration (NOAA) completed its final Environmental Impact Statement and Rules and Regulations for deep seabed mining by United States based companies. The licensing phase for exploration began in January 1982.

Several trends in the American ocean mining industry are becoming clear. Even with the inactment of the Deep Seabed Hard Mineral Resources Act the number of American companies aggressively pursuing research and development is declining. However, four United States ocean mining groups intend to apply for exploration licenses from NOAA: Ocean Minerals Company, Ocean Mining Associates, Kennecott, and Ocean Management Incorporated. The two leading companies, Ocean Minerals Company and Ocean Mining Associates, have completed their initial phase of development but have not yet proceeded with the second phase because of legal uncertainties concerning deep seabed mining in the proposed Law of the Sea (LOS) Treaty. Thus far, none of the American consortia have been able to obtain significant loans from banks, primarily because banks want legal assurances that the minerals, once mined, will belong to the companies--an assurance that they cannot yet provide.

Domestic legislation was designed to provide a stable political and legal environment so that venture capital would be more readily available to the industry. It provides assurances to United States based companies that the government stands firmly behind both exploration and, after January 1st 1988, commercial exploitation of manganese nodules in international waters. The legislation (PL 96-283) accomplishes two major goals. First, it allows UNCLOS III the opportunity to conclude an acceptable Treaty before American companies exploit the deep seabed for manganese nodules. (The change of the commercial exploitation date from 1982 to 1988, resulted in less opposition to the legislation from the Group of 77 than had been anticipated.) Second, the legislation provides legal and political assurances to the industry that the government is in favor of a strong domestic ocean mining program.

Because of the complexities of interdependence and the role of international organizations in shaping a comprehensive LOS Treaty, many years may pass before a Treaty enters into force for the United States. The United States should, therefore, use this time to continue negotiations for a more acceptable comprehensive Treaty--especially since such a treaty will set precedents for the management of other resource commons. Whether current domestic legislation and a reciprocal state arrangement remain interim in nature, or become legal guidelines for long-term ocean mining, will depend upon the final wording and acceptability of the Treaty text.

If demand for the minerals in ocean nodules increases, or if supply disruptions occur for political reasons, then their prices will rise. If this happens ocean mining will become more profitable, and United States based ocean miners will energetically pursue their plans for full-scale operations. However, if the American companies do not maintain their research and development efforts, they may lose future contracts to French, German, and Japanese competitors. Because the governments of France, Germany, and Japan work closely with their ocean mining industries, it is possible that those countries could end up supplying the United States with minerals obtained from the deep seabed. Therefore, a careful study should be made over the next ten years to determine how well United States ocean mining companies are keeping up with their foreign competitors. If they fall behind, then financial incentives such as additional tax breaks and depreciation allowances should be made available to keep R&D levels high enough so that when ocean mining does become profitable, American companies will be in a strong competitive position.

All the United States based ocean mining companies have declined the joint government-industry ties and direct subsidies that some countries have initiated to enhance their ocean mining capabilities. There is little doubt that if the American ocean mining industries felt it was beneficial for a closer working relationship with government, they would lobby for them. Instead, they have lobbied past and present Administrations for the elimination of unacceptable provisions in the LOS Treaty. In addition, Congressmen were successfully lobbied for the passage of domestic interim legislation favorable to industries needs. American corporations traditionally have shunned close ties with government. Rather, their goals have been to ensure that the regulations surrounding a particular industry are conducive to the maximization of profit. In these respects, the ocean mining industry is typical of corporate activity in the United States.

As a policy issue, ocean mining is unique in several aspects. It has, for example, created land-based versus sea-based competition for mineral exploitation. Land-based supplies of the metals contained in manganese nodules will be sufficient to meet demand for at least the next two decades. Consequently, low prices will not attract significant business investments in ocean mining. The petroleum industry, which is also involved in mineral exploitation, seeks both sea and land-based supplies; but due to the high price and limited supply of oil, there is little competition between sources from the land or sea. Another unique aspect of the ocean mining industry is that it has been put into the position (given the current provisions of the LOS Treaty), of financing, and providing technology for its international competitor--the Enterprise. Other resource industries have never had to contend with such a situation before. And, because American based ocean mining consortia may be directly competing with land-based producers of nickel, copper, cobalt, and manganese by the turn of the century, corporate activities are closely linked with the nation's foreign policy, especially those policies that deal with Third World producer demands for a NIEO and basic North-South economic relations.

It is likely that a hardening in United States Soviet relations and a less conciliatory policy toward non-OPEC Third World countries will occur during the

Reagan Administration and, perhaps, throughout the decade. These changes would increase pressures on policy makers in Washington, D.C. to take a harder line on Group of 77 demands for a New International Economic Order (NIEO), transfer of technology, and access to revenues derived from resource commons exploitation.

OCEAN MINING UNDER THE REAGAN ADMINISTRATION

Overall, the outlook for assistance to the American ocean mining interests from the Reagan Administration appears good. Given the President's concern with national security and access to strategic minerals, it is probable that the Administration will do as much as possible to enhance the goals of the deep seabed mining industry in the United States. The review of the United States stance at UNCLOS III clearly reflected the new conservative and assertive ideology of the Reagan Administration. At the same time, it is unlikely that more direct forms of assistance will be made to the industry in the form of loan guarantees or direct subsidies.

The Administration probably will not push for a speedy conclusion of the present LOS Treaty negotiations in 1982, despite threats from the Group of 77 that a Treaty will be signed without United States participation if necessary. If Treaty negotiations are prolonged, the government will have to help provide an alternative international legal framework for ocean mining companies. Consequently, in order to help the industry obtain loan guarantees from banks and provide broad policy support, the Administration may support a strong reciprocating state arrangement with the "like-minded" nations. Such an arrangment would help provide assurances about access rights to the nodules for both industry and banks.

The Office of Ocean Minerals and Energy (OME) was created in 1980, following passage of PL 96-283. This office has set up the legal structure of a domestic ocean mining licensing program. Because PL 96-283 does not allow commercial mining until 1988, permit claims for exploitation will not be made until later in the decade. OME plans to have final rules on commercial recovery regulations by that time. Those rules will reflect political and industrial developments over the next two or three years. The Office of Ocean Minerals and Energy is sensitive to the needs of United States ocean mining companies. It has attempted to create a domestic structure for deep seabed mining that the companies feel is needed for a beneficial interim mining program. That program includes governmental legal and political support which is designed to minimize economic uncertainties for the consortia. Consequently, OME intends to focus more on industry's needs for investment security over the next several years.

Although there was a complete change in the Chairmanship of Senate Committees, and several Committee changes in the House in 1980, the general endorsement of deep seabed mining legislation that prevailed in the 96th and 97th Congresses will likely prevail in the 98th. It is too early to predict whether specific ocean mining legislative and policy changes will be sought by the current Congress. The major concern throughout Washington for the near future is how best to design and live with the dramatic budget cuts undertaken by the Reagan Administration. Significant cuts in NOAA's budget will certainly have consequences for the implemention of PL 96-283. The Office of Ocean Minerals and Energy has been, and will continue to be, on a very tight budget. How successful NOAA and OME will be in carrying out their policy tasks remains to be seen. If the national security aspects of ocean mining are stressed, then more funding may become available to ensure a strong ocean mining program.

POLYMETALLIC SULFIDE ORE DEPOSITS

Recent disclosures by NOAA and the United States Geological Survey (USGS) of the discovery of potentially valuable deposits of polymetallic sulfides (PMS) along oceanic spreading centers have generated interest in both government and industry. Estimates on one such deposit have suggested that the in situ value of the metals contained in the deposit could approach several billion dollars.[1] Further, it has been indicated that these discoveries could mark a "dramatic turnaround" in the global assessment of accessible mineral deposits.[2] The degree to which these preliminary evaluations are accurate, given prevailing economic, political and legal constraints, requires further study.

Legal and political problems raised by PMS discoveries fall into three possible scenarios concerning jurisdiction over the resource: (1) exploration and exploitation within United States jurisdiction; (2) exploitation in international waters given a Law of the Sea Treaty; and (3) exploitation in international waters without United States participation in such a treaty.

Current finds off the coasts of Washington and Oregon indicate that large deposits of polymetallic sulfides may be found within 200 miles of the United States coast. Legislation along the lines proposed by Congressman John Breaux to establish a 200-mile exclusive economic zone would place such deposits within the bounds of United States jurisdiction. Another course of action would be for the President to use his executive powers to unilaterally declare--by Presidential Proclamation--the creation of a 200-mile EEZ in the same way President Truman claimed United States control of the outer continental shelf (out to the 200 meter isobath) in 1945.

On the international level, expectations of another great source of wealth and resources from the oceans could lead to a new set of questions for both the United States and developing countries at UNCLOS III. If the treaty is ratified by the United States and enters into force, rules for mining the deposits in international waters will have to be worked out alongside those for manganese nodules. Interesting policy questions are raised. For example, could the exploitation of the resource allow for the inclusion on the Council (the executive organ of the International Seabed Authority) of a wider range of metal importing and exporting countries than is presently outlined in the LOS Treaty text? Further, how will the other provisions which are negotiated on the basis of data from studies on manganese nodules, be influenced by future developments of other metalliferous sediments? Treaty articles dealing with production controls and the transfer of marine technology clearly deserve study in this new context.

Another issue that may influence ocean law and policy concerns the location of the PMS deposits. For example, could the deposits, particularly highly localized ones, contribute to "creeping jurisdiction"? It is plausible that PMS deposits situated more than 200 miles from shore could be influential in the decision by a country to extend coastal jurisdiction beyond 200 miles. For instance, if deposits in the Juan De Fuca and Gorda spreading areas are found to be both within 200 miles and just beyond that limit, there could be increasing pressure to extend United States economic jurisdiction.

Assessments of the extent to which these political and legal problems will become critical in the short-term will depend in part on the magnitude of PMS deposits' estimated economic value, a prospective value will in turn be influenced by the degree to which their eventual exploitation is likely to be burdened by costly legal and political transactions.[3]

SUMMARY

The support that the United States government has shown by passing PL 96-283, promotes the interests of the industry and helps ensure future American access to the resources of the deep seabed as well as other resources considered to be part of the global commons. United States concessions on deep seabed mining to the Group of 77 at UNCLOS III in the late 1970s now appear to be of questionable value to the nation's long-term security and economic interests in the eyes of a growing number of policy makers. While a comprehensive LOS Treaty probably is still desired by the government, a more favorable industry position is likely to be pushed by the American negotiators at UNCLOS III and in similar international forums throughout the 1980s.

United States ocean mining companies would be aided a great deal if the Reagan Administration's plans to provide a minimum price for domestic sources of cobalt becomes effective. In essence, this policy subsidizes the creation of a domestic supply source. Concern about United States vulnerability to the loss of foreign materials intensified in mid-1981 with warnings by Secretary of State Alexander M. Haig, Jr. and others that the Soviet Union had launched a "resource war" against the United States and its allies. It was also during this time that the Administration took a harder line vis-a-vis the developing nations (Group of 77) at UNCLOS III on deep seabed mining issues.[4] Politically motivated supply disruptions and an upturn in worldwide economic activity over the next ten years would do much to determine how soon the exploitation of manganese nodules on the deep seabed becomes a reality and not just a possiblity one or two steps removed from the realm of science fiction.[5]

The intrinsic values of the manganese nodules themselves may not be of great economic or military importance to the United States; however, the precedents which are established for the nodules will determine strategies for other resource exploitation in international waters (i.e. sulfide ore deposits), Antarctica, and outer space. For this important reason the Reagan Administration has sought significant changes in the LOS Treaty text. There is no question that the final form and jurisdiction of the International Seabed Authority will have wide and long-term impacts on international organizations and institutions responsible for various North-South economic and resource related problems.

The signing of a Law of the Sea Treaty is possible in 1982 or 1983 if both the United States and the Group of 77 are serious in their efforts to reach agreement. If agreement is reached between the Reagan negotiating team and the developing countries at UNCLOS III, then a Treaty will be ratified more readily by the United States Senate.[6] This would not have been the case for the Treaty text that was agreed to, but not signed, by the Carter Administration in late 1980. Industry spokesmen lobbied very hard to influence the Reagan Administration's review process of UNCLOS III. They have been successful up to a point. What this technologically innovative industry considers "acceptable" and what the Administration may end up signing, for broader political reasons, may not be exactly the same. It is a safe bet, however, that the goals of the industry strike a very receptive chord within the Reagan Administration.

In the long run the ocean mining companies realize the need for an international legal framework for the exploitation of the deep seabed. But they and a growing number of Third World governments also realize that the framework must allow for sufficient access to the resources in order to attract investments to pay for development of the technology necessary for full-scale operations. Jeffry J. Amsbaugh, President of Ocean Mining Associates, sums up his viewpoints about the proposed LOS Treaty and ocean mining this way:

> The best of all worlds, undoubtedly, would be a comprehensive universal acceptable treaty. However, we can easily do without the 'comprehensive' and 'universal' but cannot do without 'acceptable.'[7]

The ocean mining industry is indeed innovative, yet it faces several unusual problems that are frequently overlooked. It is breaking new technological ground, but continued development is constrained by both investment and legal uncertainties. The industry promises to one day supply vast amounts of the world's needs for several crucial minerals, yet the success of its operations between 1990 and 2000 may lower market prices and overall profitability. Exactly how much profitability is affected by additional supplies of these metals will depend on demand, technological innovation, and substitutability.

In sum, the ocean mining industry in the United States has enjoyed continued support from the government for access to the deep seabed. Business and market conditions as well as international legal problems have altered the make-up of several international consortia. It is possible that a reciprocating state arrangement between the United States, France, Great Britain, West Germany, and Japan, will allow ocean mining to begin by the mid-1990s, even if a LOS Treaty has not yet entered into force at that time. A reciprocating state arrangement between "like-minded" states should provide agreement on the following issues: mutually recognized rights to specific mine sites; an agreed framework for dispute settlement; environmental protection measures; and regulations relating to safety of life and property at sea.[8] See Appendix 16 for a breakdown of national involvement in the ocean mining consortia.

The Deep Seabed Hard Mineral Resources Act is detailed enough to serve as enabling legislation for American seabed miners well into the 1980s and beyond. The possibility remains, however, that an acceptable LOS Treaty will be agreed upon.[9] If that happens it would still be necessary to utilize the provisions of PL 96-283 during the time period necessary for such a treaty to enter into force. PL 96-283 provides a legal framework for ocean mining groups in the United States to apply for licenses, it makes provision for NOAA to set and monitor environmental regulations, and the Act will assist in the formation and operation of reciprocating state arrangements. Without positive steps being taken during this interim period, United States ocean mining companies might lose their momentum and hence competitive edge with foreign groups.

During the time required for the Treaty to enter into force the Preparatory Commission for the International Seabed Authority and the International Tribunal for the Law of the Sea could use the on-going ocean mining experience gained under PL 96-283 as a valuable working model for the implementation of its own specific rules, regulations, and procedures.[10] If some form of grandfather rights protection becomes part of the Treaty text (in return for technological and financial assistance from the ocean mining companies and/or their governments to the early Enterprise or its precursor), then a closer and more productive "working" relationship between the ocean mining companies and the Authority could result. For example, some form of "joint venture" could take place during the interim period before the Treaty entered into force.

Some ocean mining companies in the United States have indicated a willingness to let the Authority or its Enterprise buy into a consortium. Training would be provided to personnel representing the Authority, industry money could be put into some form of escrow account for later use by the Enterprise, and technology and equipment could be made available for sale once it is completed. This willingness is based on the premise that the Preparatory Commission be given full power by the Authority to negotiate with the companies and that arrangements worked out in the interim period (such as giving guaranteed access and tenure rights to companies in return for industry cooperation to assist the Enterprise) will provide firm contracts before and after the Treaty enters into force.[11]

If some form of agreement could be worked out like the one suggested above, it would help alleviate the fears that the industry has concerning lack of guaranteed access and tenure. It would also provide a mechanism to help ensure that the Enterprise would be competitive with the companies once the Treaty enters into force and ocean mining actually begins.[12] In this way the knowledge gained from the actual work experience of the companies, and the environmental and other regulatory mechanisms of their governments, during the interim period could prove especially beneficial for the goals of the International Seabed Authority.

In the final analysis, market and profitability levels, and an acceptable LOS Treaty are the factors which will determine the success or failure of the ocean mining industry. When world demand and prices increase for the metals in manganese nodules ocean mining will become a more profitable venture. When that occurs investment capital will be more readily available. Research and development will then surge ahead.

The United States is faced with three inter-linked program phases in the development of domestic and international deep seabed mining policy between 1982 and approximately 1985. The first involves completion of the domestic licensing program which will formalize terms, conditions, and restrictions for ocean mining groups based in the United States--which began in January 1982.

The second phase involves the negotiations and formal structure of a reciprocating state arrangement. These negotiations have already begun and will overlap various aspects of the domestic licensing program. Areas of concern include environmental regulations and dispute settlement mechanisms.

The third phase in the process will be the Preparatory Commission (PrepCom) negotiations, which may begin in 1983 and are important enough to demand careful planning and coordination with the two programs that are already under way. Two immediate questions come to mind: What type of input can or should the United States have in determining the final rules and regulations of ocean mining during the PrepCom negotiations? What negotiating tactics should the like-minded nations use to influence those regulations? The answers to the questions and the success of negotiating these phases will help determine long-term political and economic aspects of ocean resource exploitation beyond national jurisdiction.

President Reagan's official statement on the Law of the Sea was made January 29, 1982 to the United Nations. The statement reflected the conclusions of his review process which began in March 1981. The President's statement made clear that: "while most provisions of the Draft Convention are acceptable and consistent with United States' interests, some major elements of the deep seabed mining regime are not acceptable." He went on to state that the United States would return to the UNCLOS III negotiations to work with other countries to achieve an acceptable Treaty. The statement contained specific changes the Administration felt were necesssary to correct the "unacceptable elements and to achieve" a balanced Treaty.[13]

Finally, it is increasingly clear that Third World countries will have to wait longer than they had hoped for significant changes in the international economic order to provide them with a redistribution of the world's wealth. How successfully Third World governments meet the increasing economic and social demands of their growing populations remains to be seen. In the long run, instability in the Third World will create increasing instability for the entire international system. In an era when the developed nations are struggling to achieve real economic growth and striving to maintain levels of national security vis-a-vis the Soviet Union, it is unlikely that an international policy for sharing global commons will meet with much active support.

FOOTNOTES

CHAPTER 7

1. Strategic Materials Management, (Nautilus Press, Washington, D.C.) November 1, 1981.

2. New York Times, October 7, 1981.

3. Kurt Shusterich, Jim Broadus, and Robert Bowen are undertaking an economic, political, and legal analysis of deep sea polymetallic sulfide ore deposits, in the Marine Policy and Ocean Management Program at the Woods Hole Oceanographic Institution (1982/1983).

4. See, International Herald Tribune, June 16, 1981, pp. 5,7; Washington Post, March 14, 1981; and Business Week, September 7, 1981, p. 46.

5. See, United States, Congress, House, U.S. Minerals Vulnerability: National Policy Implications, A Report prepared by the Subcommittee on Mines and Mining of the Committee on Interior and Insular Affairs, 96th Cong., 2nd sess., 1981; and U.S. Congress, House, Sub-Sahara Africa: Its Role in Critical Mineral Needs of the Western World, A Report prepared by the Subcommittee on Mines and Mining of the Committee on Interior and Insular Affairs, 96th Cong., 2nd sess., 1981.

6. U.S. Ambassador to UNCLOS III, James L. Malone made this and other points, regarding the likelihood of U.S. ratification, in a Department of State statement released August 5, 1981. The statement was made by Malone in a Plenary Meeting of UNCLOS III at the second session of the 11th meeting of UNCLOS III in Geneva, August 5, 1981.

7. From a letter by Jeffry K. Amsbaugh to James L. Malone, U.S. Ambassador to UNCLOS III, date June 2, 1981. Emphasis in original.

8. PL 96-283, The Deep Seabed Hard Mineral Resources Act, Section 118, 31 USC 1428.

9. Discussions with individuals in the Office of Ocean Minerals and Energy and the State Department (September and December 1981), indicate that a reciprocating state "arrangement" (and not necessarily a regime) was very likely. Its nature will be less stringent than

a "regime" but will still provide a means to work out operational issues (i.e. conflicting areas of exploitation) once deep seabed mining is undertaken.

10. The workings of the Preparatory Commission remain to be negotiated, as does protection of investments made prior to final Treaty ratification. Former UNCLOS III Ambassador Elliot Richardson addresses these issues in, "Concluding the Law of the Sea Conference: Critical Remaining Steps," The Columbia Journal of World Business 15 (Winter 1980): 42-44.10

11. Based on discussions with Edward Dangler, Ocean Minerals Company (Lockheed), October and December, 1981.

12. With deep seabed resources agreed to be the "common heritage of mankind," negotiators at the Law of the Sea Conference constructed a "mega-mineral contract" for seabed development and arranged the financing of a new international mining entity--the Enterprise. The financial aspects of the proposed Treaty build on trends in developing country mineral contracts. To ensure a fair system that will work well in the face of economic and technical uncertainty, the financial provisions contain such innovations as inflation accounting and revenue sharing based on a discounted cash flow criterion. These aspects of ocean mining are addressed by, James K. Sebenius and Mati L. Pal, "Evolving Financial Terms of Mineral Agreements: Risks, Rewards and Participation in Deep Seabed Mining," The Columbia Journal of World Business, op cit., pp. 75-83.

13. President Reagan announced that his administration would seek to attain a Treaty that: "will not deter development of any deep seabed mineral resources to meet national and world demand; will assure national access to these resources by current, and future qualified entities, to enhance U.S. security of supply, to avoid monopolization of the resources by the operating arm of the international Authority, and to promote the economic development of the resources; will provide a decision-making role in the deep seabed regime that fairly reflects and effectively protects the political and economic interests and financial contributions of participating states; will not allow for amendments to come into force without approval of the participating states, including in our case the advice and consent of the Senate; will not set other undesirable precedents for international organizations; and will be likely to receive the advice and consent of the Senate. In this regard, the convention should not contain provisions for the mandatory transfer of private technology and participation by and funding for national liberation movements. The United States

remains committed to the multilateral Treaty process for reaching agreement on Law of the Sea. If working together at the conference we can find ways to fulfill these key objectives, my Administration will support ratification." President Reagan's Statement on Law of the Sea, presented to the United Nations, January 29, 1982.

Appendices

APPENDIX 1

PRINCIPAL CHEMICAL AND PHYSICAL CHARACTERISTICS OF MANGANESE NODULES

Parameter	Nature and Extent of Variability
Size	Range generally about 0.5 cm to 10 cm in diameter.
External shape	Most frequently are spheroidal ("peas" to "cannon-balls"), ellipsoidal ("potatoes"), discoidal or tabular (including "hamburgers," slabs), and polybucleate (intergrowths of spheroids or ellipsoids which produce forms resembling grape clusters).
Surface texture	Usually consists of small, closely spaced hemispherical protrusions (mammillae), which give nodule surface a rough to knobby appearance, depending upon mammillae size.
Character of nucleus	Can be any solid surface, such as rock or shark's tooth. Often dictates external shape of nodule.
Nature of ferro-manganese oxide crust	Thickness variable from only a stain to about 5 cm. Typically deposited as concentric growth laminations. May also pratically be a replacement of an easily-altered volcanic nucleus.

Mineralogy	Nodules usually consist of a mixture of authigenic minerals (including manganese and iron oxides, montmorillonite and phillipsite) and clastic minerals (especially quartz and feldspar). Most important are those oxides chemically precipitated on the seafloor--extremely fine-grained manganese oxides (todorokite, birnessite, δ-MnO$_2$) and amorphous hydrated ferric oxyhydroxide.
Chemical composition	Average composition of ore-grade nodules found southeast of Hawaii = Manganese 25-30%, Iron 6%, Nickel 1.5%, Copper 1.3%, and Cobalt 0.25% by weight. Composition quite variable geographically. Typically retain 20-30% water even after air-drying.
Apparent density	1.4-1.5 g/cm^3.
Porosity	50-60%.

Source: Modified from W.J. Raab and M.A. Meylan, 1977, Morphology (Ch. 5), in G.P. Glasby, ed., Marine Manganese Deposits, (Amsterdam: Elsevier, 1977).

APPENDIX 2

USES OF NODULE METALS

The principle uses of the metals contained in deepsea nodules are briefly reviewed below. This outline will help provide an overview of the general economic value of the resource. Some of these minerals have substitutes, however, which can affect their value in times of supply disruption.

Nickel is used in the manufacture of stainless steel, nickel and chromium platings, nickel alloys and steel castings, and also for petroleum refining and ceramics.

Copper is used in electrical equipment, such as transmission lines, electric motors, generators and transformers, and for plumbing supplies. It is also used to make such automobile parts as brakes, radiators, heaters, and carburetors.

Cobalt is used in high strength steel alloys, from which items like industrial magnets and gas turbines are made. Cobalt is also used in telephones. Although not itself naturally radioactive, a man-made isotope of this metal is used for radiation treatment and research.

Manganese is used in all iron and steel products to prevent brittleness caused by sulfur and other impurities, and to impart various qualities of strength and hardness. Steel cannot be made without it.

APPENDIX 3

FINDINGS AND PURPOSES OF PUBLIC LAW 96-283

(June 28, 1980)

[AN ACT: To establish an interim procedure for the orderly development of hard mineral resources in the deep seabed, pending adoption of an international regime relating thereto, and for other purposes]

SECTION 1. SHORT TITLE.

This Act may be cited as the "Deep Seabed Hard Minerals Resources Act."

SEC. 2. FINDINGS AND PURPOSES.

(a) Findings--The Congress finds that--
(1) the United States' requirements for hard minerals to satisfy national industrial needs will continue to expand and the demand for such minerals will eventually exceed the available domestic sources of supply;

(2) in the case of certain hard minerals, the United States is dependent upon foreign sources of supply and the acquisition of such minerals from foreign sources is a significant factor in the national balance-of-payments position;

(3) the present and future national interest of the United States requires the availability of hard mineral resources which is independent of the export policies of foreign nations;

(4) there is an alternate source of supply, which is significant in relation to national needs, of certain hard minerals, including nickel, copper, cobalt, and manganese, contained in the nodules existing in great abundance on the deep seabed;

(5) the nations of the world, including the United States, will benefit if the hard minerals resources of the deep seabed beyond limits of national jurisdiction can be developed and made available for their use;

(6) in particular, future access to the nickel, copper, cobalt, and manganese resources of the deep seabed will be important to the industrial needs of the nations of the world, both developed and developing;

(7) on December 17, 1970, the United States supported (by affirmative vote) the United Nations General Assembly Resolution 2749 (XXV) declaring inter alia the principle that the mineral resources of the deep seabed are the common heritage of mankind, with the expectation that this principle would be legally defined under the terms of a comprehensive international Law of the Sea Treaty yet to be agreed upon;

(8) it is in the national interest of the United States and other nations to encourage a widely acceptable Law of the Sea Treaty, which will provide a new legal order for the oceans covering a broad range of ocean interests, including exploration for the commercial recovery of hard mineral resources of the deep seabed;

(9) the negotiations to conclude such a Treaty and establish the international regime governing the exercise of rights over, and exploration of, the resources of the deep seabed, referred to in General Assembly Resolution 2749 (XXV) are in progress but may not be concluded in the near future;

(10) even if such negotiations are completed promptly, much time will elapse before such an international regime is established and in operation;

(11) development of technology required for the exploration and recovery of hard mineral resources of the deep seabed will require substantial investment for many years before commercial production can occur, and must proceed at this time if deep seabed minerals are to be available when needed;

(12) it is the legal opinion of the United States that exploration for and commercial recovery of hard mineral resources of the deep seabed are freedoms of the high seas subject to a duty of reasonable regard to the interests of other states in their exercise of those and other freedoms recognized by general principles of international law;

(13) pending a Law of the Sea Treaty, and in the absence of agreement among states on applicable principles of international law, the uncertainty among potential investors as to the future legal regime is likely to discourage or prevent the investments necessary to develop deep seabed mining technology;

(14) pending a Law of the Sea Treaty, the protection of the marine environment from damage caused by exploration or recovery of hard mineral resources of the deep seabed depends upon the enactment of suitable interim national legislation;

(15) a Law of the Sea Treaty is likely to establish financial arrangements which obligate the United States or United States citizens to make payments to an international organization with respect to exploration or recovery of the hard mineral resources of the deep seabed; and

(16) legislation is required to establish an interim legal regime under which technology can be developed and the exploration and recovery of the hard mineral resources of the deep seabed can take place until such time as a Law of the Sea Treaty enters into force with respect to the United States.

(b) Purposes--The Congress declares that the purposes of this Act are--

(1) to encourage the successful conclusion of a comprehensive Law of the Sea Treaty, which will give legal definition to the principle that the hard mineral resources of the deep seabed are the common heritage of mankind and which will assure, among other things, nondiscriminatory access to such resources for all nations;

(2) pending the entering into force of such a Treaty, to provide for the establishment of an international revenue-sharing fund the proceeds of which shall be used for sharing with the international community pursuant to such Treaty;

(3) to establish, pending the ratification, by and entering into force with respect to, the United States of such a Treaty, an interim program to regulate the exploration for and commercial recovery of hard mineral resources of the deep seabed by United States citizens;

(4) to accelerate the program of environmental assessment of exploration for the commercial recovery of hard mineral resources of the deep seabed and assure that such exploration and recovery activities are conducted in a manner which will encourage the conservation of such resources, protect the quality of the environment, and promote the safety of life and property at sea; and

(5) to encourage the continued development of technology necessary to recover the hard mineral resources of the deep seabed.

SEC. 3. INTERNATIONAL OBJECTIVES OF THIS ACT.

(a) Disclaimer of Extraterritorial Sovereignty-- By the enactment of this Act, the United States--

(1) exercises its jurisdiction over United States citizens and vessels, and foreign persons and vessels otherwise subject to its jurisdiction, in the exercise of the high seas freedom to engage in exploraton for, and commercial recovery of, hard mineral resources of the deep seabed in accordance with generally accepted principles of international law recognized by the United States; but

(2) does not thereby assert sovereignty or sovereign or exclusive rights or jurisdiction over, or the ownership of, any areas or resources in the deep seabed.

(b) Secretary of State. (1) The Secretary of State is encouraged to negotiate successfully a comprehensive Law of the Sea Treaty which, among other things, provides assured and nondiscriminatory access to hard mineral resources of the deep seabed for all nations, gives legal definition to the principle that the resources of the deep seabed are the common heritage of mankind, and provides for the establishment of requirements for the protection of the quality of the environment as stringent as those promulgated pursuant to this Act.

(2) Until such a Treaty is concluded, the Secretary of State is encouraged to promote any international actions necessary to adequately protect the environment from adverse impacts which may result from any exploration for and commercial recovery of hard mineral resources of the deep seabed carried out by persons not subject to this Act.

SEC. 4 DEFINITIONS

For purposes of this Act, the term--
(1) "commercial recovery" means--
    (A) any activity engaged in at sea to recover any hard mineral resource at a substantial rate for the primary purpose of marketing or commercially using such resource to earn a net profit, whether or not such net profit is actually earned;
    (B) if such recovered hard mineral resource will be processed at sea, such processing; and
    (C) if the waste of such activity to recover any hard mineral resource, or of such processing at sea, will be disposed of at sea, such disposal;
(2) "Continental Shelf" means--
    (A) the seabed and subsoil of the submarine areas adjacent to the coast, but outside the area of the territorial sea, to a depth of 200 meters or, beyond that limit, to where the depth of the superjacent waters admits of the exploitation of the natural resources of such submarine area; and
    (B) the seabed and subsoil of similar submarine areas adjacent to the coast of islands;
(3) "controlling interest," for purposes of paragraph 14(C) of this section, means a direct or indirect legal or beneficial interest in or influence over another person arising through ownership of capital stock, interlocking directorates or officers, contractual relations, or other similar means, which substantially affect the independent business behavior of such person;
(4) "deep seabed" means the seabed, and the subsoil thereof to a depth of ten meters, lying seaward of and outside--
    (A) the Continental Shelf of any nation; and
    (B) any area of national resource jurisdiction of any foreign nation, if such area extends beyond the Continental Shelf of such nation and such jurisdiction is recognized by the United States;
(5) "exploration" means--
    (A) any at-sea observation and evaluation activity which has, as its objective, the establishment and documentation of--
        (i) the nature, shape, concentration, location, and tenor of a

          hard mineral resource; and
             (ii)   the environmental, technical, and other appropriate factors which must be taken into account to achieve commercial recovery; and
          (B)   the taking from the deep seabed of such quantities of any hard mineral resource as are necessary for the design, fabrication, and testing of equipment which is intended to be used in the commercial recovery and processing of such resource;

    (6)   "hard mineral resource" means any deposit or accretion on, or just below, the surface of the deep seabed of nodules which include one or more minerals, at least one of which contains manganese, nickel, cobalt, or copper;

    (7)   "international agreement" means a comprehensive agreement concluded through negotiations at the Third United Nations Conference on the Law of the Sea, relating to (among other matters) the exploration for and commercial recovery of hard mineral resources and the establishment of an international regime for the regulation thereof;

    (8)   "licensee" means the holder of a license issued under title I of this Act to engage in commercial recovery;

    (9)   "permittee" means the holder of a permit issued under title I of this Act to engage in commercial recovery;

    (10)   "person" means any United States citizen, any individual, and any corporation, partnership, joint venture, association, or other entity organized or existing under the laws of any nation;

    (11)   "reciprocating state" means any foreign nation designated as such by the Administrator under section 118;

    (12)   "Administrator" means the Administrator of the National Oceanic and Atmospheric Administration;

    (13)   "United States" means the several States, the District of Columbia, the Commnwealth of Puerto Rico, American Samoa, the United States Virgin Islands, Guam, and any other Commonwealth, territory, or possession of the United States; and

    (14)   "United States citizen" means--
          (A)   any individual who is a citizen of the United States;
          (B) any corporation, partnership, joint venture, association, or other entity organized or existing under the laws of any of the United States; and

(C) any corporation, partnership, joint
venture, association, or entity (whether
organized or existing under the laws of any
of the United States or a foreign nation)
if the controlling interest in such entity
is held by an individual or entity
described in subparagraph (A) or (B).

APPENDIX 4

Security of Supply and Availability of the Four Major Minerals Contained in Manganese Nodules

United States nickel supply is mainly provided by Canada, Australia, and New Caledonia, all of which are regarded as highly reliable. Several developing nations could provide supplementary supplies should the need arise. Nickel can be substituted for cobalt in certain uses.

Copper mining in the United States is a solid industry with large reserves that assure continued strength. In addition to the large reserves, approximately 40 percent of the copper used in this country is recycled. Recycling and substitutes could help meet world demand for copper if one of the major sources of supply--Chile, Zaire, Zambia--were unable to market either processed ore or processed metal.

Cobalt is produced as a by-product of nickel and copper mining so it is not possible to significantly increase its supply except at high cost. Because of the high cobalt content of its copper ore, Zaire is able to supply over 50 percent of the world demand for cobalt. Revenues from the sale of copper and cobalt are essential to the government of that country, so the mines are an attractive target to forces that wish to weaken or remove the government. To a large extent the cobalt markets in Zaire are controlled by ex-colonial ties in Europe (Union Miniere of Belgium), but attacks from internal or external forces might change this situation. If supplies from Zaire were cut off, other sources would not be able to make up the loss. Consequently, higher prices would result. In addition, new sources of the mineral would be actively sought as there are some industrial uses of cobalt that cannot be substituted by other minerals such as nickel.

Manganese is principally found in Brazil, Gabon, Australia, South Africa, India and the Soviet Union. The security of supply for manganese presents the most crucial long-term problem for the United States. The distribution of high-grade reserves indicates that in the future, South Africa and the Soviet Union will be the major producers of manganese, as the other producers deplete their high-grade ore and are left with a lower grade and less profitable product. Because of its own growing demands, Brazil no longer exports as much of this mineral as it once did. As some of the other more advanced Third World mineral rich states expand their economies they will be using a larger portion of their reserves for their own needs thereby increasing costs for other nations. By the end of the century, it is possible that the South African manganese production may be subject to disturbance from political forces--either by anti-government forces or by the government. In addition, the Soviet Union cannot be relied upon as a secure source of manganese. As yet there is no substitute for this mineral which is found in all steel products. The trends in the development of manganese mines are shown in Table 1.

Studies by private consulting firms and by the Departments of Commerce and Interior have clearly stated that the value of ocean mining to the national security of the United States is in its potential to supply manganese that would reduce dependence on potentially unreliable sources. Studies indicate that ocean mining has the potential to become a major source of nickel and cobalt also.

Manganese is the major constituent of seabed nodules; and although some of the ocean mining companies do not plan to process this mineral, it deserves special attention for analysis. Franz Dykstra, a Mining Geologist and Mineral Economist, stated in testimony before the Senate that manganese is the classic example of a strategic/critical raw material. This refers to a metal or mineral without which the welfare of the United States' economy would be in jeopardy--and for which the United States is dependent on remote sources or those subject to preclusion.[1]

Under the Strategic and Critical Materials Stockpiling Act, the General Services Administration acquires, manages, and maintains strategic and critical materials to protect the United States from dependence on foreign supplies in time of national emergency. All four of the major minerals in ocean nodules have been identified as critical materials. Manganese requirements are tied directly to iron and steel production; cobalt, because of its use in the basic tools industry and especially because of its use in high-temperature resistant alloys for jet engines, is vital to defense efforts; copper and nickel demand grown more rapidly in time of war than does the economy as a whole.

Because we cannot produce steel without manganese, United States requirements for it will increase as world steel production increases. The current Free World consumption of manganese as metal equivalent is about 4.5 million tons per year. This amounts to approximately one million tons per year less than reported current production capacity, indicating a surplus. Dykstra points out, however, that if we relate realistic production capabilities (current and projected) to announced increases in world steel production, we can anticipate a modest shortage by 1987, becoming critical by the turn of the century.

TABLE 1

Distribution of Manganese Ore Production[1]

Country	1970	1975	1980	1985
USSR	38%	39%	37%	37%
South Africa	15	18	19	18
Gabon	8	10	10	11
Brazil	10	8	7	7
Australia	4	7	7	6
China	5	5	5	6
India	9	6	5	4
Other	11	7	10	10

Source: C. R. Tinsley, "Manganese Gains Depend on Rate of Recovery in Steel Industry," Engineering and Mining Journal Vol. 178, No. 3, p. 99.

[1] Because the grade of ore varies with location, this table does not indicate the distribution of metal production. This information (for year 1975) is given in Table 9.

This assumes that there will be no political or other
interruption of supply. The pervading optimism that no
such shortage is imminent reflects several misapprehen-
sions, according to several resource analysts.[2]

The abundance of manganese ore from nodules indicates that just a few large-scale ocean mining operations,
plus landbased sources, should be able to meet worldwide
demands for that metal. It should be noted, however, that
commercial grade manganese ore is about 48-50 percent,
while the manganese content of nodules is only approximately 25-30 percent. Both the government and industry
agree that it is necessary to begin ocean mining as soon
as possible to ensure production of all the minerals
contained in seabed nodules, especially as their supply
becomes more critical in the next two decades. For a
summary of findings on manganese supply and dependency
see Tables 2 and 3.

TABLE 2

FREE WORLD – MANGANESE

PROVEN & ACCESSIBLE SUPPLY vs PROJECTED DEMAND – ALL USES
(Annual Basis)

(In thousands of tons)
Contained Mn

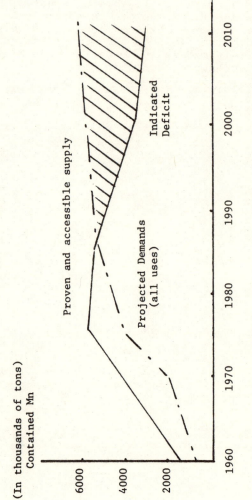

Proven and accessible supply

Projected Demands
(all uses)

Indicated
Deficit

1960   1970   1980   1990   2000   2010

6000

4000

2000

Note: No provisions made for erstwhile exporters becoming importers––
as for example – COMECON, India, Brazil

Source: Franz R. Dykstra, Prepared statement before the Subcommittee on
Energy Research and Development of the Senate Committee on Energy and
and Natural Resources, March 29, 1979.

TABLE 3

U.S. MANGANESE DEPENDENCY

(SHOWN AS PERCENT OF ESTIMATED REQUIREMENTS)

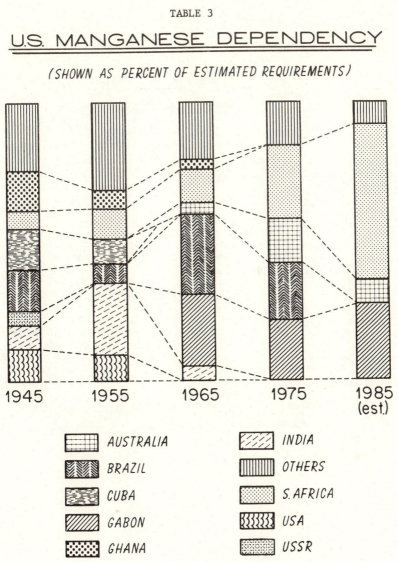

AUSTRALIA		INDIA	
BRAZIL		OTHERS	
CUBA		S. AFRICA	
GABON		USA	
GHANA		USSR	

Note: U.S. imports both manganese ore and alloys. Several importers of alloys derive their raw materials from the same source as the U.S.--France, Norway, Japan, for example. Others ship both alloys and ore to the U.S.--South Africa, Mexico, Brazil, India, for example.

The above constitutes an estimate of net imports by ultimate source.

Source: Franz R. Dykstra, Prepared statement before the subcommittee on Energy Research and Development of the Senate Committee on Energy and Natural Resources, March 29, 1981.

FOOTNOTES

APPENDIX 4

1. Prepared statement of Franz R. Dykstra, U.S, Congress, Senate, Committee on Energy and Natural Resources, Hearings on S.493, Deep Seabed Mineral Resources Act, before a subcommittee of the Senate Committee on Energy and Natural Resources, 95th Cong. 1st sess., 1979.

2. Briefly these include: (1) Confusion between the definitions of measured, economically recoverable "reserves" and intangible or extrapolated "reserves." (2) The tendency of suppliers to assuage any concern by optimistic reports as to their production capabilities and/or assured reserves. (3) The almost unique complexity of defining a manganese "ore," which precludes the conventional practice of increasing reserves as a direct proportional function of price. Dykstra defines an "ore" as a rock from which a specific metal or mineral may be economically extracted. A "reserve" is an identifiable and measurable volume of "ore." He claims that it is impossible to estimate "resources" without defining them as to potential costs, values once recovered, quality or technological developments--categories which he says are frequently confused, ignored or misintrepreted. See, Dykstra, Hearings.

APPENDIX 5

Ocean Mining Systems

The most significant mechanical system developed
for ocean mining is the continuous line bucket (CLB)
method. It involves a series of dredge baskets hung by
cable from the surface vessel or vessels. See Figure 1.
The cable is submerged in a loop fashion and is continu-
ously rotated as successive buckets dig, fill up, move
forward and are lifted to the surface for dumping.
Although the flexible cable is fairly adaptable to
currents and variable topography, potential material loss
at significant depth and in heavy currents is said to
exceed that of hydraulic methods; it may therefore not be
a viable method.
The cable forms a loop that passes through the
ship's bow and stern, with the bottom end of the loop
touching the ocean floor. By rotating the cable through
this loop, and moving the ship at right angles to the
plane of the rotating loop, the buckets/baskets are
dragged across the bottom and nodules are gathered in a
path that is traced by the movement of the ship. The
basic principle of operation, as outlined in Figure 1,.
may be modified with the addition of a container ship as
part of the loop.
Hydraulic methods of recovering nodules represent
a more sophisticated technology. The airlift pump system
being developed by Ocean Mining Associates involves the
pumping of air into a long (i.e. 15,000 foot) flexible
pipe attached by a shorter, rigid pipe to the dredgehead
which is dragged along the ocean floor. See Figure 2.
Lift is created when the injected air expands in the pipe
and forces the lighter water-air mixture to rise. This
suction system forces both water and the deposits of
nodules to the surface without significant sediment
disturbance. The material is forced upwards, outflows
are collected and separated at the surface, and new
material rushes in at the pipe base. The quantity of
nodules lifted with this system depends on the area
swept, the nodule concentration, and the efficiency of
the pickup system. This three-phase airlift system
involves the injection of compressed air into the vertical
pipe at a specific depth. The air bubbles rise to the
surface, reducing the average water density in the pipe.
The pressure differential between the bottom and the top
of the pipeline then causes a flow of water to enter the
lowest portion of the pipe. The nodules are then carried

227

Figure 1

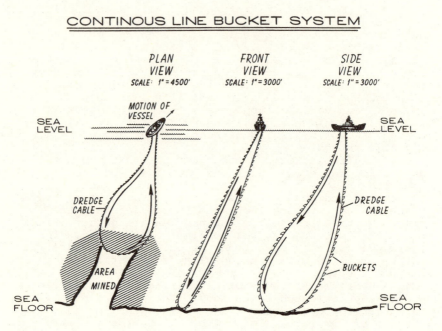

CONTINOUS LINE BUCKET SYSTEM

(Cable diameter and buckets not drawn to scale.)

Source: John L. Mero, "Potential Economic Value of Ocean Floor Manganese Nodule Deposits," in David R. Horn, ed., Ferromanganese Deposits on the Ocean Floor, (Washington D.C.: National Science Foundation, Internationa Decade of Ocean Exploration, 1972).

FIGURE 2

HYDAULIC LIFT SYSTEM

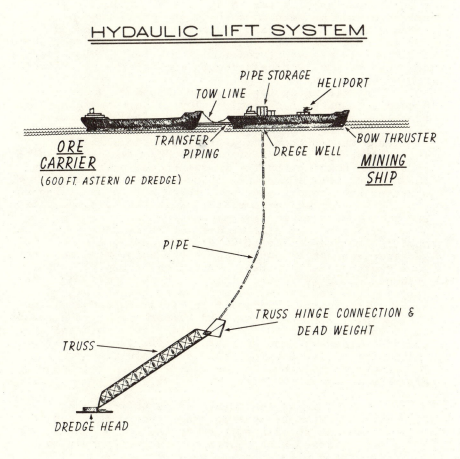

Source: Based on information from Ocean Mining Associates.

into the pipe and up to the surface. (Figure 3 is a photograph of Ocean Mining Associate's test mining device. This piece of equipment is much smaller than the final device which will be used on the seafloor to collect nodules.)

A second hydraulic system is reported to be favored by Kennecott Copper Corporation. This two-phase submerged multi-stage system uses a hydraulic pump to create a continuous upsurge of water in an attached flexible pipeline extended from the mining ship to the dredgehead on the ocean floor. Nodules are dislodged from the seabed and carried upwards in the suction pipe to the surface, where the minerals are separated from the water. This system has been seriously considered by most of the major ocean mining consortia.

The mining system being developed by Ocean Minerals Company (Lockheed) employs a bottom, self-propelled mining vehicle, completely remote-controlled, that moves slowly on the ocean bottom and scoops up nodules. This bottom "crawler," sends nodules up to an intermediate pumping station through a flexible conduit pipe. The pumping station is suspended in the water a few hundred feet above the bottom crawler. From the station, nodules are sent up a three-mile pipe string to the mining ship at the surface. Both the pumping station and bottom crawler/miner are un-manned robots.

The pipe has a great deal of resistance to moving rapidly in three miles of water. Because the pipe represents about as much drag as the ship, both must be move together as a system. Therefore, the pipe is not attached directly to the miner on the bottom. The link coupling between the miner and the buffer (pumping station) is several hundred feet of reinforced and flexible hose. Like the miner, the buffer has its own sensors as to where it is. The miner is left free to crawl forward, sideways, and backward--at its own pace within the limits of its flexible hose and cable tether.

Conrad Welling, Senior Vice President of Ocean Minerals Company, explains that:

> All the equipment--ship, buffer, and miner--must be able to "know" where they are in relation to one another, to the bottom and to the wave-tossed ocean surface. Each component is equipped with sonar to measure distances and angles involved. The miner, on the bottom, must also locate rich nodule beds, go to them, and crawl through them in what might be called an intelligent fashion. So, the miner has television cameras and powerful lights as well.

The experimental test bottom miner is the size of a small house and weighs approximately 100 tons. (See

231

Figure 3
TEST MINER DEVELOPED BY OCEAN MINING ASSOCIATES

Photograph courtesy of Ocean Mining Associates, Glouster Point, Virginia

Figure 4.) The three-mile string of pipe that brings the nodules to the surface ship is nearly two feet in diameter and weighs approximately seven million tons. The pumping station (buffer) weighs about 100 tons and is 25 feet square and 65 feet high. While the size of this equipment is large, full-scale operations will require larger dimensions. The working miner, for example, will be approximately 100 feet wide instead of the 30 foot width of the pilot model. The pipe string will also be wider and most likely heavier. To accommodate the full-scale equipment a much larger ship (than the already impressive Glomar Explorer--see Figure 5--that Lockheed has been using for test runs) will be needed. Such a ship may approach 1,000 feet or more in length and be the size of a super-tanker. Thus far, Lockheed has spent over $100 million dollars to develop its experimental system. The working system is estimated to require an investment of $1 billion dollars.

Figure 4

TEST MINER DEVELOPED BY OCEAN MINERALS COMPANY

Test Miner in "Moonpool" of the Glomar Explorer.
Photograph courtesy of Ocean Minerals Company (Lockheed),
Mountain View, California.

Figure 5

Glomar Explorer

Used in deep seabed mining tests

References

For further information see, John R.W. Black, The Recovery of Metals from Deepsea Manganese Nodules and the Effects on the World Cobalt and Manganese Markets, (Boston: Charles River Associates, Inc., 1980), pp. 21-36.

For more information on the technology and equipment being developed by Ocean Minerals Company, see Conrad G. Welling, "Mining the Ocean," a series on underwater natural resources in Port Soundings, August through November 1980. This series includes material on, "The Oceans' Waiting Mineral Resources," (August); "The Massive Technology for Ocean Mining," (September); "Ocean Mining: The Ships and Ports," (October); and "Ocean Minerals and World Politics," (November). The articles present an excellent account of the many factors involved in deep seabed mining from an industry standpoint.

I would like to thank Mr. Conrad Welling and Mr. Edward Dangler of Ocean Minerals Company (Lockheed), and Mr. Jeffry Amsbaugh of Ocean Mining Associates for their assistance in providing technical information and photographs of their respective ocean mining systems and test miners.

APPENDIX 6

REMOTE CONTROLLED VEHICLE (SHUTTLE)
FOR INDUSTRIAL COLLECTION OF MANGANESE NODULES

Part I

INDUSTRIAL NODULE EXPLOITATION SCHEME:
DEEP SEA MINING BY SELF-CONTAINED SHUTTLES

Part II

SEA FLOOR EXPERIMENTAL SHUTTLE VEHICLE:
PLA PROGRAMME

Projects Under Development by the French Consortia,

AFERNOD

INDUSTRIAL NODULE EXPLOITATION SCHEME

DEEP SEA MINING BY SELF-CONTAINED SHUTTLES

by J. VERTUT (C.E.A.) and J.P. MOREAU (C.F.D.)

*

March 1980

I - Project of an experimental remote-controlled vehicle for industrial collection of ores

This project of an experimental vehicle for the industrial collection of ores (called V.E.R.A.) is under study at C.E.A. and FRANCE-DUNKERQUE Shipyard.

For industrial exploitation, the shuttles will serve two purposes :

— mining : collection of nodules on the sea-bed
— transportation : transfer of nodule from the floor to the surface.

A - Basic principles

The industrial shuttle is balanced by ballast (waste from Metallurgical Processing Plant). Ballast is used for the several stages of the cycle : descent (diving), displacement on sea-bed (dredging), ascent.

The shuttle is in equi-pressure. It is propelled on the sea-bed by Archimedean screwed thrusters.

B - Technical description *(see fig. 1)*

— Characteristics :
```
Length...........................24    m
Breadth..........................12    m
Height...........................  7.50 m
Mass when empty ..................550 tonnes
```

— Dredging :

Modular dredge design has been chosen. The structure is made of light alloy (type AG5) - (12 elements of 1-metre wide dredge heads).

— Storage :

Storage containers are standardized (nodules/waste).

. 2 x 9 standardized silos - capacity = 300 m3
. size of one silo : 2.30 x 1.70 x 4.50 m
. capacity for nodules : 250 tonnes.

— Transfers :

Nodules are transferred by : mechanical means during loading after collecting
                              mechanical and hydraulic means during discharging into surface
                              support

. Waste is transferred by hydraulic and mechanical means during the filling operation at the surface support and by mechanical means during discharge on the sea-bed (dredging stage).

. Shuttle/surface support transfers are controlled from the surface support.

. Waste now chosen are granules (without efflorescence).

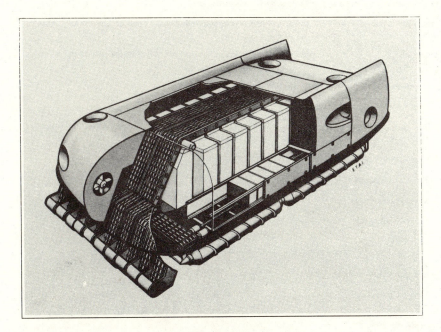

Fig. 1 : **Industrial Shuttle (V.E.R.A.)**

— **Propulsion** :

. The vehicle is propelled on the sea-bed by 4 independent trains of Archimedean screws (length = 7 m ; diameter = 0.80 m ; installed power = 350 kW).

. Homing on to the underwater ports of the surface support is made possible by 4 vertical and 4 horizontal thrusters. These nozzle propeller type thrusters have an installed power of 550 kW.

— **Energy balance** :

The energy consumed during the dredging/transfer/propulsion and homing operations is about 1,200 kWh i.e. a mass of abt. 50 t (with reserve) of installed batteries.

Let us mention that the energy (dredging, mooring) used for raising one tonne of nodules to the surface is only 4.8 kWh.

— **Buoyancy** :

The shuttle is in equi-pressure. Its weight in the water is small due to buoyancy foam (specific gravity chosen now : 0.68 - foam mass : 430 tonnes).

— **Instrumentation** :

The positioning systems, the systems for the auxiliaries, the controls of the actuators and the monitoring systems are contained in two scientific containers which can withstand a pressure of 600 bars.

II - Project for a mining platform with underwater shuttle port

The industrial plant for the mining of polymetallic nodules consists of a surface support and underwater remote controlled vehicles.

— The surface support is a semi-submersible platform with dynamic positioning situated on the mining site (at ± 150 m). This platform has three functions :

. underwater port for the remote-controlled shuttles (at — 40 m)
. temporary storage
. maintenance of the shuttles.

— The underwater remote-controlled vehicle of the V.E.R.A. type described above collect the nodules through systematic dredging operations (programmed dredging with wide mesh).

A - Management principle of industrial mining *(see fig. 2)*

— The shuttles operate on the mining fields.

— Mining parameters :

. Surface density of nodules . . . .   7 to 10 kg/mm2
. Dredging rate. . . . .   0,70 to 0.75
. Dredging speed . . . .   0.5 m/sec.
. Sweeping rate of mining fields. 0.70

— Management criteria :

. Dredging hours :

Hours per day   24
Days per annum 300/330

. Storage capacity of surface support. . . . . .   59 000 tonnes

. Ascent/descent speed of shuttles . . . .   from 0.4 to 0.7 m/sec. according to the angle of incidence (0° to 45°)

. Hydraulic transfer rate between a shuttle
and the surface support. . . . .   62 kg/sec.

— Two management schemes for systematic dredging are given below.

. The full cycle of an industrial shuttle takes 7.30 to 8 hours (departure from surface-support, descent, dredging, ascent, approach, homing and discharge).

1. For 8 operating shuttles and 3 underwater ports :

— the daily capacity is about 6,000 tonnes
— the occupancy coefficient of the ports is about 60 %
— the occupancy coefficient of the mining fields is about 45 %.

2. For 14 operating shuttles and 4 underwater ports :

— the daily capacity is about 10,500 tonnes
— the occupancy coefficient of the ports is about 85 %
— the occupancy coefficient of the mining fields is about 80 %.

Fig. 2 : Principle of Industrial Mining

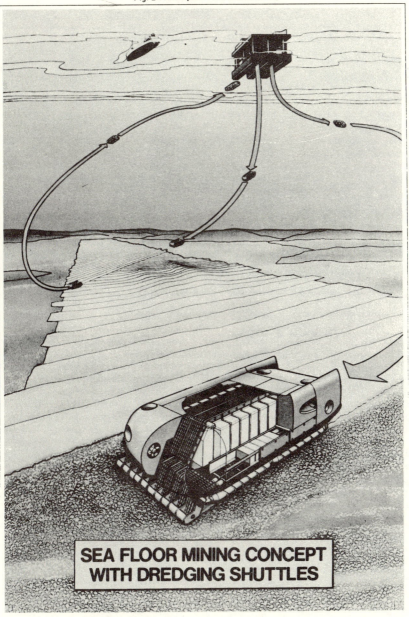

SEA FLOOR MINING CONCEPT
WITH DREDGING SHUTTLES

Selecting of industrial mining strategy has permitted to simulate the managing of a mining plant, to define the desired number of shuttles and ports for the collection. These elements have permitted to define a marine mining platform and underwater port for remote-controlled vehicle.

B - Surface-support *(see fig. 3)*

— Main particulars :

Length.	± 100 m
Breadth.	± 100 m
Overall height	± 100 m
Operating water-draught	56 m
Survival water-draught.	49 to 51 m
Air space.	44 m
Displacement.	140 000 T, abt.
Light weight	55 000 T
Storage for nodules/waste.	59 000 T
Installed power	40 000 kW, abt.
Personnel.	150 to 180 people

— This semi-submersible platform comprises :

. 4 underwater ports (minus 40 m) for remote-controlled vehicles.

. Facilities, maintenance and accommodation on air deck (2 levels).

. Ports and air deck are serviced by 2 elevators.

. There can be 17 complete shuttles (13 on air deck and 4 in ports).

. Nodules and waste are stored in standardized equipressurized containers under the floats. They are transferred hydraulically (principle of constant load basin).

. Batteries are transferred under water.

C - Conclusions

The industrial application of these future underwater techniques is to be significant in deep off-shore mining : development of certain components such as buoyancy materials, composite structures, deeply immersed electric motors, fuel or dry batteries, positioning of machines in addition to the construction of mining ships and remote-controlled modular vehicles.

Due to their unremitting determination to find the best solution, through the structure of their design departments and research divisions, thanks to their cooperation with Public bodies and various Private Companies, the French Atomic Energy Commission (C.E.A.) and the FRANCE-DUNKERQUE Ship-yard of the EMPAIN-SCHNEIDER Group are particularly qualified to play their part in the research and development of the techniques designed to solve the everyday problems which sea-workers have to cope with.

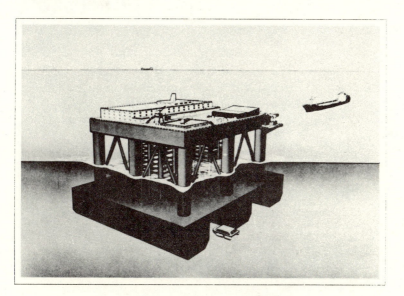

Fig. 3 : Mining Platform and Underwater Ports

If you would like to know more information, please contact :

FRENCH ATOMIC ENERGY COMMISSION
C. E. N. SACLAY
P.O. Box 2
91190 GIF-SUR-YVETTE

Phone : (1) 941.80.00
Telex : 690 641 F

FRANCE-DUNKERQUE SHIPYARD
C. F. D.
P.O. Box 1-503
59381 DUNKERQUE CEDEX

Phone : (28) 65.97.00
Telex : 820 010 F

A F E R N O D

SEA FLOOR EXPERIMENTAL SHUTTLE VEHICLE

*

PLA PROGRAMME

by J. VERTUT   (C.E.A.)
J.P. MOREAU (C.F.D.)

French Atomic Energy Commission

C. E. A.

France-Dunkerque Shipyard

C. F. D.

March 1980

1. HISTORY

1972 — C.E.A. was started the studies of the dredging facilities and carrier-vehicles for collecting and raising the nodules to the surface.

1974 — C.F.D. joined in C.E.A. for the study and construction of an underwater experimental shuttle vehicle which foreshadows the first experimental dredgers of the forthcoming underwater industrial mining plant.

1975 — A first feasibility model (300 kg in weigh ; 1 m wide) was built and tested on low cohesion simulated sea beds, so called PLA 1 : first generation remote-controlled vehicle.

1977 — After adding buoyancy (syntactic foam), this PLA 1 model (*see fig. 1*) was tested on a piece of ground that was very much similar to the deep occur sea-bed made of soft and sticky material, in shallow water with University of Perpignan Cooperation, as port of the study of the two 250 mm diameter Archimedean screws to sediment interaction, and tested on reconstituted (bentonite) sea-beds in C.N.E.X.O. model test basin (*see fig. 2*).

Fig. 1 : First Generation Remote-controlled Vehicle — PLA 1 model with syntactic foam

These many trials were conducted in model basins and in situ, with a view to achiev ing in-depth studies of the Archimedean screw thrusters.

Fig. 2 : Trials of PLA 1 in C.N.E.X.O. model basin
(screw prints are visible top)

1978 — Further tests were carried out at MONTEYNARD (a hydro-electric dam), at SALSES (in situ) and at BREST (C.N.E.X.O. model basin) on reconstituted sea-beds and on sandy sediments in shallow water :

- trafficability trials
- manœuvring tests with cable control system.

As a result of these, it was ascertained that Archimedean screws were an ideal solution for ground bearing and also for propelling heavy vehicles on sea floors of low cohesion.

— Taking these results into consideration, it was decided to design and build a prototype vehicle of the second generation —so called PLA 2 - 6000 m— for deep sea operations (20.000 ft.) on nodules fields to test propulsion, trafficability and dredge nodules. And so, it is intented to collect and bring up about 200 kilos of nodules at a time (see fig. 3).

This new vehicle combines the hydro-dynamics possibility to glide during descent and ascent stages thanks a limited of negative or positive buoyancy and Archimedean screw propulsion on sea floor.

Fig. 3 : Second Generation Remote-controlled Vehicle PLA 2 - 6000 m (20,000 ft.)

2. PLA 2 - 6000 M PROJECT

2.1. Introduction

The experimental shuttle vehicle is a 1/4 scale model of an industrial nodule mining shuttle vehicle, with a full scale limited width dredge module, including transfer and storage.

The vehicle glides down, lands automatically, moves on sea floor to dredge, stores nodules sample and refects excess during long experimental test ; then it takes off and glides up to surface.

The whole operation is programmed ; experiment date is recorded on tape. In case of incident, it can be released to surface thanks a positive buoyancy.

Pay load is either an experimental dredge module or any scientific or technological package.

Studies and trials are being conducted by the C.E.A. and C.F.D. : behaviour of the vehicle in water (hydro-dynamic study) ; instrumentation ; specific trials and associated structure and mechanics (construction study).

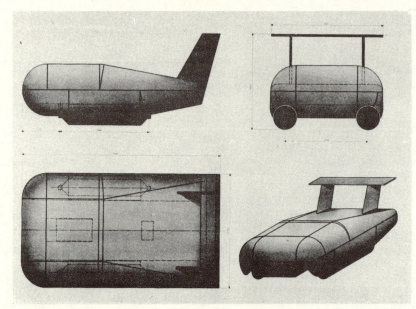

Fig. 4 : PLA 2 basic shape

2.2 Hydro-dynamic study

The behaviour of the vehicle in water has been studied by a dynamic scale model several shapes were determined.

A lines drawing study was determined a first shape who tested in ship model basin (*see fig. 4*).

A preliminary dynamical testing study was made with a balanced scale model. Gliding dynamic forces was tested in descent and ascent, with different trim due to extra fore ballast weight and extra buoyancy (*see fig. 5*).

The extra fore ballast weight is hooked at fore end of the vehicle and automatically released when it lands.

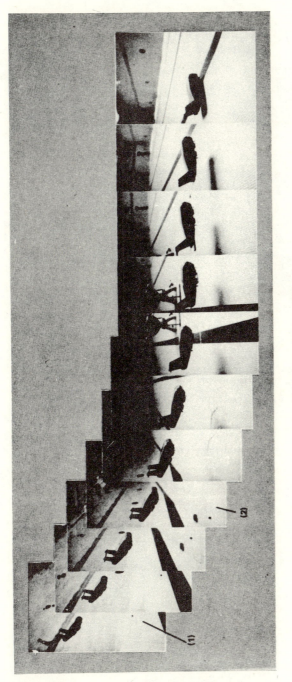

Fig. 5 : Diving-in strategy of PLA 2
(Scale model : 1/8)

Steering capability tests were carried out on a 1/8th scale model with a view to investigating the diving-in strategy

Descent and landing stages : 1) descent ballast weight
2) weight released

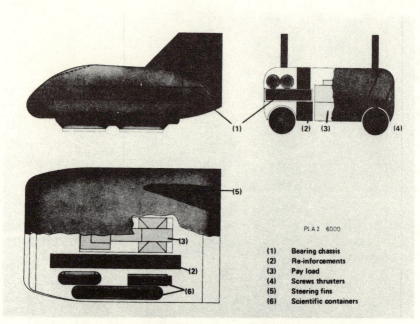

Fig. 6 : PLA 2 final shape

Weight value and rope length are enable to control soft landing in different ways : a 5-% extra buoyancy is sufficient for ascent at a 2-knots speed.

An improved shape is designed. This final shape will be tested in 1979/80 (see fig. 6).

2.3. Construction study

— Associated structure and mechanics (see fig. 7) :

. A basic feature in this vehicle is that the structure is made of buoyant material, as a bearing chassis with central opening for pay load and four re-inforcements (buoyancy : FM 200 syntactic foam, specific gravity : 0,68)

. Dry batteries in marine type containers and instrumentation in scientific containers

. the fore buoyant block received cameras and recording unit.

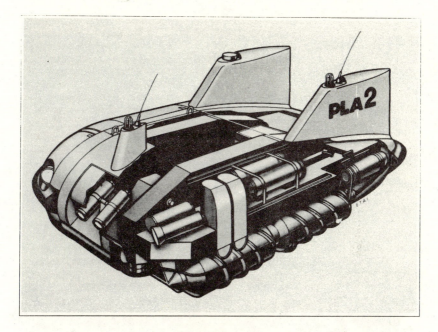

Fig. 7 : **PLA 2 open view**

— Pay load :

   . The center pay load can be an experimental dredge unit, or any scientific package

   . The front pay load can be an instrument package or a manipulator.

— Main particulars :

   . Sizes :   Length : 5,400 m   — 16' abt.
                    Width   : 3,600 m   — 12' abt.
                    Height : 1,200 m (underfins) — 4' abt.

   . Total mass : about 6 tonnes
   . Dynamical mass including water : 15 tonnes
   . Ballast mass : 400 kg (880 lbs)
   . Module pay load : 200 kg (storage hoppers)
   . Sea floor weight : 50 daN (110 lbs)
   . Sea floor velocity : 0,5 m s^{-1} (1 kn)
   . Autonomy : about 2 hours, moving on the sea floor.

— Propulsion : propelled on the sea bed by 2 Archimedean screws with welded thread :

   . Diameter : 650 mm ; Length : 2,000 m

   . 2 motor./reducing sets D.C 2,2 kW each

   . Energy supplied by motorized dry batteries (2 x 120 accumulators).

— Instrumentation : two scientific containers are provided for readings (16 sensors) film shooting (3 cameras + lighting spot). Control of actuators and data processing.

Fig. 8 : **Industrial applications of deep-sea remote-controlled vehicle**

The PLA 2 vehicle is a forerunner of the industrial shuttle for the collecting of polymetallic nodules. It will be used to experiment various technological solutions such as the steering, positioning, dredging and control systems...

The development of a vehicle capable of working on sea-beds of various characteristics offers a wide range of possibilities in addition to the collecting of nodules.

The current surveys have brought to light the possible technological applications of these vehicles for Deep-sea Off-shore Work. Let us mention a few projects and perspectives (see fig. 8 and 9) :

— Underwater ore and aggregate mining with a **dredge-head** adapted to the remote-controlled vehicle (1) ;
— Reading of sea-bed mechanics with **penetrometer or core** adapted to the remote-controlled vehicle (2) ;
— Supervision of off-shore work, pipe-line with a **camera** (3) ;
— Continued subsurface exploration and miscellaneous work on low cohesion sea-beds ;
— Specific work requiring great accuracy or hazardous work with a **telemanipulator** adapted to the remote-controlled vehicle (4) ;
— Replacement of human operators in a hostile marine environment ;
— Deep-sea oil mining of vast amplitude which requires a lot of remote-controlled unmanned machines.

Fig. 9

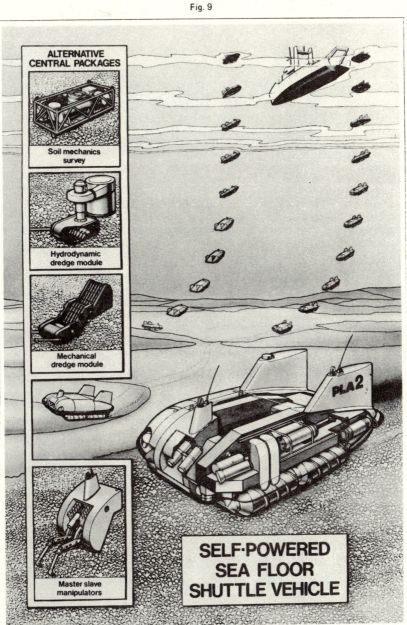

ALTERNATIVE CENTRAL PACKAGES

Soil mechanics survey

Hydrodynamic dredge module

Mechanical dredge module

Master slave manipulators

PLA2

SELF·POWERED SEA FLOOR SHUTTLE VEHICLE

APPENDIX 7

PROCESS FOR THE SMELTING OF MANGANESE NODULES

The Kennecott group has developed a Cuprion
Process for extracting the metal values from the
nodules. This process is based on leaching the nodules
with an ammonical solution containing cupric ions to
dissolve copper, nickel, cobalt, and molybdenum. The
metals are extracted by liquid ion exchange, electrowinning, and chemical means. This process allows the
recovery of manganese as a ferromanganese product from
the leach tailings. This process has one of the lowest
costs, is the most energy-efficient, and has proved
workable through the pilot-plant stage.

The system most likely to be used by Ocean Mining
Associates (OMA) is the Hydrochloric Acid (HCl) Leach
Process. This process was originally patented by Deepsea
Ventures, Inc., and later inherited by U.S. Steel and
others upon the acquisition of Deepsea Ventures. The
process uses aqueous HCl to reduce and dissolve the metal
values that are recovered by liquid ion exchange and
electrowinning. Successful pilot plants using this
method have been built at Glouster Point, Virginia. OMA
has brought up over 150 tons of nodules for use in these
plants.

OMA might also choose the Sulfuric Acid Leach
Process or a Union Minere process that recovers only the
metal oxides or sulfides. There is also a possibility
that OMA might opt to license Kennecott's Cuprion Process.

Ocean Management Inc., is using a pyrometallurgical
process to smelt the nodules to recover nickel, copper,
and cobalt as a matte which then uses pressure leaching,
liquid ion exchange, and electrowinning to recover the
metals. As of early 1980, however, OMI had ceased its
research and development on ocean mining.

Ocean Minerals Company (Lockheed), has been planning a $4 million pilot plant on the island of Hawaii.
OMC is highly secretive of their ocean mining and processing technology. They are believed, however, to be
developing a process based on sulfuric acid leaching.
This process would recover nickel, copper, and cobalt and
leave manganese in the tailings with the option for later
recovery.

The French group, led by the Centre National pour
l' Exploration des Oceans (CNEXO), have been considering
three nodule processes since 1975: the pyrometallurgical,

an unknown hydrometallurgical process, and as yet undefin-
ed technique. They have yet to decide on a choice.*

---

*For a good summary of the smelting process see, John
Black, The Recovery of Metals from Deepsea Manganese
Nodules and the Effects on the World Cobalt and Manganese
Markets, (Boston: Charles River Associates, Inc., 1980),
pp. 36-76.

APPENDIX 8

HIGHLIGHTS OF THE UNITED NATIONS CONFERENCE ON THE LAW OF
THE SEA FROM 1958 THROUGH 1982

1958   UNCLOS I--Produced 4 Conventions (Treaties on
        ocean law of the Territorial Sea, High Seas,
        Continental Shelf, and Fishing.

1960   UNCLOS II--Failed to agree on the limits of
        coastal state (nation) jurisdiction (rights)
        over offshore waters and seabed.

1967   Ambassador Arvid Pardo of Malta issued his call
        to action on the seabed beyond national
        jurisdiction before the United Nations General
        Assembly (UNGA).

1968   Permanent Committee on the Peaceful Uses of the
        Seabed and the Ocean Floor Beyond the Limits of
        National Jurisdiction--the Seabed Committee--was
        established. Its role was to explore the
        possibilities of establishing an international
        regime (laws) and machinery (organization) to
        govern seabed exploitation in the interests of
        humankind, taking into special consideration the
        interests and needs of the developing nations.

1969   UNGA approves a moratorium resolution banning
        seabed mining until the international regime is
        established. The United States and several
        other industrially advanced nations vote against
        the resolution.

1970   UNGA approves a Declaration of Principles on the
        seabed beyond national jurisdiction as the
        common heritage of humankind and calls for the
        convening of UNCLOS III on all unsettled aspects
        of international law.

1971-   Seabed Committee continues its preparatory 1972
        work for UNCLOS III and divides its now expanded
        agenda into sub-committee I on the seabed beyond
        national jurisdiction, sub-committee II on
        traditional uses of the sea such as fishing and
        navigation and on the limits of coastal nation
        jurisdiction, and sub-committee III on the
        environment and marine scientific research.

1973   In December UNCLOS III met for 3 weeks in New
        York to determine its rules of procedure.

1974   UNCLOS III met for 10 weeks in Caracas,
        Venezuela, during the Summer. 138 nations stated
        their positions on all the issues before the
        Conference. The sub-committees became full com-
        mittees. Committee II produced a Main Trends
        document listing several alternate provisions on
        all its agenda items.

1975   UNCLOS III met for 8 weeks in Geneva and produced
        the Single Negotiating Text (SNT) which included
        only one formulation selected by the Committee
        chairmen on each subject before the Conference.
        (A negotiating text is a procedural device to
        serve as a basis for negotiation and does not
        suggest that any nation wholeheartedly supports
        its provisions. That is, it is not considered a
        widely approved negotiated document.)

1976   UNCLOS III met for 8 weeks in New York in the
        Spring and for 7 weeks in the Fall. The first
        session resulted in a Revised Single Negotiating
        Text (RSNT).

1977   UNCLOS III met for 8 weeks in New York and pro-
        duced the Informal Composite Negotiating Text
        (ICNT) whose aim was to get rid of inconsistent
        language in the RSNT and to revise a number of
        articles so that they were generally more
        acceptable.

1978   UNCLOS III met for 8 weeks in Geneva in the
        Spring and for 4 weeks in New York in the Fall.
        Seven Negotiating Groups (NGs) were formed to
        focus on the "hard core" issues yet to be
        resolved. The NGs recommended a number of
        changes in their subject areas. According to
        the rules agreed upon in 1978, these changes were
        not to be included in any revised ICNT unless
        they were "presented to the plenary (full member-
        ship of the conference) and found from the wide-
        spread and substantial support prevailing in
        plenary, to offer a substantially improved
        prospect of consensus." (Only the work of NG5
        met this standard by the end of 1978, although
        the work of NG4 had remained unchanged since.
        NG4 dealt with access by land-locked and
        geographically disadvantaged nations to fish in
        coastal nations' 200-mile economic zones. NG5
        worked on settlement of disputes arising from
        NG4's allocation process.)

1979   UNCLOS III met for 6 weeks in Geneva in the Spring and for 6 weeks in New York in the Summer. The Working Group of 21 was established to coordinate work on seabed mining matters and Committee III concluded its work on the environment. After the Geneva meeting the ICNT/Revision 1 was produced. Additional modifications emerged from the New York meeting and Final Clauses discussions began in depth. The Conference set itself a firm schedule to conclude its work in 1980.

1980   UNCLOS III met for 5 weeks in New York in the Spring and produced the ICNT/Revision 2. It is composed of 303 articles, 8 annexes which amplify certain provisions in the articles. Committee III concluded its work on marine scientific research. The Negotiating Groups established in 1978 were abolished. The 5 week Summer meeting in Geneva came close to producing a final revision but did not formally adopt a draft LOS Convention as planned. U.S. Ambassador Elliot Richardson resigned as head of the American delegation shortly after the Geneva conference stating agreement was near. Final session was set for 1981.

1981   The tenth session of UNCLOS III, met in New York (March/April), and Geneva (August). "Draft convention on the Law of the Sea" issued. Final session was set for 1982. The Reagan Administration replaced the top U.S. negotiators and began its "review process."

1982   The eleventh session met in New York (March/April), and Geneva (August). The Group of 77 had threatened to sign a Treaty even if the U.S. did not. The Reagan Administration completed it's "review" and made a public statement January 29th which declared that the United States would return to the negotiations and seek constructive changes in the text on seabed mining. A Convention (Treaty) may be signed in Caracas, Venezuela. It will then be up to each national government which signs the Treaty to approve or ratify it. Sixty nations will have to do this before the Treaty enters into force. This may take several years.

APPENDIX 9

THE NATIONAL OCEAN INDUSTRIES ASSOCIATION:
A LIST OF "FAIR AND REASONABLE" TERMS
FOR TECHNOLOGY TRANSFER

(1) Establish a price--in specie, in kind, or in other appropriate form--which provides a fair return to the owner for the transfer of the technology and any related services provided and which may be based on factors such as the cost of developing the technology (including direct research and development costs, overhead and other indirect costs, and taking into account the cost of the total development effort including unsuccessful projects), the risk to which the owner was exposed in developing the technology, the uniqueness of the technology, the profit or benefits to be derived or passed on by the Enterprise [the recipient] and a reasonable profit to the owner;

(2) provide security for payments by means of letters of credit or other devices;

(3) limit the use of the technology by the Enterprise to exploration and exploitation of the deep seabed;

(4) provide for termination of the agreement in the event of substantial breach of the agreement;

(5) require that the Enterprise provide to the owner, on an exclusive or non-exclusive basis and without royalties, any improvements which it makes in the technology transferred to it (known as 'grantbacks');

(6) ensure appropriate protection and proper handling of leased equipment;

(7) protect the secrecy of the technology, including restrictions on sub-licensing or assigning the technology to third parties;

(8) require indemnification by the Enterprise to the owner in the event the Enterprise causes damage to others by misuse of the technology and the owner is held liable;

(9) make appropriate provisions for the protection of the Enterprise in its use of technology, such as warranties as to the validity of any patent;

(10) ensure that if there are any warranties of new technology, they take into account the untested nature of the technology;

(11) provide for a commercial arbitration mechanism to adjudicate any disputes arising within the scope of the contract for the transfer of technology including questions of financial or other damages to be awarded.

APPENDIX 10

DRAFT CONVENTION ON THE LAW OF THE SEA
(DRAFT TREATY TEXT 1981)

SECTION 5. THE AUTHORITY

SUBSECTION A. GENERAL

Article 156
Establishment of the Authority

1. There is hereby established the International
Sea-Bed Authority which shall function in accordance with
the provisions of this Part.

2. All States Parties are *ipso facto* members of
the Authority.

3. The seat of the Authority shall be at Jamaica.

4. The Authority may establish such regional
centres or offices as it deems necessary for the performance of its functions.

Article 157
Nature and fundamental principles of the Authority

1. The Authority is the organization through which
States Parties shall organize and control activities in
the Area, particularly with a view to administering the
resources of the Area, in accordance with this Part.

2. The powers and functions of the Authority shall
be those expressly conferred upon it by the relevant
provisions of this Convention. The Authority shall have
such incidental powers, consistent with the provisions of
this Convention, as are implicit in and necessary for the
performance of these powers and functions with respect to
activities in the Area.

3. The Authority is based on the principle of the
sovereign equality of all its members.

4. All members, in order to ensure to all of them
the rights and benefits resulting from membership, shall
fulfill in good faith the obligations assumed by them in
accordance with this Part.

Article 158
Organs of the Authority

1. There are hereby established as the principal organs of the Authority, an Assembly, a Council and a Secretariat.

2. There is hereby established the Enterprise, the organ through which the Authority shall carry out the functions referred to in article 1970, paragraph 1.

3. Such subdidiary organs as may be found necessary may be established in accordance with this Part.

4. The principal organs shall each be responsible for exercising those powers and functions which have been conferred upon them. In exercising such powers and functions each organ shall avoid taking any action which may derogate from or impede the exercise of specific powers and functions conferred upon another organ.

SUBSECTION B. THE ASSEMBLY

Article 159
Composition, procedure and voting

1. The Assembly shall consist of all the members of the Authority.

2. The Assembly shall meet in regular session every year and in such special sessions as may be determined by the Assembly, or convened by the Secretary-General at the request of the Council or of a majority of the members of the Assembly.

3. Sessions shall take place at the seat of the Authority unless otherwise determined by the Assembly. At such sessions, each member shall have one representative who may be accompanied by alternates and advisers.

4. The Assembly shall adopt its own rules of procedure. It shall elect its President and such other officers as may be required, at the beginning of each regular session. They shall hold office until the new President and other officers are elected at the next regular session.

5. Each member of the Assembly shall have one vote.

6. All decisions on questions of substance shall be taken by a two-thirds majority of the members present

and voting, provided that such majority includes at least
a majority of members participating in that session of
the Assembly. When the issue arises as to whether the
question is one of substance or not, the question shall
be treated as one of substance unless otherwise decided
by the Assembly by the majority required for questions of
substance.

7. Decisions on questions of procedure, including
the decision to convene a special session of the Assembly,
shall be made by a majority of the representatives present
and voting.

8. When a matter of substance comes up for voting
for the first time, the President may, and shall, if
requested by at least one-fifth of the members of the
Assembly, defer the question of taking a vote on such
matter for a period not exceeding five calendar days.
This rule may be applied only once on the matter, and
shall not be applied so as to defer questions beyond the
end of the session.

9. A majority of the members of the Assembly
shall constitute a quorum.

10. Upon request in writing to the President
sponsored by not less than one-quarter of the members of
the Authority for an advisory opinion on the conformity
with this Convention of a proposed action before the
Assembly on any matter, the Assembly shall defer its vote
on that matter and shall request the Sea-Bed Disputes
Chamber for an advisory opinion thereon. Voting on that
action shall be deferred pending delivery of the advisory
opinion by the Chamber. If the advisory opinion is not
received by the final week of the session in which it is
requested, the Assembly shall decide when it will meet to
vote upon the deferred matter.

Article 160
Powers and functions

1. The Assembly, as the sole organ of the
Authority consisting of all the members, shall be considered the supreme organ of the Authority to which the other
principal organs shall be accountable as specifically
provided for in this Convention. The Assembly shall have
the power to establish general policies in conformity with
the relevant provisions of this Convention on any question
or matter within the competence of the Authority.

2. In addition, the powers and functions of the
Assembly shall be:

(a) Election of the members of the Council in accordance with article 161;

(b) Election of the Secretary-General from among the candidates proposed by the Council;

(c) Election, upon the recommendation of the Council, of the members of the Governing Board of the Enterprise as well as the Director-General of the Enterprise;

(d) Establishment, as appropriate, of such subsidiary organs as may be found necessary for the performance of its functions in accordance with the provisions of this Part. In the composition of such subsidiary organs due account shall be taken of the principle of equitable geographical distribution and of special interests and the need for members qualified and competent in the relevant technical questions dealt with by such organs;

(e) Assessment of the contributions of members to the administrative budget of the Authority in accordance with an agreed general assessment scale based upon the scale used for the regular budget of the United Nations until the Authority shall have sufficient income from other sources for meeting its adminstrative expenses;

(f) Consideration and approval of the rules, regulations and procedures of the Authority, and any amendments thereto, provisionally adopted by the Council pursuant to article 162, paragraph 2 (n). These rules, regulations and procedures shall relate to prospecting, exploration, and exploitation in the Area, the financial management and internal administration of the Authority, and, upon the recommendation of the Governing Board of the Enterprise, the rules, regulations and procedures for the transfer of funds from the Enterprise to the Authority;

(g) Consideration and approval of the budget of the Authority on its submission by the Council;

(h) Examination of periodic reports from the Council and from the Enterprise and of special reports requested from the Council and from any other organs of the Authority;

(i) Initiation of studies and recommendations for the purpose of promoting international co-operation concerning activities in the Area and encouraging the progressive development of international law relating thereto and its codifications;

(j) Deciding upon the equitable sharing of financial and other economic benefits derived from activities in the Area, consistent with the provisions of this Convention and the rules, regulations and procedures of the Authority;

(k) Consideration of problems of a general nature in connection with activities in the Area in particular for developing States, as well as of such problems for States in connection with activities in the Area as are due to their geographical location, including land-locked and geographically disadvantaged countries;

(l) Establishment, upon the recommendation of the Council on the basis of advice from the Economic Planning Commission of a system of compensation as provided in article 151, paragraph 4;

(m) Suspension of members pursuant to article 185;

(n) Discussion of any question or matter within the competence of the Authority and decisions as to which organ shall deal with such question or matter not specifically entrusted to a particular organ of the Authority, consistent with the distribution of powers and functions among the organs of the Authority.

APPENDIX 11

DRAFT CONVENTION ON THE LAW OF THE SEA
(DRAFT TREATY TEXT 1981)

SECTION 5. THE AUTHORITY
SUBSECTION C. THE COUNCIL

Article 161
Composition, procedure and voting

1. The Council shall consist of 36 members of the
Authority elected by the Assembly, the election to take
place in the following order:

(a) Four members from among the eight States
Parties which have the largest investments in
preparation for and in the conduct of activities
in the Area, either directly or through their
nationals, including at least one State from the
Eastern (Socialist) region;

(b) Four members from among those States
Parties which, during the last five years for which
statistics are available, have either consumed more
than 2 percent of total world consumption or more
than 2 percent of total world imports of the
commodiites produced from the categories of
minerals to be derived from the Area, and in any
case one State from the Eastern (Socialist)
European region:

(c) Four members from among countries which
on the basis of production in areas under their
jurisdiction are major exporters of the categories
of minerals to be derived from the Area, including
at least two developing countries whose exports of
such minerals have a substantial bearing upon their
economies;

(d) Six members from among developing States,
representing special interests. The special
interests to be represented shall include those of
States with large populations, States which are
land-locked or geographically disadvantaged, States
which are major importers of the categories of
minerals to be derived from the Area, and least
developed States;

(e) Eighteen members elected according to the principle of ensuring an equitable geographical distribution of seats in the Council as a whole, provided that each geographical region shall have at least one member elected under this subparagraph. For this purpose the geographical regions shall be Africa, Asia, Eastern Europe (Socialist), Latin America and Western Europe and others.

2. In electing the members of the Council in accordance with paragraph 1, the Assembly shall ensure that:

(a) Land-locked and geographically disadvantaged States are represented to a degree which is reasonably proportionate to their representation in the Assembly;

(b) Coastal States, especially developing States, which do not qualify under paragraph 1 (a), (b), (c), and (d) are represented to a degree which is reasonably proportionate to their representation in the Assembly;

(c) Each group of States and Parties to be represented on the Council is represented by those members, if any, which are nominated by the group.

3. Elections shall take place at regular sessions of the Assembly, and each member of the Council shall be elected for a term of four years. In the first election of members of the Council, however, one half of the members of each category shall be chosen for a period of two years.

4. Members shall be eligible for reelection; but due regard shall be paid to the desirability of rotating seats.

5. The Council shall function at the seat of the Authority, and shall meet as often as the business of the Authority may require, but not less than three times a year.

6. Each member of the Council shall have one vote.

7. (a) Decisions on questions of procedure shall be taken by a majority of the members present and voting;

(b) Decisions on questions of substance arising under the following provisions shall be taken by a two-thirds majority of the members present and voting, provided that such majority

includes a majority of the members of the
Council: article 162, paragraph 2(f); article
162, paragraph 2(g); article 162, paragraph 2(h);
article 162, paragraph 2(i); article 162,
paragraph 2(m); article 162, paragraph 2(o);
article 162, paragraph 2(u); article 189;

(c) Decisions on questions of substance
arising under the following provisions shall be
taken by a three-fourths majority of the members
present and voting, provided that such majority
included a majority of the members of the Council;
article 162, paragraph 1; article 162, paragraph
2(a); article 162, paragraph 2(b); article 162,
paragraph 2(c); article 162, paragraph 2(d);
article 162, paragraph 2(e); article 162,
paragraph 2(k); article 162, paragraph 2(p);
article 162, paragraph 2(q); article 162,
paragraph 2(r); article 162, paragraph 2(s);
article 162, paragraph 2(t) in cases of
non-compliance by a contractor or a sponsor:
article 162, paragraph 2(v) provided that orders
issued under this subparagraph may be binding for
no more than thirty days unless confirmed by a
decision taken in accordance with subparagraph
(d); article 162, paragraph 2(w); article 162,
paragraph 2(x); article 162, paragraph 2(y);
article 263, paragraph 2, article 174, paragraph
3; article 11 of annex IV:

(d) Decisions on questions of substance
arising under the following provisions shall be
decided by consensus: article 162, paragraph
2(1); article 162, paragraph 2(n); adoption of
amendments to Part XI;

(e) For the purpose of subparagraph (d), the
term "consensus" means the absence of any formal
objection. Within fourteen days of the submission
of a proposal to the Council the President shall
ascertain whether there would be an objection to
the proposal if it were put to the Council for
adoption. If the President of the Council ascer-
tains that there would be an objection to a
proposal before the Council, he shall constitute a
Conciliation Committee consisting of not more than
nine members, with himself as Chairman, for the
purpose of reconciling the differences and producing a proposal which can be adopted by consensus.
The President shall establish the said committee
work expeditiously and report to the Council within
fourteen days. If the Conciliation Committee is
unable to recommend a proposal which can be adopted

by consensus it shall in its report, set out the grounds on which a proposal is being opposed;

(f) Decisions not listed above which the Council is authorized to take by the rules, regulations and procedures of the Authority or otherwise shall be taken pursuant to the subparagraphs of this article specified in the rules, regulations and procedures or, if not specified therein, then pursuant to the subparagraph determined by the Council if possible in advance, by the majority required for questions under subparagraph (d);

(g) When the issue arises as to whether a question is within subparagraphs (a), (b), (c) or (d), the question shall be treated as being within the subparagraph requiring the higher or highest majority as the case may be, unless otherwise decided by the Council by the said majority.

8. A majority of the members of the Council shall constitute a quorum.

9. The Council shall establish a procedure whereby a member of the Authority not represented on the Council may send a representative to attend a meeting of the Council when a request is made by such member, or a matter particularly affecting it is under consideration. Such a representative shall be entitled to participate in the deliberations but not to vote.

Article 162
Powers and functions

1. The Council is the executive organ of the Authority, having the power to establish in conformity with the provisions of this Convention and the general policies established by the Assembly, the specific policies to be pursued by the Authority on any questions or matters within the competence of the Authority.

2. In addition, the Council shall:

(a) Supervise and co-ordinate the implementation of the provisions of this Part on all questions and matters within the competence of the Authority and invite the attention of the Assembly to cases on non-compliance;

(b) Propose to the Assembly a list of candidates for the election of the Secretary-General;

(c) Recommend to the Assembly candidates for election as members of the Governing Board of the Enterprise as well as the Director-General of the Enterprise;

(d) Establish, as appropriate, and with due regard to economy and efficiency, in addition to the Commissions provided for in article 163, paragraph 1, such subsidiary organs as may be found necessary for the performance of its functions in accordance with the provisions of this Part. In the composition of such subsidiary organs, emphasis shall be placed on the need for members qualified and competent in the relevant technical matters dealt with by such organs provided that due account shall be taken of the principles of equitable geographical distribution and of special interests;

(e) Adopt its rules of procedure including the method of selecting its president;

(f) Enter into agreements with the United Nations or other international organizations on behalf of the Authority and within its competence, subject to approval by the Assembly;

(g) Examine the reports of the Enterprise and transmit them to the Assembly with its recommendations;

(h) Present to the Assembly annual reports and such special reports as the Assembly may require;

(i) Issue directives to the Enterprise in accordance with article 170;

(j) Approve plans of work in accordance with article 6 of annex III. The Council shall act upon each plan of work within sixty days of its submission by the Legal and Technical Commission at a session of the Council in accordance with the following procedures:

>   (i) If the Commission recommends the approval of a plan of work, it shall be deemed to have been approved by the Council if no Council member submits to the President within fourteen days a specific written objection alleging non-compliance with the requirements of article 6 of

annex III. In the event that there is an objection, the conciliation procedure contained in article 161, paragraph 7(e), shall apply. If, at the end of the conciliation process, the objection to the approval of the plan of work is still maintained, the plan of work shall be deemed to have been approved by the Council unless the Council disapproves it by consensus among its members excluding the State or States, if any, making the application or sponsoring the applicant;

(ii) If the Commission recommends the disapproval of a plan of work or does not make a recommendation, the Council may decide to approve the plan of work by a three-fourths majority of the members present and voting, provided that such majority includes a majority participating in that session;

(k) Exercise control over activities in the Area in accordance with article 153, paragraph 4, and the rules, regulations and procedures of the Authority;

(l) Adoption of the recommendation of the Economic Planning Commission necessary and appropriate measures in accordance with article 150, subparagraph (g), to protect against adverse economic effects specified therein;

(m) Make recommendations to the Assembly on the basis of advice from the Economic Planning Commission for a system of compensation or other measures of economic adjustment assistance as provided in article 151, paragraph 4;

(n) (i) Recommend to the Assembly rules, regulations and procedures on the equitable sharing of financial and other economic benefits derived from activities in the Area and the payments and contributions made pursuant to article 82, taking into particular consideration the interests and needs of the developing States and peoples who have not attained full independence or other self-governing status;

(ii) Adopt and supply provisionally, pending approval by the Assembly, the rules, regulations and procedures of the Authority, and any amendments thereto, taking into account the recommendations of the Commission or other subordinate organ concerned. These rules, regulations and procedures shall relate to prospecting, exploration and exploitation in the Area, the financial management and internal administration of the Authority. Such rules, regulations and procedures shall remain in effect on a provisional basis until approval by the Assembly or by the Council in the light of any views expressed by the Assembly.

(o) Review the collection of all payments to be made by or to the Authority in connection with operations pursuant to this Part;

(p) Make the selection among applicants for production authorization pursuant to article 7 of annex III for the production authorization referred to in article 151, where such selection is required by those provisions;

(r) Make recommendations to the Assembly concerning policies on any question or matter within the competence of the Authority;

(s) Make recommendations to the Assembly concerning suspension of the privileges and rights of membership for gross and persistent violations of the provisions of this Part upon a finding of the Sea-Bed Disputes Chamber;

(t) Initiate on behalf of the Authority proceedings before the Sea-Bed Disputes Chamber in cases on non-compliance;

(u) Upon a finding by the Sea-Bed Disputes Chamber on proceedings resulting from subparagraph (t), notify the Assembly and make recommendations with respect to measures to be taken unless otherwise decided;

(v) Issue emergency orders, which may include orders for the suspension or adjustment of operations, to prevent serious harm to the marine environment arising out of any activity in the Area:

(w) Disapprove areas for exploitation by contractors or the Enterprise in cases where substantial evidence indicates the risk of serious harm to the marine environment;

(x) Establish a subsidiary organ for the elaboration of draft financial rules, regulations and procedures relating to:

(i) financial management in accordance with articles 171 to 175; and

(ii) financial arrangements in accordance with article 13 and article 17, paragraph 1(c), of annex II.

(y) Establish appropriate mechanisms for directing and supervising a staff of inspectors who shall inspect activities in the Area to determine whether the provisions of this Part, the rules, regulations and procedures prescribed thereunder, and the terms and conditions of any contract with the Authority are being complied with.

APPENDIX 12

A DESCRIPTION OF ANTARCTICA AND ITS MAJOR RESOURCES
AND ENVIRONMENTAL PROBLEMS

Comprising about 9 percent of the land surface of
the earth, Antarctica is a circumpolar continent of 13.5
million km^2. The Southern Ocean which surrounds the
continent is about 36 million km^2 or approximately 10
percent of the world's oceans. The Antarctic Convergence
is a zone where the cold and low-saline waters of the
Southern Ocean meet the warmer and higher saline waters
of the southern parts of the Atlantic, Pacific, and
Indian Oceans. The Antarctic Convergence is also known
as the Polar Front Zone and generally lies between 50°
and 60° south latitude.
The continental shelf surrounding Antarctica is
exceptionally narrow and deep. Its average width is only
30 km and its depth at the outer margin ranges from under
500 meters. Because of the weight of the continental ice
cap, the shelf fringing the Antarctic continent is four
to five times deeper than other continental shelves. Sea
ice overlies all of the shelf for nine to ten months of
the year. During the austral summer, much of it is
broken into pack ice and moves northward, leaving open
sea above the shelf. The pressure of several years'
accumulation of the ice in certain areas makes ship
passage impossible at times.
The Antarctic ice sheet covers 98 percent of the
land surface of the continent leaving only about 260,000
km^2 of nonglacial terrain on which direct geological
observations are possible. This ice sheet averages about
2,300 meters thick, but in some places it has been
measured up to 4,000 meters. Geographically, the
continent has been divided into East Antarctica, West
Antarctica, and the Antarctic Peninsula. Temperatures
are very severe. The mean annual temperature on the polar
plateau of East Antarctica is -50°C and in the coastal
regions is about -15°C. The North and West sides of the
Antarctic Peninsula are much warmer, but still average
-10°C to -35°C. The coasts of the peninsula average
around 0°C. Antarctica is known as the windiest continent
on earth. The strong winds which are common to the coasts
are due to the strong catabatic--mountain--winds that flow
from the interior. The winds are less intense on the
northern and western sides of the Antarctic Peninsula.
The winds also pick up ice and loose snow and create
"snow storms." Actually, Antarctica is a desert with one

of the world's lowest precipitation levels. This brief
physical description of Antarctica helps to highlight the
extreme logistical problems that will be encountered in
any type of resource exploration and exploitation of the
area.

ANTARCTIC RESOURCES

The resources of the Antarctic can be divided into
two categories: living and non-living. A further
division can be made between those resources that are
identified and those that are undiscovered or potential.
Though a detailed analysis of Antarctic resources is
beyond the scope of this study, the major marine (i.e.
living) and mineral resources can be briefly described
here.

Living Resources

The major marine forms in Antarctica are krill,
seals, whales, birds, and fish. As a resource, however,
krill harvesting has presented the most significant economic and political problems thus far. It is likely that
the decline in the whale population (a natural predator
of krill) has caused the krill population to expand so
that a "surplus" exists. The opportunity thus exists to
use this "surplus" as a source of food for human consumption. On the other hand, biological knowledge about krill
leaves us in considerable doubt as to the amount that
could be harvested without hurting other krill consumers
such as whales, penguins, seals, squid, and fish. Despite
these doubts, the harvesting of krill is becoming a
thriving industry. The combined annual catches by the
Soviet Union, Poland, West Germany, Japan, Taiwan, Korea,
Argentina, and Chile are on the order of 80 to 90 thousand
metric tons.

None of Antarctica's development issues has raised
problems as immediate as the harvest of krill. Until
recently, krill had never been harvested commercially
because of its inaccessibility and the relative abundance
of other fisheries. But now these clouds of crustaceans
in Antarctica's waters are regarded as one of the last
major undeveloped sources of marine protein. Shrimp-like,
and only about three inches long, the krill swarm in very
large quantities throughout the southern ocean. How close
to which shores around Antarctica these swarms occur,
however, has raised many difficult resource management
issues.[1] For example, Antarctic Treaty powers which
make territorial claims, also claim 200-mile EZZs off the
continent and around islands. Non-claimant nations do
not acknowledge these claims within the Treaty's jurisdiction. The claimant States believe they have economic,
and therefore fishing control within these 200-mile

economic zones.

Mineral Resources

There are no mineral deposits in Antarctica which
are likely to be of economic value in the near future.
With the rapid advances in mining technology that have
occurred over the last decade and the changing political
circumstances which have substantially increased oil costs
over the past few years, however, there is increasing
pressure to find mineral resources which can be economically exploited. It is already possible to identify the
most likely regions where mineral prospecting might occur
in the future.

Land Based Mineral Resources. The Scientific
Committee on Antarctic Research (SCAR) carried out a study
of the Environmental Impact Assessment of Mineral Resource
Exploration and Exploitation in Antarctica (EAMREA) which
called attention to potential resource areas. The EAMREA
Group found that, given known geological information, four
regions on the Antarctic continent could be targets of
future exploration. See Table 1.

According to present geological information, the
potential mineral resources on land include only the
metallic minerals listed in Table 1. It is also highly
unlikely that there will be land-based drilling for petroleum resources. In fact only the continental shelf of
West Antarctica appears to have a hydrocarbon resource
potential.[2] Although hard mineral occurrences have been
discovered throughout various locations in Antarctica,
their magnitude and quality have not been determined, so
they should not be thought of as mineral reserves. Among
the mineral occurrences discovered, only iron and coal
have actually been found in quantity. But the low grade
and remote location of the iron and coal make exploitation
economically unfeasible, even in the case of coal for
local use.

TABLE 1
Areas of Antarctica Most Likely to Attract Mineral
Exploration

Area	Minerals
Antarctic Peninsula	Copper, Molybdenum
Dufek Massif	Chromium, Platinum, Copper
Transantarctic Mountains	Copper, Lead, Zinc, Silver, Tin, Gold
Prince Charles Mountains	Iron
Continental Shelf of West Antarctica	Petroleum

Mineral Potential of the Continental Shelf. Over
the past few years, continental shelves have been the
sites of exploration for hydrocarbons around the world.
This has resulted in several major discoveries from which
substantial quantities of oil and natural gas have been
produced. Even though the Antarctic continental shelf is
geologically poorly known, it has become the primary area
for current and future hydrocarbon exploration. One area
of the shelf has undergone several surveys and exploratory
drilling by the Glomar Challenger. These studies were
carried out in the Ross Sea, where methane, ethane, and
ethylene have been discovered in quantities that indicate
potentially exploitable resources. Other parts of the
continental shelf that may be of interest include both
sides of the Antarctic Peninsula and the Amery Ice Shelf
in East Antarctica. The United States, in its report to
the Special Preparatory Meeting of the Antarctic Treaty
nations in Paris in June 1976, stated: "...it appears
that the Antarctic continental shelf could contain
potentially recoverable oil in the order of magnitude of
tens of billion barrels...."[3] Hydrocarbons are now
being produced from offshore fields off the coasts of
Australia and Argentina. Whether a geological connection
between the producing regions in these fields actually
exists is unknown. But because both Australia and South
America in past geological time were all part of Gondwana-
land (a huge super continent), the possibility of such
extensions cannot be ignored.

Available data are insufficient to establish the
economic probabilities of recoverable deposits of petroleum. A document presented by the United States Antarctic
delegation and used in Congressional hearings in 1979,
explained that the combination of water depth, ice conditions, severe weather, transportation costs, and short
annual working time imply production costs of such
magnitude that other areas will be more attractive to
industrial exploitation for some time. But industrial
mineral resource activities, such as exploratory drilling,
blasting, and supply transportation, which normally
precede industrial exploitation, could begin at any
time.[4]

Manganese Nodules. The valuable metal content of
manganese nodules declines progressively with distance
from the equator, and those on the Antarctic seabed have
significantly less valuable metal content than nodules
found elsewhere. Unless high-grade nodules can be found
in economically significant numbers, they will not be of
commercial interest for the forseeable future.

Icebergs. The abundance of Antarctic icebergs and
their particular shape has led to the idea that suitable
bergs could be towed by oceangoing tugs to parts of the

world that are water deficient. Further studies will have
to be made. Current studies have concerned transportation
to Australia and Saudi Arabia.

Environmental Concerns

Land Based. The United States has adopted a policy
of favoring development with strong environmental controls
administered jointly by the treaty powers. Under such a
policy any nation would be free to apply to the Treaty
members for exploration rights. There would have to be
unanimous consent by all members before such rights were
given. Critics of the United States have noted that this
would be to the advantage of American industrial corporations who control much of the technology required to work
in the harsh environment of the Antarctic. Actually,
three American oil companies--Gulf, Exxon, and Atlantic
Richfield--regularly advise the Administration on Antarctic development through the State Department and the
Arctic Advisory Committee.

The possibility of effective environmental control
has been discounted by critics of the treaty because of
the organization's use of a consensus rule, whereby all
nations must agree to any regulation before its adoption.
Such a procedure, the critics say, virtually guarantees
that strict environmental measures will be vetoed by one
or another of the thirteen participating nations. But as
John Negroponte, head of the United States delegation to
negotiations on the commercial exploitation of Antarctica,
has pointed out, the widely recognized success of the
treaty powers in prohibiting nuclear testing and military
intrusion in Antarctica was achieved through a consensus
rule.

While special protective measures may be necessary
to maintain the environmental balance of certain unique
ecosystems, it is possible that exploratory drilling
activities, whether conducted for scientific purposes or
for resource evaluation, can be conducted in a manner that
will maintain the integrity of the environment in
Antarctica.[5] The fragile and simplified ecosystem which
is characteristic of the Antarctic, however, is highly
vulnerable to physical disturbance. Mineral exploitation
would be much more disruptive of this ecosystem than
exploration. In one study addressing the likely consequences of land-based mineral exploitation, the following
points were made.
(1) The major impacts would be mostly geographically restricted and would probably include:
- the deposit of rock waste and spoil on land;
- dust over inland ice altering its reflec-
tivity (albedo) and perhaps causing melting,
with unknown effects on the world's weather;
- local air pollution;

(2)   In addition, three broader-ranging effects
were noted involving:
-    air pollution;
-    ice melting;
-    the injection of fine tailings into Antarctic
     bottom water, which feeds all the world's
     oceans.[6]
The major ecological concern of land-based oil
drilling is to prevent blow-outs. Exploratory drilling
does not appear to present nearly as many potential
ecological problems as would the production stage. The
major impact areas would include the construction of a
base, ship moorings, pipeline heads, oil storage tanks,
and an airstrip.

     Offshore. Production drilling for oil on the
continental shelf would have to be underwater--either
deep enough not to be a risk from iceberg scour, or sunk
into the seabed. Even if a way could be devised to drill
for the hydrocarbons safely, the oil or gas would have to
be transported to land for storage. Because there are
few ice-free areas along the coasts of Antarctica, and
because what little there is accounts for much of
Antarctica's mineral, plant, and animal life, there is a
likelihood that environmental damage would occur. The
damage could come from a ruptured pipeline or tank, a
well blow-out, or a tanker spill.

OVERVIEW

     Mineral resource exploration on the Antarctic
continent could and should be permitted to continue if it
is carried out under the same environmental guidelines
that have governed similar activities in the past with
the limitations imposed by the Antarctic Treaty. Most
studies of the Antarctic also conclude that exploration
of the continental shelf should be permitted given the
same conditions. Deep water drilling technology, including the use of marine risers and blow-out preventers,
should be a sufficient safeguard for exploratory drilling.
     The protection of undersea hydrocarbons, however,
presents more difficult technical and environmental
problems. It is likely that a period of ten years would
elapse between the time of discovery and production of
hydrocarbons on the continental shelf. As yet no major
finds have been discovered. Better drilling technology
and a better understanding of the marine ecosystem in
Antarctic water will help to minimize risks and provide a
more precise basis for decisions on the safety of offshore
production. If there is any likelihood of even moderate
ecosystem disruption whether on land or offshore, due to
hydrocarbon or mineral production, then those activites

must be stopped. The pristine and therefore scientifi-
cally important continent of Antarctica is worth more to
mankind in its present form than all its potential mineral
resources.[7]
Especially since 1979, American environmental
groups have attempted to persuade the United States
government that the risks of economic development in the
Antarctic are so high that the continent should be placed
in the category of a world preserve. While this request
has been declined, State Department officials concede that
the development issue entails the first major challenge
to the harmony of the treaty that has prevailed since
1959. In short, the development issue raises the question
of who owns Antarctica. For twenty years the members have
been able to sidestep this question, but it has never been
solved and now has come back to create several major
resource management problems.
Evidence of increasing interest in the potential
exploitation of resources in Antarctica by developing
states was highlighted in January 1982 when a scientific
expedition of twenty scientists from India landed
(January 9, 1982) in East Antarctica on the coast of
Queen Maud Land. India has long argued that Antarctica
should be considered the "common heritage of mankind."
The United States and other Treaty members are eager to
prevent that concept from applying to Antarctica.
The expedition was particularly interested in
studying the effect of Antarctica and its surrounding
seas on monsoons in India and in gathering information on
krill. India may attempt to obtain full membership in
the Treaty or attempt to promote Third World interests
for a broad sharing of the resources. Should India push
for the latter, new political problems will make agreement on a regime for minerals exploitation more
difficult.[8]

FOOTNOTES

APPENDIX 12

1. Final Report, The Antarctic Krill Resource: Prospects for Commercial Exploitation, Tetra Tech Report TC-903, February 1978. Prepared for the U.S. Department of State; see also, the Antarctic Conservation Act of 1978, (Public Law 95-541), National Science Foundation, August.

2. James H. Zumberge, "Mineral Resources and Geopolitics in Antarctica," American Scientist 67, (January-February 1979): 68-77.

3. U.S. Report to the Special Preparatory Meeting of the Antarctic Treaty Nations, in Paris, June 28, 1976. (Unpublished document available from the U.S. Department of State).

4. U.S., Congress, Senate, Committee on Energy and Natural Resources, Hearings on the Oversight of U.S. Activites in Antarctica, before the Senate Committee on Energy and Natural Resources, 96th Cong., 1st sess., 1979.

5. James H. Zumberge, American Scientist 67.

6. See, "Antarctica and its Resources," Earthscan Press Briefing Document 21, p. 34.

7. James H. Zumberge, American Scientist 67: 74-75.

8. "Expedition From India Arrives in Antarctica," New York Times, February 16, 1982, p. C2.

THE ANTARCTIC TREATY

The Governments of Argentina, Australia, Belgium, Chile, and the French Republic, Japan, New Zealand, Norway, the Union of South Africa, the Union of Soviet Socialist Republics, the United Kingdom of Great Britain and Northern Ireland, and the United States of America,

Recognizing that it is in the interest of all mankind that Antarctica shall continue forever to be used exclusively for peaceful purposes and shall not become the scene or object of international discord;

Acknowledging the substantial contributions to scientific knowledge resulting from international cooperation in scientific investigation in Antarctica;

Convinced that the estabishment of a firm foundation for the continuation and development of such cooperation on the basis of freedom of scientific investigation in Antarctica as applied during the International Geophysical Year accords with the interests of science and the progress of all mankind;

Convinced also that a treaty ensuring the use of Antarctica for peaceful purposes only and the continuance of international harmony in Antarctica will further the purposes and principles embodied in the Charter of the United Nations;

Have agreed as follows:

Article I

1. Antarctica shall be used for peaceful purposes only. There shall be prohibited, _inter alia_, any measures of a military nature, such as the establishment of military bases and fortifications, the carrying out of military maneuvers, as well as the testing of any type of weapons.

2. The present treaty shall not prevent the use of military personnel or equipment for scientific research or for any other purpose.

Article II

Freedom of scientific investigation in Antarctica and cooperation toward that end, as applied during the International Geophysical year, shall continue, subject to the provisions of the present treaty.

Article III

1.   In order to promote international cooperation
in scientific investigation in Antarctica, as provided
for in Article II of the present treaty, the Contracting
Parties agree that, to the greatest extent feasible and
practicable:

> (a)   information regarding plans for
> scientific programs in Antarctica shall be
> exchanged to permit maximum economy and efficiency
> of operations;
> (b)   scientific personnel shall be exchanged
> in Antarctica between expeditions and stations;
> (c)   scientific observations and results from
> Antarctica shall be exchanged and made freely
> available.

2.   In implementing this article, every encouragement shall be given to the establishment of cooperative
working relations with those Specialized Agencies of the
United Nations and other international organizations
having a scientific or technical interest in Antarctica.

Article IV

1.   Nothing in the present treaty shall be inter-
preted as:

> (a)   a renunciation by any Contracting Party
> of previously asserted rights of or claims to
> territorial sovereignty in Antarctica;
> (b)   a renunciation or diminution by any
> Contracting Party of any basis of claim to
> territorial sovereignty in Antarctica which it may
> have whether as a result of its activites or those
> of its nationals in Antarctica, or otherwise;
> (c)   prejudicing the position of any Contract-
> ing Party as regards its recognition or
> non-recognition or any other State's rights of or
> claim or basis of claim to territorial sovereignty
> in Antarctica.

2.   No acts or activities taking place while the
present treaty is in force shall constitute a basis for
asserting, supporting or denying a claim to territorial
sovereignty in Antarctica or create any rights of sovereignty in Antarctica. No new claim, or enlargement of an
existing claim, to territorial sovereignty in Antarctica
shall be asserted while the present treaty is in force.

Article V

1. Any nuclear explosions in Antarctica and the disposal there of radioactive waste material shall be prohibited.

2. In the event of the conclusion of international agreements concerning the use of nuclear energy, including nuclear explosions and the disposal of radioactive waste material, to which all of the Contracting Parties whose representatives are entitled to participate in the meetings provided for under Article IX are parties, the rules established under such agreements shall apply in Antarctica.

Article VI

The provisions of the present treaty shall apply to the area south of 60° South Latitude, including all ice shelves, but nothing in the present treaty shall prejudice or in any way affect the rights, or the exercise of the rights, of any state under international law with regard to the high seas within that area.

Article VII

1. In order to promote the objectives and ensure the observance of the provisions of the present treaty, each Contracting Party whose representatives are entitled to participate in the meeting referred to in Article IX of the treaty shall have the right to designate observers to carry out any inspection provided for by the present article. Observers shall be nationals of the Contracting Parties which designate them. The names of observers shall be communicated to every other Contracting Party having the right to designate observers, and like notice shall be given of the termination of their appointment.

2. Each observer designated in accordance with the provisions of paragraph 1 of this article shall have complete freedom of access at any time to any or all areas of Antarctica.

3. All areas of Antarctica, including all stations, installations and equipment within those areas, and all ships and aircraft at points of discharging or embarking cargoes or personnel in Antarctica, shall be open at all times to inspection by any observers designated in accordance with paragraph 1 of this article.

4. Aerial observation may be carried out at any time over any or all areas of Antarctica by any of the

Contracting Parties having the right to designate observers.

5. Each Contracting Party shall, at the time when
the present treaty enters into force for it, inform the
other Contracting Parties, and thereafter shall give them
notice in advance, of:

(a) all expeditions to and within
Antarctica, on the part of its ships or nationals,
and all expeditions to Antarctica organized in or
proceeding from its territory;
(b) all stations in Antarctica occupied by
its nationals; and
(c) any military personnel or equipment
intended to be introduced by it into Antarctica
subject to the conditions prescribed in paragraph
2 of Article 1 of the present treaty.

Article VIII

1. In order to facilitate the exercise of their
functions under the present treaty, and without prejudice
to the respective positions of the Contracting parties
relating to jurisdiction over all other persons in
Antarctica, observers designated under paragraph 1 of
Article VII and scientific personnel exchanged under
subparagraph 1(b) of Article III of the treaty, and
members of the staffs accompanying any such persons, shall
be subject only to the jurisdiction of the Contracting
Party of which they are nationals in respect of all acts
or ommissions occurring while they are in Antarctica for
the purpose of exercising their functions.

2. Without prejudice to the provisions of paragraph 2 of this article, and pending the adoption of
measures in pursuance of subparagraph 1(e) of Article IX,
the Contracting Parties concerned in any case of dispute
with regard to the exercise of jurisdiction in Antarctica
shall immediately consult together with a view to reaching a mutually acceptable solution.

Article IX

1. Representatives of the Contracting Parties
named in the preamble to the present treaty shall meet at
the City of Canberra within two months after the date of
entry into force of the treaty, and thereafter at suitable
intervals and places, for the purpose of exchanging
information, consulting together on matters of common
interest pertaining to Antarctica, and formulating and
considering, and recommending to their governments,
measures in furtherance of the principles and objectives

of the treaty, including measures regarding:

      (a)   use of Antarctica for peaceful purposes only;
      (b)   facilitation of scientific research in Antarctica;
      (c)   facilitation of international scientific cooperation in Antarctica;
      (d)   facilitation of the exercise of the rights of inspection provided for in Article VII of the treaty;
      (e)   questions relating to the exercise of jurisdiction in Antarctica;
      (f)   preservation and conservation of living resources in Antarctica.

2. Each Contracting Party which has become a party to the present treaty by accession under Article XIII shall be entitled to appoint representatives to participate in meetings referred to in paragraph 1 of the present article, during such time as that Contracting Party demonstrates its interest in Antarctica by conducting substantial scientific research activity there, such as the establishment of a scientific station or the dispatch of a scientific expedition.

3. Reports from the observers referred to in Article VII of the present treaty shall be transmitted to the representatives of the Contracting Parties participating in the meetings referred to in paragraph 1 of the present article.

4. The measures referred to in paragraph 1 of this article shall become effective when approved by all the Contracting Parties whose representatives were entitled to participate in the meeting held to consider those measures.

5. Any or all of the rights established in the present treaty may be exercised as from the date of entry into force of the treaty whether or not any measures facilitating the exercise of such rights have been proposed, considered or approved as provided in this article.

Article X

Each of the Contracting Parties undertakes to exert appropriate efforts, consistent with the Charter of the United Nations, to the end that no one engages in any activity in Antarctica contrary to the principles or purposes of the present treaty.

Article XI

1. If any dispute arises between two or more of the Contracting Parties concerning the interpretation or application of the present treaty, those Contracting Parties shall consult among themselves with a view to having the dispute resolved by negotiation, inquiry, mediation, conciliation, arbitration, judicial settlement or other peaceful means of their own choice.

2. Any dispute of this character not so resolved shall, with the consent, in each case, of all parties to the dispute be referred to the International Court of Justice for settlement; but failure to reach agreement on reference to the International Court of Justice shall not absolve parties to the dispute from the responsibility of continuing to seek to resolve it by any of the various peaceful means referred to in paragraph 1 of this article.

Article XII

1. (a) The present treaty may be modified or amended at any time by unanimous agreement of the Contracting Parties whose representatives are entitled to participate in the meetings provided for under Article IX. Any such modification or amendment shall enter into force when the depositary government has received notice from all such Contracting Parties that they have ratified it.

   (b) Such modification or amendment shall thereafter enter into force as to any other Contracting Party when notice of ratification by it has been received by the depositary government. Any such Contracting Party from which no notice of ratification is received within a period of two years from the date of entry into force of the modification or amendment in accordance with the provisions of subparagraph 1(a) of this article shall be deemed to have withdrawn from the present treaty on the date of the expiration of such period.

2. (a) If after the expiration of thirty years from the date of entry into force of the present treaty, any of the Contracting Parties whose representatives are entitled to participate in the meetings provided for under Article IX so requests by a communication addressed to the depositary government, a conference of all the Contracting Parties shall be held as soon as practicable to review the operation of the treaty.

(b) Any modification or amendment to the present treaty which is approved at such a conference by a majority of the Contracting Parties there represented, including a majority of those representatives who are entitled to participate in the meetings provided for under Article IX, shall be communicated by the depositary government to all the Contracting Parties immediately after the termination of the conference and shall enter into force in accordance with the provisions of paragraph 1 of the present article.

(c) If any such modification or amendment has not entered into force in accordance with the provisions of subparagraph 1 (a) of this article within a period of two years after the date of this communication to all the Contracting Parties, any Contracting Party may at any time after the expiration of that period give notice to the depositary government of its withdrawal from the present treaty; and such withdrawal shall take effect two years after the receipt of the notice by the depositary government.

Article XIII

1. The present treaty shall be subject to ratification by the signatory states. It shall be open for accession by any state which is a member of the United Nations, or by any other state which may be invited to accede to the treaty with the consent of all the Contracting Parties whose representatives are entitled to participate in the meetings provided for under Article IX of the treaty.

2. Ratification of or accession to the present treaty shall be effected by each state in accordance with its constitutional processes.

3. Instruments of ratification and instruments of accession shall be deposited with the Government of the United States of America, hereby designated as the depositary government....

Signed at Washington, December 1, 1959

APPENDIX 14

DESCRIPTIONS OF THE "TRUSTEESHIP SOLUTION" AND A "JOINT
ANTARCTIC RESOURCE JURISDICTION"

TRUSTEESHIP

James N. Barnes, Director of the Center for Law
and Social Policy in Washington, D.C., and a member of the
United States Antarctic negotiating team, has suggested
that a Trusteeship for Antarctica would require the
following points:

-- That both claimants and non-claimants
   renounce any territorial claims they have
   asserted or might assert in the future.
-- That the Treaty Parties explicitly take into
   consideration the interests of the international community in all decisions, particularly those regarding resources.
-- That the Parties' deliberations be conducted
   in the open.
-- That representatives of appropriate international organizations be invited to participate as members or observers.
-- That the technology for exploiting living
   resources in the Antarctic be made available
   on a fair basis to interested countries.
-- That the Southern Ocean, except for 200-mile
   zones around islands north of 60° South as to
   which there is no dispute over sovereignty,
   be declared a common heritage.

There are certain potential benefits of a Trusteeship solution that warrant a closer look at this proposal.
With appropriate provisions for the use of resources,
sharing of benefits, and environmental protection, it
could satisfy the interests of the world community on all
pertinent levels. More specifically, if all territorial
claims were removed the Parties would eliminate the most
serious reasons for hostility among themselves. The
Parties would therefore be in a better position to
concentrate on the goals of the living resources and
minerals negotiations. These goals are the conservation
of resources, protection of the environment, and production of scarce resources, if done safely. As trustees,
the thirteen Parties would have powers similar to those

290

which accompany ownership, as well as the collective
capacity to exercise their control in a reasonable way.
A Trusteeship solution would keep the Antarctic Treaty
intact, with its crucial environmental, scientific and
access limitation arrangements. With the Parties acting
as trustees over resources on behalf of all nations
presumably many of the deficiencies of the Living
Resources Convention (which exists to protect national
juridical and fishing interests) would be remedied.
Areas for modification would include voting, interim
measures, agreement on national catch and effort limitations and area allocations, support for a permanent
scientific staff to advise the commission, joint enforcement and effective dispute resolution.
     The Trusteeship "solution" is an attempt by Barnes
to offer a creative and bold design for the management of
Antarctica. One of the major premises of this solution,
however, is very questionable: that claimant Parties give
up their territorial claims of sovereignty. For this
reason, it is unlikely that the Trusteeship solution as
outlined by Barnes would be accepted by the claimant
states. On the other hand, as the enforcement of measures
already outlined in the Treaty (and the Marine Living
Resources Convention) have become more politicized because
of greater demands for exploitation made on Antarctic
resources, all Parties may agree to a Trustee-like
arrangement. If they do not, they face the likelihood of
the Antarctic Treaty falling apart, probable environmental
damage, and increased pressure from nations outside the
Treaty to get a part of the action--in short, a total
mismanagement of the continent and its resources might
result.

JOINT ANTARCTIC RESOURCE JURISDICTION

     One of the more elaborate and well considered
approaches to the resource management problems of
Antarctica is a Joint Antarctic Resource Jurisdiction
(JARJ), proposed by Frank C. Alexander, Jr.[1] He
recommends that the Consultative Parties declare joint
exclusive resource jurisdiction over the continent and
the continental shelf of Antarctica. The approach was
designed to be acceptable to claimant and non-claimant
states as well as to the entire international community.
In addition, it is meant to be implemented pursuant to
the Antarctic Treaty procedures and in a way that would
leave the Treaty intact.
     The main features of a JARJ are worth consider-
ing. According to this plan, a study would be conducted
to determine environmental effects of hydrocarbon exploitation. Areas that were found to be suitable for commercial activities would then be leased to any interested

state. Revenues generated from the leasing of the areas
would go to the twelve original Consultative Parties on
an equal basis. Revenues obtained from taxes levied on
exploitation would go to both the twelve Consultative
Parties and into a trust fund created to aid less developed countries (which would be administered by the United
Nations).

Another aspect of this proposal is that the
Antarctic Ocean would retain the status of high seas.
This would allow all states to participate in the new
treaty regulating the living resources of Antarctica. A
Joint Antarctic Resource Jurisdiction declaration would
induce all interested parties to attempt to reach an
Antarctic resource agreement. Under the JARJ, all states
would exercise high seas freedom in the Southern Ocean.
And, because it would assure jurisdiction over the
continental shelf of Antarctica, UNCLOS III would be able
to extend the scope of its jurisdiction to all waters
and submerged lands of the Treaty area--except the
continental shelf. This proposal has appeal to most Third
World countries. The United States, however, has been
opposed to the inclusion of the seabed--within the
Antarctic Treaty area--under the jurisdiction of the
International Seabed Authority.[2]

The non-Consultative Party developing states would
benefit directly from the revenue provisions of the
JARJ. In addition, all states would continue to have a
chance to engage in scientific pursuits in the Treaty
area, as well as the opportunity to accede to the Treaty
and attain consultative status upon meeting the proper
requisites. Other aspects of this approach appeal to both
claimant and non-claimant Treaty states. The JARJ
proposal does not pretend to meet the needs of all states
in an ideal resource regime. But it does offer aspects
of a regime framework which could be implemented that
protects the environment, establishes an Antarctic non-
living resource regulatory mechanism, preserves the
Treaty, and could be sufficiently acceptable to the
international community as a whole.[3]

FOOTNOTES

APPENDIX 14

1. See, Frank C. Alexander, Jr., "A Recommended Approach to the Antarctic Resource Problem," University of Miami Law Review 33, (December 1978): 371-425.

2. For connections between UNCLOS III and the future management of Antarctic resources, see Julia Rose, "Antarctic Condominium: Building a New Legal Order for Commercial Interests," Marine Technology Society Journal 10 (January 1976): 19-27; Deborah Shapley, "Antarctic Problems: Tiny Krill to Usher in New Resource Era," Science 196 (April 1977): 503-5-5; and Barbara Mitchell and Richard Sandbook, The Management of the Southern Ocean, (London: International Institute for Environment and Development, 1980). See especially sections 3 and 11.

3. Frank C. Alexander, Jr., University of Miami Law Review 33. M.C.W. Pinto, a leading Third World delegate at UNCLOS III, has noted that Alexander's approach (the J.A.R.J.) favors the Consultative Party states too much for it to appeal to the Group of 77. See, M.C.W. Pinto, "The International Community and Antarctica," University of Miami Law Review 33 (December 1978): 475-487.

APPENDIX 15

MAJOR ISSUES INVOLVED IN OUTER SPACE RESOURCE USE

REMOTE SENSING

The current United States remote sensing program
has no major international restrictions on its use or the
dissemination of data received. The funding and the
benefits are in the exclusive hands of the United States
Government for commercial and military use. There is,
however, increasing Third World pressure to control the
sensing of their territory and to share in the benefits
of remote sensing if agreement is given to compile data
about their countries. Before there is agreement to share
this data, the United States would prefer to have a sharing of the costs involved as well. Sharing the resource
information requires training Third World personnel and
providing the necessary technical equipment.

The primary management problem of the remote
sensing of the earth from outer space concerns the
distribution of the data acquired. Nations differ a
great deal in their ability to process and analyze the
data. Consequently, some of the less developed countries
(LDCs) have expressed fear that other countries may be
able to use the data to gain economic, political, or
military advantage over them. The usual argument is that
national sovereignty over information about countries is
diminished by remote sensing from satellites.[1]

With a management framework that insures data
distribution to nations that want it, and economic protection of the holders of the technology that provides
that data, remote sensing can be of immense service to
all mankind. The knowledge required to utilize the data
could also be made available through an international
organization so that information may be used by many
countries. The rich nations could provide the funds and
technology for the placement of satellites in orbit.
Joint international financing, however, would enable the
cost to be distributed. This might result in less
duplication of satellites and make the technologically
advanced nations more inclined to assist in the distribution and benefits of the resource data returned. (The
use of military surveillance satellites would obviously
remain a purely nationalist program.)

DIRECT BROADCASTING VIA SATELLITE

The major controversy surrounding this issue is whether recipient states have the right to determine whether they should be the targets of broadcasts, and whether they should be able to control the content of such broadcasting. There are very few arguments for permitting direct telecommunications broadcasting without recipient approval. If the broadcasts were unintentional, bilateral negotiations could be carried out to settle matters, if an international legal framework were set up to provide mechanisms for dispute settlement. Broadcasts of this sort may be due to the close geographic proximity of selected and non-selected target areas. The chances of peaceful negotiation over broadcast spillover would be greater if there was a legal framework to which all nations could refer.[2]

MARITIME COMMUNICATIONS SATELLITE SYSTEMS

The principal issue here concerns the institution for managing the system. Preferably, operational responsibility should be lodged by each country in whatever entities-private, governmental, or mixed--that can carry out the tasks of maritime communications most efficiently. The role of COMSAT (Communications Satellite Corporation), in the INTELSAT organization provides a good model for this type of arrangement. In whatever organization is formed, the voting could be weighted both on the grounds of investment and levels of use in some sort of executive council; and on the basis of one member, one vote in the assembly. The assembly of such an organization could be granted broad authority for policy and budget and the council should be given operational flexibility.[3] The proposed International Seabed Authority has a structure similar to the one proposed here. This framework could work successfully for both resource commons if developed and developing countries perceive they have more to gain from working together than not. Actually it would probably work better for the maritime satellite system because it is much more resource-specific than an International Seabed Authority which is part of a much broader ocean resource use management framework.

AIR WAVE FREQUENCY AND ORBITAL PATHS

Because of the increasing use of air wave frequency and orbital satellite paths, issues of allocation and accountability have arisen which are similar to those arising from the use of scarce ocean resources. Both

resource areas involve questions of scarcity and demands
by the Third World for a change in the way the resources
are utilized and allocated. In other words, Third World
countries are demanding access to resources they do not
at present have the technology to fully exploit. It is
important for them to ensure future access. It is also
important that the United States and other technologically
advanced states continue to have free access to air wave
and geo-stationary orbits. This is particularly so as
new technological developments increase the benefits
derived from these resources. Both space and land
electronic communications have grown exponentially over
the last two decades. This has put new demands on the
radio spectrum. Also, the growth in space and satellite
activity has put increased pressure on policy makers for
dealing with the management of geo-stationary orbits
around the equator that satellites use for increasingly
important remote sensing and navigation purposes.
     Thus far, the present system for allocating fre-
quencies and orbital uses has been relatively successful.
It involves a high degree of international accountability
among the major users, and has managed to solve most
allocation problems. Beginning at the 1977 World
Administrative Radio Conference (WARC), however, increased
concern over the future distribution of the resources and
their efficient use has occurred.
     In an age of "instant information," one of the
World's most vital and most limited resources is the
electromagnetic spectrum. This spectrum contains the
frequencies on which radio, telephone, television, military and other signals are broadcast around the globe.
The developed nations (particularly the United States),
have long dominated the use of the spectrum. The 1979
WARC meeting witnessed a strong challenge to that control
by the developing contries. When WARC met in 1959,
eighty-seven countries attended; in 1979 there were an
additional sixty-five delegations--almost all of them from
the Third World.[4]
     Most of the major issues facing WARC over the next
twenty years carry rich-versus-poor country overtones.
For example, although the developed countries account for
only 10 percent of the world's population they control 90
percent of the spectrum--which they obtained on a first
come, first served basis. New technology, however, has
placed new demands on the air waves. The rich countries
want more shortwave stations broadcasting to listeners
overseas. Representatives from the developed nations
argue that even without redistributing the spectrum, new
technology can squeeze in more broadcasting resources.
Delegates from the poorer countries claim they cannot
afford new, narrow-band technology. They also maintain
that an expanded shortwave radio band will interfere with
their telephone service, which also uses shortwave.

Consequently, the Third World is demanding more shortwave stations of their own--even though they may not have the technology or need to utilize the air space at the present time.

In 1976, the nations of Brazil, Colombia, Congo, Ecuador, Indonesia, Kenya, Uganda, and Zaire signed the Declaration of Bogota, in which these equatorial nations laid claim to the geo-stationary orbit, e.g. the twenty-four hour orbit that lies 35,900 kilometers above the equator. But the United States and Soviet Union have denounced the Declaration and stated that the geo-stationary orbit is in free space, under the terms of the 1967 Outer Space Treaty.

FOOTNOTES

APPENDIX 15

1. Among the major potential benefits of remote sensing
are: mapping areas of the world that are difficult to
map by conventional methods; geologic mapping of land
masses as one of the initial steps toward commercial
exploration for minerals and fossil fuels; monitoring
land use in rural and urban areas as well as coastal
zones; monitoring geologic hazards and assessing the
results of natural disasters; forecasting crop yields;
surveying soils; surveying water resources; identifying
the ecological condition of water; monitoring hydrometeor-
ological conditions in the atmosphere and on the earth's
surface and subsurface to facilitate control of ocean
resources and pollution; or gathering data on ocean
navigational movements. See, Dag T. Gjessing, Remote
surveillance by electromagnetic waves for air, water,
land, (Ann Arbor, Michigan: Ann Arbor Science
Publishers, 1978); Fredrick Ira Ordway III, Carsbie C.
Adams, and Mitchell R. Sharpe, Dividends from Space, (New
York: Crowell Press, 1972); and Ocean Wave Sensors: A
bibliography with abstracts, Audrey S. Hundermann, ed.,
(Springfield, Va.: United States Department of Commerce,
National Technical Information Service, 1977).

2. Three alternatives to the existing regime covering
direct broadcasting via satellites have been offered by
Seyom Brown et al. These are a consultative regime, a
prior consent regime, and an agreement regime. The
Agreement regime offers the best alternative to balance
the often contrary objectives of insuring a free exchange
of ideas and information while maintaining accountability
in the field of space broadcasting. See Seyom Brown et
al., Regimes for the Ocean, Outer Space, and Weather,
(Washington, D.C.: The Brookings Institution, 1977), pp.
134-135 and 160-164.

3. Brown et al., Regimes, pp. 169-174, 100.

4. See, Newsweek, October 8, 1979, p. 52; and "Opening
Shots in the Battle for the Airwaves," The Economist,
Sept. 29, 1979, pp. 91-92.

APPENDIX 16

NATIONAL INVOLVEMENT IN THE DEEP
SEABED MINING CONSORTIA

Deep seabed mining consortia involving United States firms including dates of consortia formation.

Nation	Kennecott Corp. (1/74) *Sohio & BP	Ocean Mining Associates (OMA) (11/74)	Ocean Management (Inc.) (OMI) (5/75)	Ocean Minerals Company (OMCO) (11/74)
United States	Kennecott Corp. Noranda Exploration, Inc.	Deepsea Ventures, Inc. (Tenneco and *) *Essex Minerals Co. (U.S. Steel) *Sun Ocean Ventures, Inc. (Sun Oil)	Sedco, Inc.	Ocean Minerals Inc. (Lockheed Missiles & Space Co., Billiton**; BRW***) AMOCO Ocean Minerals Co.,(Standard Oil Co. of Indiana) Lockheed Systems Co., Inc. (Lockheed Corp.)
Belgium		*Union Seas, Inc. (Union Miniere)		
Canada			INCO, Ltd.	
Italy		*Samin Ocean Inc. (Subsidiary of Italian Govt.)		

Japan	Mitsubishi Corp.		
Netherlands		Deep Ocean Mining Co., Ltd.	**Billiton B.V. (Royal Dutch Shell)
			***BRW Ocean Minerals (Royal) Bas Kalis Westminster Group N.V.)
United Kingdom	R.T.Z. Deep Sea Mining Enterprises, Ltd.		
	Consolidated Gold Fields, Ltd.		
	BP Petroleum Dev., Ltd.		
West Germany	AMR		

NOTE: Asterisks show relationship of subsidiaries to their parent companies.

Source: Deep Seabed Mining, Report to Congress, U.S. Dept. of Commerce, National Oceanic and Administration, Office of Ocean Minerals and Energy. December 1981.

For additional information, see Summary Tables of Major Deepsea Mining Investors, prepared by the Ocean Economics and Technology Branch of the Department of International Economic and Social Affairs (original document, U.N. Publication ST/ESA/107) March 1982.

Selected Bibliography

BOOKS

Alexander, Lewis M., ed. The Law of the Sea: Needs and Interests of Developing Nations: Proceedings of the Seventh Annual Conference of the Law of the Sea Institute. Kingston, Rhode Island: University of Rhode Island, 1973.

Allen, Scott, and Craven, John P., eds. Alternatives in Deepsea Mining: Proceedings of the Workshop on Alternatives in Deepsea Mining, December 1978, Ka'u, Hawaii, Law of the Sea Institute Workshop. Honolulu: University of Hawaii, 1979.

Amacher, Ryan C., and Sweeney, Richard, eds. The Law of the Sea: U.S. Interests and Alternatives. Washington, D.C.: American Enterprise Institute for Public Policy Research, 1976.

Arrow, Dennis W. "The Customary Norm Process and the Deep Seabed." Ocean Development and International Law 9 (1/2, 1981): 1-60.

Barkenbus, Jack N. Deep Seabed Resources: Politics and Technology New York: Free Press, 1979.

Bergsten, C. Fred, ed. The Future of International Economic Order: An Agenda for Research. Lexington, Mass.: D.C. Heath, 1973.

_____. Managing International Economic Interdependence: Selected Papers of C. Fred Bergsten, 1975-1976. Lexington, Mass.: D.C. Heath, 1977.

Bhagwati, Jagdish N., ed. The New International Economic Order: The North-South Debate. Cambridge, Mass.: MIT Press, 1977.

Black, John R.H. The Recovery of Metals from Deepsea Manganese Nodules and the Effects on the World Cobalt and Manganese Markets. Boston, Mass.: Charles River Associates, 1980.

Borgese, Elisabeth Mann, ed. Pacem in Maribus. New York: Dodd, Mean and Co., 1979.

304

_____. and Ginsburg, Norton, eds. Ocean Yearbook 1.
Chicago: University of Chicago, 1979.

Bosson, Rex, and Bension, Varon. The Mining Industry and
the Developing Countries. New York: Oxford
University Press, 1977.

Brandt, Willy. North-South: A Program for Survival, The
Report of the Independent Commission on Inter-
national Development Issues. Cambridge, Mass.:
MIT Press, 1980.

Brown, Seyom; Cornell, Nina W.; Fabian, Larry L.: and
Weiss, Edith Brown. Regimes for the Ocean, Outer
Space, and Weather. Washington, D.C.: The
Brookings Institution, 1977.

Diederich, Franz; Muller, Wolfgang; and Schneider,
Wolfgang. Analysis of the MIT Study of Deep Ocean
Mining--Critical Remarks on Technologies and Cost
Estimates. Aachen: Research Institute for
International Technology-Economic Co-operation,
Technical University, 1979.

Eckert, Ross D. The Enclosure of Ocean Resources:
Economics and the Law of the Sea. Stanford:
Hoover Institution Press, 1979.

Emery, K.O. "Geological Limits of the 'Continental
Shelf'." Ocean Development and International Law
10 (1/2, 1981): 1-12.

Frank, Richard A. Deepsea Mining and the Environmental
Regulation of Deepsea Mining. Washington, D.C.:
The American Society of International Law, 1976.

Frazer, J.Z., and Fish, M.B. Geological Factors Related
to Characteristics of Seafloor Manganese Nodule
Deposits. Prepared for the U.S. Department of the
Interior, Bureau of Mines. University of
California: Scripps Institution of Oceanography.
1980.

_____, and Wilson, L.L. Manganese Nodule Deposits in
the Indian Ocean. University of California:
Scripps Institution of Oceanography, 1979.

Friedheim, Robert L., ed. Managing Ocean Resources: A
Primer. Boulder: Westview Press, 1979.

Gamble, John K. Jr., Maritime Policy, Lexington, Mass.:
Lexington Books, 1977.

Gjessing, Dag T. Remote Surveillance by Electromagnetic Waves for Air, Water, Land. Ann Arbor, Michigan: Ann Arbor Science Publishers, 1978.

Glasby, G.P. Marine Manganese Deposits. Amsterdam: Elsevier Publishing Company, 1977.

Granger, John V. Technology and International Relations. San Francisco: W.H. Freeman and Company, 1979.

Hansen, Roger D. Beyond the North-South Stalemate. New York: McGraw Hill, 1979.

Hardin, Garrett, and Baden, John, eds. Managing the Commons. San Francisco: W.H. Freeman and Company, 1977.

Hardy, Michael et al. A New Regime for the Oceans (1976). Trilateral Task Force on the Oceans. The Trilateral Papers, Report Number 9. New York: New York University Press, 1976.

Hollick, Ann L. U.S. Foreign Policy and the Law of the Sea. Princeton, New Jersey: Princeton University Press, 1981.

_____, and Osgood, Robert. New Era of Ocean Politics. Baltimore: The Johns Hopkins University Press, 1974.

Horn, David R., ed. Ferromanganese Deposits on the Ocean Floor. Washington D.C.: National Science Foundation, 1972.

Hundermann, Audrey S., ed. Ocean Wave Sensors: A Bibliography with Abstracts. Springfield, Va.: United States Department of Commerce. National Technical Information Service, 1977.

Interfutures, Facing the Future: Mastering the Probable and Managing the Unpredictable. Paris: Organization for Economic Cooperation and Development, 1979.

Janis, Mark W. Sea Power and the Law of the Sea. Boston: Lexington Books, 1976.

Jessup, P., and Taubenfeld, H. Controls For Outer Space and the Antarctic Analogy. New York: Columbia University Press, 1959.

Juda, Lawrence. Ocean Space Rights. New York: Praeger, 1975.

Keohane, Robert O., and Nye Joseph S., eds. Transnational Relations and World Politics. Cambridge, Mass.: Harvard University Press, 1972.

_____, and Nye, Joseph. Power and Interdependence: World Politics in Transition. Boston: Little, Brown and Company, 1977.

Kildow, Judith, ed. Deepsea Mining: Selected Papers From a Series of Seminars Held at M.I.T. in December 1978 and January 1979. Cambridge, Mass.: MIT Press, 1980.

Krasner, Stephen D. Defending the National Interest: Raw Materials Investments and U.S. Foreign Policy. Princeton: Princeton University Press, 1979.

Kronmiller, Theodore G., ed. The Lawfulness of Deep Seabed Mining. Vols. 1 and 2. Dobbs Ferry, New York: Oceana, 1980.

Larson, David, ed. Major Issues of the Law of the Sea. Durham: University of New Hampshire, 1976.

Luard, Evan. The Control of the Sea-Bed. London: Heinesmann, 1974.

Magoffin, Ralph Van Deman. The Freedom of the Seas. Translation of Hugo Groitus, Mare Liberum, 1618. New York: Oxford University Press, 1916.

Manganese Nodules--Metals from the Sea. Metallgesellschaft A.G. Revised Activities. Edition 18. 1975.

Mangone, Gerard. Marine Policy for America. Boston: Lexington Books, 1977.

Mansfield, Eswin. Industrial Research and Technological Innovation: An Econometric Analysis, 1st ed. New York: Norton, 1968.

McLaughlin, Martin, M. The United States and World Development: Agenda 1979. New York: Praeger, 1979.

Mero, John L. The Mineral Resources of the Sea. Amsterdam: Elsevier Press, 1965.

Miles, Edward, and Gamble, John King, eds. Law of the
Sea: Conference Outcomes and Problems of
Implementation, Proceedings of the Law of the Sea
Institute, Tenth Annual Conference, June 22-25,
1976. Cambridge, Mass.: Ballinger, 1977.

Mineral Development in the Eighties: Prospects and
Problems. A Report Prepared by a Group of
Committee Members of the British-American
Committee. National Planning Association, U.S.A.,
1976.

Mitchell, Barbara, and Sandbrook, Richard. The
Management of the Southern Ocean. International
Institute for Environment and Development.
London: IIED, 1980.

Nyhart, J.D. et al. Deep Ocean Mineral Mining: A
Computer Model for Investigating Costs, Rates of
Return, and Economic Implications of Some Policy
Options, revised edition. The M.I.T. Marine
Industry Collegium Opportunity Brief 12. The
M.I.T. Sea Grant Program, 1978.

Ordway, Fredrick Ira, III; Adams, Carsbie C.; and Sharpe,
Mitchell R. Dividends From Space. New York:
Crowell Press, 1972.

Pardo, Arvid. The Common Heritage of Mankind. Valetta,
Malta: University of Malta Press, 1975.

_____, and Borgese, Elisabeth Mann. The New
International Economic Order and the Law of the
Sea. Occasional Paper 4. International Ocean
Institute, Santa Barbara: Center for the Study of
Democratic Institutions, 1976.

Ramesh, Jairam, and Weiss, Charles, Jr. Mobilizing
Technology for World Development. Published for
the International Institute for Environment and
Development and the Overseas Development Council.
New York: Praeger, 1979.

Ross, David A. Introduction to Oceanography, 2nd edition.
New Jersey: Prentice Hall, 1977.

Schoahler, Jacob. Invention and Economic Growth.
Boston: Harvard University Press, 1966.

Tilton, John E. The Future of Nonfuel Minerals.
Washington, D.C: The Brookings Institution, 1977.

Wirsing, Robert G., ed. International Relations and the Future of Ocean Space. Columbia: University of South Carolina Press, 1974.

Wooster, Warren S., ed. Freedom of Oceanic Research. New York: Crane, Russak, 1973.

ARTICLES

Adede, A.O. "The Group of 77 and the Establishment of the International Sea-Bed Authority." Ocean Development and International Law 7 (1979): 31-64.

_____. "Toward the Formulation of the Rule of Delimitation of Sea Boundries Between States with Adjacent or Opposite Coastlines." Virginia Journal of International Law 19 (Winter 1979): 207-256.

Agrait, Luis E. "The Third United Nations Conference on the Law of the Sea and Non-Independent States." Ocean Development and International Law 7 (1979): 19-30.

Alexander, Lewis M., and Robert D. Hodgson. "The Impact of the 200-Mile Economic Zone on the Law of the Sea." San Diego Law Review 12 (1975): 569-599.

_____. "The Role of the Geographically-Disadvantaged States in the Law of the Sea." San Diego Law Review 13 (1976): 558-582.

_____. "Regionalism as an Approach to Marine Science and Technology Transfer." Marine Technology Society Journal 13 (June-July 1979): 30-34.

_____. "The New Geography of the World's Oceans Before and After Law of the Sea." The Columbia Journal of World Business 15 (Winter 1980): 6-16.

Alexander, Frank C. Jr. "A Recommended Approach to the Antarctic Resource Problem." University of Miami Law Review 33 (December 1978): 371-425.

"Antarctica and its Resources," Earthscan Press Briefing 21.

Auburn, G.M. "United States Antarctic Policy." Marine Technology Society Journal 12 (February-March 1978): 31-36.

Barkenbus, Jack N. "How to Make Peace on the Seabed." Foreign Policy 25 (Winter 1976/77): 211-220.

Benjamin, Mark M. and Andrew Felmy. "Trace Metal Exchange Between Ferromanganese Nodules and Artificial Seawater." Marine Mining 3 (Numbers 1-2, 1981): 151-184.

Biggs, Gonzalo. "Deep Seabed Mining and Unilateral Legislation." Ocean Development and International Law 8 (1980): 223-257.

Borgese, Elisabeth Mann. "A Constitution for the Oceans: Comments and Suggestions Regarding Part XI of the Informal Composite Negotiating Text." San Diego Law Review 15 (1978): 371-408.

Breaux, John, "Technology Transfer: A Case Study of the Inequality of the New International Economic Order." Marine Technology Society Journal 13 (April-May 1979): 19-23.

_____. "The Diminishing Prospects for an Acceptable Law of the Sea Treaty." Virginia Journal of International Law 19 (Winter 1979): 257-297.

Brown, Seyom, and Larry L. Fabian. "Toward Mutual Accountability in the Nonterrestrial Realms." International Organization 29 (Summer 1975): 877-389.

Burke, William T., "Critical Changes in the Law of the Sea." The Columbia Journal of World Business 15 (Winter 1980): 17-21.

Chan, Augustine T., and George C. Anderson. Environmental Investigation of the Effects of Deep-Sea Mining on Marine Phytoplankton and Primary Productivity in the Tropical Eastern North Pacific Ocean." Marine Mining 3 (Numbers 1-2, 1981): 121-150.

Charney, Jonathan I. "Law of the Sea: Breaking the Deadlock." Foreign Affairs 55 (1977): 598-629.

Clingan, Thomas A., Jr., "Environmental Problems and the New Order of the Oceans." The Columbia Journal of World Business 15 (Winter 1980): 45-51.

Cooper, Richard N. "An Economists View of the Oceans." Journal of World Trade Law 9 (July/August 1975); 357-373.

Cruickshank, Michael. "Deep Seabed Mining and Developing Countries: Considerations of Distributional Factors." Marine Technology Society Journal 13 (April-May 1979): 5-8.

Curlin, James W. "With an Eye for the Future: An Appraisal of the Status of U.S. Ocean Policy in the 1970's." Marine Technology Society Journal 13 (February-March 1979): 3-8.

da Costa, Joao F. "Applying a New Concept of Development." Marine Technology Society Journal 13 (June-July 1979): 3-7.

Dam, Kenneth W. "The Evolution of North Sea Licensing Policy in Britain and Norway." Journal of Law and Economics 19 (1974): 213-263.

Darman, Richard. "The Law of the Sea: Rethinking U.S. Interests." Foreign Affairs 56 (January 1978): 373-395.

Demsetz, Harold. "Toward a Theory of Property Rights." American Economic Review, Papers and Proceedings 57 (May 1967): 347-359.

Denman, D.R. "Minerals, mining and maritime management." Ocean Management 7 (June 1981): 25-40.

Derkmann, K.J., R. Fellerer, and H. Richter. "Ten years of German exploration activities in the field of marine raw materials." Ocean Management 7 (June 1981): 1-8.

Dickey, Margaret Lynch. "Freedom of the Seas and the Law of the Sea: Is What's New for Better or Worse?" Ocean Development and International Law 5 (1978): 23-26.

Dhalal, Hasjim. "Application to the Asian Region of the Law of the Sea Conference Resolution." The Indonesian Quarterly 8 (April 1980): 3-15.

_____. "The Developing Countries and the Law of the Sea Conference." The Columbia Journal of World Business 15 (Winter 1980): 22-29.

Eisma, D., H. van Hoorn, and A. J. Jong. "Concepts for Sea-Use Planning in the North Sea." Ocean Management 5 (1979).

"Europe's Battle for the Sky." The Economist. July 19, 1980, pp. 93-94.

Ferreima, Penelope Simoes. "The Role of African States the Development of the Law of the Sea at the Third United Nations Conference." Ocean Development and International Law 7 (1979): 89-130.

Friedheim, Robert, and Robert E. Bowen. "Assessing the State of the Art in National Ocean Policy Studies: An Organizing Paper for an NSF

Workshop." Ocean Development and International Law 7 (1979): 179-220.

Freidheim Robert L., and William J. Durch. "The International Seabed Resources Agency Negotiations and the New International Economic Order." International Organization 31 (Spring 1977): 343-384.

Friedheim, Robert L., and Robert E. Bowen. "Neglected Issues at the Third United Nations Law of the Sea Conference." Ocean Management 5 (1979): 309-339.

Gamble, John King, Jr. "Where Trends the Law of the Sea?" Ocean Development and International Law 10 (Numbers 1-2, 1981): 61-92.

Goncalves, Maria Eduarda. "Concepts of Marine Region and the New Law of the Sea." Marine Policy 3 (October 1979): 255-263.

Gullard, John. "Developing Countries and the New Law of the Sea." Oceans 22 (Spring 1979): 36-42.

Haas, Ernst B. "Is there a Hole in the Whole: Knowledge, Technology, Interdependence, and the Construction of International Regimes." International Organization 29 (August 1975): 827-876.

_____. "Why Collaborate? Issue-Linkage and International Regimes." World Politics 32 (April 1980): 357-405.

Hansen, Roger D. "The Political Economy of North-South Relations: How Much Change?" International Organization 29 (August 1975): 921-947.

Hardy, Michael. "The Implications of Alternative Solutions for Regulating the Exploitation of Seabed Minerals." International Organization 31 (Spring 1977): 313-342.

Harry, Ralph L. "The Antarctic Regime and the Law of the Sea Convention: An Australian View." Virginia Journal of International Law 21 (Summer 1981): 727-744.

Hirch, Fred. "Is There a New International Economic Order?" International Organization 30 (Summer 1976): 521-531.

313

Hirota, Jed. "Potential Effects of Deep-Sea Minerals Mining on Macrozooplankton in the North Equatorial Pacific. Marine Mining 3 (Numbers 1-2, 1981): 19-58.

Hopkins, Raymond F. "The International Role of 'Domestic' Bureaucracy." International Organization 30 (Summer 1976): 405-432.

Howe, James W. "Power in the Third World." Journal of International Affairs 29 (1975): 113-127.

Hollick, Ann L. "Seabeds Make Strange Politics." Foreign Policy 9 (Winter 1972/73): 148-170.

_____. "United States and Canadian Policy Processes in Law of the Sea." San Diego Law Review 12 (April 1975): 518-552.

Huddle, Franklin P. "U.S. Materials Policy: A Legislative Approach." Resources Policy (March 1978): 2-12.

"Into the Space Club." The Economist. July 26, 1980, p. 40.

Jacovides, Angreas. "Three Aspects of the Law of the Sea--Islands, Delimitation and Dispute Settlement." Marine Policy 3 (October 1979): 278-288.

Joyner, Christopher C. "The Exclusive Economic Zone and Antarctica." Virginia Journal of International Law 21 (Summer 1981): 691-725.

Juda, Lawrence. "UNCLOS III and the New International Economic Order." Ocean Development and International Law 7 (1979): 221-256.

Jumars, Peter A. "Limits in Predicting and Detecting Benthic Community Responses to Manganese Nodule Mining." Marine Mining 3 (Numbers 1-2, 1981): 213-229.

Kaye, Lawrence Wayne. "The Innocent Passage of Warships in Foreign Territorial Seas: A Threatened Freedom." San Diego Law Review 15 (1978): 573-602.

Kimball, Lee. "Implications of the Arrangements Made for Deep Sea Mining for Other Joint Exploitations." The Columbia Journal of World Business 15 (Winter 1980): 52-61.

Kingham, J.D., and D.M. McRae. "Competent International Organizations and the Law of the Sea." Marine Policy 3 (April 1979): 106-132.

Knight, H. Gary. "Introduction." Law of the Sea X. San Diego Law Review 15 (April 1978): 365-370.

Koers, Albert. "Participation of the European Economic Community in a New Law of the Sea Convention." American Journal of International Law 73 (1979): 426-443.

Krueger, Robert B., and Myron H. Nordquist. "The Evolution of the 200-Mile Exclusive Economic Zone: State Practice in the Pacific Basin." Virginia Journal of International Law 19 (Winter 1979): 321-400.

Laist, David, and John T. Epting. "Perspectives on an Ocean Management System." Ocean Development and International Law 7 (1979): 257-298.

La Que, F.L. "Different Approaches to International Regulation of Exploitation of Deep-Ocean Ferromanganese Nodules." San Diego Law Review 15 (April 1978): 477-492.

Larson, David. "Security, Disarmament and the Law of the Sea." Marine Policy 3 (January 1979): 40-56.

Lavelle, J.W., and E. Ozturgut. "Dispersion of Deep-Sea Mining Particulates and Their Effect on Light in Ocean Surface Layers." Marine Mining 3 (Numbers 1-2, 1981): 185-212.

Lavelle, J.W., E. Ozturgut, S.A. Swift, and B.H. Erickson. "Dispersal and Resedimentation of the Benthic Plume from Deep-Sea Mining Operations: A Model with Calibration." Marine Mining 3 (Numbers 1-2, 1981): 59-94.

Lee, Roy S. "The Enterprise: Operational Aspects and Implications." The Columbia Journal of World Business 15 (Winter 1980): 62-74.

Leff, Nathaniel. "Changes in the American Climate Affecting the NIEO Proposals." The World Economy 2 (January 1979): 91-98.

_____. "Technology Transfer and U.S. Foreign Policy: The Developing Countries." Orbis 23 (Spring 1979): 145-165.

315

Lenoble, J.P. "Polymetallic nodule resources and reserves in the North Pacific from the data collected by AFERNOD." Ocean Management 7 (June 1981): 9-24.

Levy, Jean-Pierre. "The Evolution of a Resource Policy for the Exploitation of Deep Sea-bed Minerals." Ocean Management 5 (April 1979): 49-73.

Linebaugh, Ruth M. "Ocean Mining in the Soviet Union." Marine Technology Society Journal 14 (February-March 1980): 20-24.

Lynch, William C. "The Nepal Proposal for a Common Heritage Fund: Panacea or Pipedream?" California Western International Law Journal 10 (Winter 1980): 25-52.

Manley, Robert H. "Developing Nation Imperatives for a New Law of the Sea: UNCLOS I and III as Stages in the International Policy Process." Ocean Development and International Law 7 (1979): 9-18.

Marjoram, Tony. "Nodules and Scandinavia--Mining Opportunities." Marine Policy 3 (October 1979): 313-315.

McCloskey, Paul, Jr. "Domestic Legislation and the Law of the Sea." Syracuse Journal of International Law and Commerce 6 (1978079): 227-231.

Mero, John L. "Manganese." North Dakota Engineer 27 (1952): 28-32.

Miles, Edward. "Introduction." International Organization 31 (Spring 1977): 151-158.

_____. "The Structure and Effects of the Decision Process in the Seabed Committee and the Third United Nations Conference on the Law of the Sea." International Organization 31 (Spring 1977): 159-234.

Mink, Patsy T. "Forward" to Law of the Sea X, San Diego Law Review 15 (April 1978): 357-364.

Mitchell, Barbara, and Lee Kimball. "Conflict Over the Cold Continent." Foreign Policy 35 (Summer 1979): 125-141.

Moore, John Norton. "Some Specific Suggestions for Resolving Two Lingering Law of the Sea Problems: Packages of Amendments on 'The Status of the Economic Zone' and Marine Scientific Research."

Virginia Journal of International Law 19 (Winter 1979): 401-410.

Morris, Admiral Max K., and John W. Kindt. "The Law of the Sea: Domestic and International Considerations Arising From the Classification of Floating Nuclear Power Plants and Their Breakwaters as Artificial Islands." *Virginia Journal of International Law* 19 (Winter 1979): 299-320.

Morris, Michael A. "Have U.S. Security Interests Really Been Sacrificed?: A Reply to Admiral Hill." *Ocean Development and International Law* 4 (1977): 381-397.

Morris, Michael A., and Penelope Simoes Ferreira. "Latin America, Africa, and the Third United Nations Conferences on the Law of the Sea: Annotated Bibilography." *Ocean Development and International Law* 9 (Numbers 1-2, 1981): 101-186.

Murphy, John M. "The Politics of Manganese Nodules: International Consideration and Domestic Legislation." *San Diego Law Review* 16 (April 1979): 531-554.

"New for Old." *The Economist*. August 29, 1980, p. 60.

"Nickel: From Land and Sea." *Mining Journal* 294, March 21, 1980.

Nordquist, Myron. "Deep Seabed Mining: Who Should Pay?" *Marine Technology Society Journal* 12 (April-May 1978): 23-26.

"Ocean Mining." *The Economist*. May 31, 1980.

Osgood, Robert. "Military Implications of the New Ocean Politics." *Adelphi Papers* 122, International Institute for Strategic Studies, 1976.

Oxam, Bernard. "The Third United Nations Conference on the Law of the Sea: The Seventh Session (1978)." *American Journal of International Law* 73 (January 1979): 1-41.

_____. "The Third United Nations Conference on the Law of the Sea: The Eighth Session (1979)." *American Journal of International Law* 74 (January 1980): 1-47.

Ozturgut, Erdogan, J. W. Lavelle and B.H. Erickson. "Estimated Discharge Characteristics of a

Commercial Nodule Mining Operation." Marine
Mining 3 (Numbers 1-2, 1981): 1-18.

Pinto, M.C.W. "The International Community and
Antarctica." University of Miami Law Review 33
(December 1978): 475-487.

_____. "The Developing Countries and the Exploitation
of the Deep Seabed." The Columbia Journal of
World Business 15 (Winter 1980): 30-41.

Pirtle, Charles E. "Alternative Regimes for Harvesting
the Seabed: A Review Article." Ocean Development
and International Law 9 (Numbers 1-2, 1981):
77-100.

Press, Frank. "The United States and UNCSTD." Marine
Technology Society Journal 13 (June-July 1979):
8-11.

Raymond, Nicholas. "Sea Law: The Unpleasant Options."
Ocean World (January 1979): 4-12.

Rose, Julia. "Antarctic Condominium: Building a New
Legal Order for Commercial Interests." Marine
Technology Society Journal 10 (January 1976):
19-27.

Richardson, Elliot. "Power, Mobility and the Law of the
Sea." Foreign Affairs 58 (Spring 1980): 902-919.

_____. "Concluding the Law of the Sea Conference:
Critical Remaining Steps." The Columbia Journal
of World Business 15 (Winter 1980): 42-44.

San Diego Law Review 9 (No. 3, 1982). Special Law of the
Sea Issue.

Sebenius, James K., and Pal L. Mati. "Evolving Financial
Terms of Mineral Agreements: Risks, Rewards and
Participation in Deep Seabed Mining." The
Columbia Journal of World Business 15 (Winter
1980): 75-83.

Science 206, November 23, 1979: 915-916.

"Scramble for the Sea." The Economist, March 3, 1976.

Serfaty, Simon. "Conciliation and Confrontation: A
Strategy for North-South Negotiations." Orbis
(Spring 1978): 47-61.

Shapley, Deborah. "Antarctic Problems: Tiny Krill to Usher in New Resource Era." Science 196 (April 1977): 503-505.

Suman, Daniel Oscar. "A Comparison of the Law of the Sea Claims of Mexico and Brazil." Ocean Development and International Law 10 (Numbers 1-2, 1981): 131-174.

Suprovicz, Bohdan. "Fear Soviet Supercartel for Critical Minerals." Purchasing (November 8, 1978): 42-49.

Swing, John Temple. "Who Will Own the Oceans?" Foreign Affairs 54 (1976): 527-546.

Talwani, Manik. "Marine Research and the Law of the Sea." The Columbia Journal of World Business 15 (Winter 1980): 84-91.

Teitel, Simon. "On the Concept of Appropriate Technology for Less-Industrialized Countries." Technological Forecasting and Social Change 11 (April 1978): 349-369.

Tinsley, C.R. "Manganese Gains Depend on Rate of Recovery in Steel Industry." Engineering and Mining Journal 178 (March 1977): 98-104.

Van Hegelum, G.J.F. "The Argument for an Interim Approach." Marine Policy July 1981

Virginia Journal of International Law 22 (No. 4, 1982). Special Law of the Sea Issue

Walker, George K. "Sea Power and the Law of the Sea: The Need for a Contextual Approach." Ocean Development and International Law 7 (1979).

Walsh, Don. "Some Thoughts on National Ocean Policy: The Critical Issue." San Diego Law Review 13 (1976): 594-627.

Welling, Conrad G. "Ocean Mining Systems: Strategic Importance of Deep Ocean Mining to the United States." Mining Congress Journal. September 1976.

_____. "The Oceans' Waiting Mineral Resources." Stockton's Port Soundings, August 1980: 6-9.

_____. "The Massive Technology for Ocean Mining." Stockton's Port Soundings, September 1980: 8-11.

_____. "Ocean Mining: The Ships and Ports."
Stockton's Port Soundings, October 1980: 7-9.

_____. "Ocean Minerals and World Politics."
Stockton's Port Soundings, November 1980: 11-13.

Wooster, Warren. "Interaction in Marine Affairs."
International Organization 17 (Winter 1973);
252-275.

Young, Oran B. "Natural Resources Policy: A Modest Plea
for Political Analysis." Ocean Development and
International Law 8 (1980): 183-199.

Zumberge, James. "Mineral Resources and Geopolitics in
Antarctica." American Scientist 67 (January-
February 1979): 68-77.

GOVERNMENT DOCUMENTS

U.S. Congress. House. Committee on Merchant Marine and Fisheries. Deep Seabed Mining. Hearings before a subcommittee of the House Committee on Merchant Marine and Fisheries on H.R. 1270, H.R. 6017, H.R. 11879. 94th Cong., 1st sess., 1976.

U.S. Congress. Senate. Joint Hearings, Mining of the Deep Sea. Hearings before the Committee on Energy and Natural Resources, and the Committee on Commerce, Science, and Transportation, on S. 2053. 95th. Cong., 1st sess., 1977.

U.S. Congress. House. Committee on Merchant Marine and Fisheries. Oceanography Miscellaneous Part 2. Hearings before a subcommittee of the House Committee on Merchant Marine and Fisheries Committee on Law of the Sea Conference Briefings. 95th. Cong., 1st and 2nd sess. 1978.

U.S. Congress. House. Committee on International Relations. Deep Seabed Mineral Resources Act. Hearings before a subcommittee of the Senate Committee on Foreign Relations on H.R. 3350. 95th. Cong., 2nd sess., 1978.

U.S. Congress. Senate. Committee on Foreign Relations. Deep Seabed Mineral Resources Act. Hearings before a subcommittee of the Senate Committee on Foreign Relations on S. 2053. 95th. Cong., 2nd sess., 1978.

U.S. Congress. House. Committee on Ways and Means. The Deep Seabed Hard Minerals Resources Act. Hearings on H.R. 3350. 95th. Cong., 2nd sess., 1978.

U.S. Congress. Senate. Joint Hearings. Deep Seabed Mineral Resource Act. Hearings before a subcommittee of the Senate Committee on Energy and Natural Resources and the Committee on Commerce, Science and Transportation, on S. 493. 96th. Cong., 1st sess., 1979.

U.S. Congress. House. Committee on Merchant Marine and Fisheries. Report together with Dissenting Views before the Committee on Merchant Marine and Fisheries on H.R. 2759. 96th. Cong., 1st sess., 1979.

U.S. Congress. House. Committee on Foreign Affairs. Briefing on the Eighth Session of the Third United Nations Conference on the Law of the Sea, before a subcommittee of the Committee on Foreign Affairs. 96th. Cong., 1st sess., 1979.

U.S. Congress. House. Committee on Interior and Insular Affairs. Hearings and Report before the subcommittee on Mines and Mining. Oversight Hearings on Nonfuel Minerals Policy Review. 96th. Cong., 1st and 2nd sess., 1979.

U.S. Congress. House. Committee on Science and Technology. Hearings before a subcommittee of the House Committee on Science and Technology. 96th. Cong., 2nd sess., 1979.

U.S. Congress. House. Committee on Science and Technology. Hearings on Antarctic Issues before a subcommittee of the House Committee on Science and Technology. 96th. Cong., 1st sess., 1979.

U.S. Congress. House. Congressional Record. Deep Seabed Mining. H.R. 2759. June 9, 1980. 96th. Cong., 1st sess., 1980.

U.S. Congress. House. Report to the Committee of the Whole House. Report No. 96-411, on Deep Seabed Mining, on H.R. 2759. 96th. Cong., 1st sess., 1979.

U.S. Congress. House. Committee on Interior and Insular Affairs. U.S. Minerals Vulnerability: National Policy Implications. A Report prepared by the subcommittee on Mines and Mining of the Committee on Interior and Insular Affairs. 96th. Cong., 2nd sess., 1980.

U.S. Congress. House. Committee on Interior and Insular Affairs. Sub-Sahara Africa: It's Role in Critical Mineral Needs of the Western World. A Report prepared by the subcommittee on Mines and Mining of the Committee on Interior and Insular Affairs. 96th. Cong., 2nd sess., 1980.

U.S. General Accounting Office. Report to the Congress by the Comptroller General of the United States. The United States Mining and Mineral Processing Industry: An Analysis of Trends and Implications. October 1979.

U.S. General Accounting Office. Report to the Congress by the Comptroller General of the United States. Impediments to U.S. Involvement in Deep Ocean Mining Can Be Overcome. February 3, 1982.

322

U.S. Library of Congress. Congressional Research
Service. Ocean Manganese Nodules, 2nd ed.
Prepared for the United States Senate Committee on
Interior and Insular Affairs. February 1977.

U.S. Library of Congress. Congressional Research
Service. Science Policy Research Division.
Strategic and Critical Minerals: U.S. Import
Reliance, Stockpile Strategy and Feasibility of
Cartels. September 22, 1980.

U.S. Library of Congress. Congressional Research
Service. Science Policy Research Division. Ocean
Mining. Issue Brief number IB74024. November
1981.

U.S. Library of Congress. Congressional Research
Service. Foreign Affairs and National Defense
Division. The Law of the Sea Conference: A U.S.
Perspective. Issue Brief number IB81153. October
1981.

U.S. Department of the Interior. Manganese Nodule
Resources and Mine Site Availability. Ocean
Mining Administration. August 1976.

U.S. Congress. House Document 249. U.S. Foreign Policy
for the 1970's, Emerging Structure of Peace.
Report to Congress by Richard Nixon, President of
the United States, February 9, 1972, 92nd Cong.,
2nd sess., 1972.

U.S. General Accounting Office. Report to Congress by
the Comptroller General of the United States. The
Law of the Sea Conference Status of the Issues,
1978. March 1979.

U.S. General Accounting Office. Report to Congress by
the Comptroller General of the United States.
Impediments to U.S. Involvement in Deep Ocean
Mining Can be Overcome. EMD-82-31, February 3,
1982.

U.S. Department of Commerce. U.S. Ocean Policy in the
1970's: Status and Issues. 1978.

U.S. Department of Commerce. Cobalt, Copper, Nickel and
Manganese: Future Supply and Demand and
Implications for Deep Seabed Mining. Office of
Policy and Planning, 1979.

U.S. Department of Commerce. Deep Ocean Mining of
Manganese Nodules in the North Pacific:

Pre-Mining Environmental Conditions and
Anticipated Mining Effects. NOAA Technical
Memorandum ERL MESA-33. Marine Ecosystems
Analysis Program. Boulder, Colorado, December
1978.

U.S. Department of Commerce. Deep Seabed Mining, Final
Regulations. NOAA,Office of Ocean Minerals and
Energy. September 1981.

U.S. Department of Commerce. Deep Seabed Mining, Final
Programmatic Environmental Impact Statement, Vols.
I and II. NOAA, Office of Ocean Minerals and
Energy. September 1981.

U.S. Department of Commerce. Deep Seabed Mining, Report
to Congress. NOAA, Office of Ocean Minerals and
Energy. December 1981.

U.S. Department of Commerce. Deep Seabed Mining, Final
Technical Guidance Document. NOAA, Office of
Ocean Minerals and Energy. September 1981.

U.S. Department of Commerce. Progress Report. State of
Art Environmental Assessment of the Ocean Disposal
of Manganese Nodule Processing Rejects. Tetra
Tech Report TC-3514. Prepared for: Marine
Minerals Division, Office of Ocean Minerals and
Energy, National Oceanic and Atmospheric
Administration. November 13, 1981.

U.S. Central Intelligence Agency. Polar Regions Atlas.
U.S. Government Printing Office. January 1979.

U.S. Congress. Office of Technology Assessment.
Establishing a 200-Mile Fisheries Zone. U.S.
Government Printing Office. 1977.

U.S. Department of State. Delegation Reports on the
Third United Nations Conference on the Law of the
Sea. Sixth Session, March 21-September 15, 1978;
Eighth Session, March 19-April 27, 1979; Resumed
Eighth Session, July 16-August 24, 1979; Ninth
Session, February 27-April 4, 1980.

U.S. Department of State. Final Report. The Antarctic
Krill Resource: Prospects for Commercial
Exploitation. Tetra Tech Report TC-903. February
1978.

U.S. National Science Foundation. Antarctic Conservation
Act of 1978. Public Law 95-541. August 1979.

324

State of Hawaii. The Feasibility and Potential Impact of
    Manganese Nodule Processing in Hawaii. Center for
    Science Policy and Technology Assessment. Depart-
    ment of Planning and Economic Development. 1978.

State of Hawaii. Bibliography and Index to Literature on
    Manganese Nodules (1861-1979). Department of
    Planning and Economic Development. January 1981.

Manchester v. Massachusetts 139. U.S. 240, 257-258,
    (1890); Cunard Steamship Co. v. Mellon, 262. U.S.
    122-124, (1922); United States v. California 332.
    U.S. 33, (1946).

United Nations. United Nations Conference on Trade and
    Development. Final Act and Report. Proceedings
    of the UNCTAD. Geneva, 23 March-16 June 1964.

United Nations. G.A. Res. 2574 (XXIV), 24 UN GAOR, Supp.
    (No. 30), 11, UN Doc. A/7630. 1969.

United Nations. The United Nations Charter. Inter-
    national Trusteeship System. Articles 75-85.

United Nations. Honduras Doc. A/Conf. 62/Sr 25; Morocco
    Doc. A/Conf. 62/SR 28; Cameroon Doc. A/Conf. 62/D,
    1/:16; France Doc. in general Doc. A/C 2 SR 1650
    para. 8.

United Nations. A/Res, 2749 (XXV). 17 December 1970.

United Nations. United Nations Conference on Trade and
    Development (UNCTAD). Report of the Intergovern-
    mental Group of Experts on an International Code
    of Conduct on Transfer of Technology on its Fifth
    Session, Annex 1. UN. Doc. TD/AC. 1/15, preamble,
    art. 2. 1978.

United Nations. A/Res. 3281 (SSIX). 12 December 1974.

United Nations. Problems of Raw Materials and
    Development. UNGA. 1974.

United Nations. Centre for Economic and Social
    Information. Problems of Raw Materials and
    Development: Declaration and Programme of
    Action. Declaration RES 1 E21. Sixth Special
    Session for the U.N. General Assembly. 1 May 1974.

United Nations. A/ Conf. 62/25. 22 May, 1974.

325

United Nations. UN Environment Programme. The Cocoyoc
Declaration. Declaration A/C 2/292. Symposium on
Patterns of Resouce Use Environment and
Development Strategies. Cocoyoc, Mexico. 8-12
October 1974.

United Nations. Charter of Economic Rights and Duties.
OPI/542-75-38308. February 1975.

United Nations. Draft Treaty on the Moon and Other
Celestial Bodies. UN. Doc. A/AC. 105-1.113/Add
4. July 2, 1979.

United Nations. Third Conference on the Law of the Sea,
Eighth Session. 19 March-27 April, 1979.
Informal Composite Negotiating Text/Rev. 1. UN
Doc. A/Conf. 62/WP. 10/Rev.1 28 April, 1979.

United Nations. Third Conference on the Law of the Sea.
Resumed Ninth Session. Draft Convention on the
Law of the Sea (Informal Text). A/Conf. 62/W.P.
10/Rev 3, 22 September 1980.

United Nations. Third United Nations Conference on the
Law of the Sea: First Part of Ninth Session. New
York, 3 March-4 April. SEA/396. 4 April 1980.

United Nations. Economic Implications of Sea-Bed Mineral
Development in the International Area: Report of
the Secretary General. Doc. A/Conf. 62025. 22
May 1974.

United Nations. A Guide to the New Law of the Sea...and
to the Third United Nations Conference on the Law
of the Sea. Department of Public Information.
Press Section. Reference Paper 18. March 1979.

MISCELLANEOUS

Barnes, James N. "The Emerging Antarctic Living
Resources Convention." Paper for the Center for
Law and Social Policy. Washington, D.C. 1979.

Darman, Richard. "United States Deepsea Mining Policy:
The Pattern and the Prospects." A Paper prepared
for presentation at the M.I.T. seminar series on
Deepsea Mining and U.S. Materials/Resource
Policies. January 12, 1979.

de Soto, Alvero. Statement by Deputy Permanent
Representative of Peru to the United Nations
Office in Geneva. From proceedings of the Seminar
on Antarctic Resources and the Environment.
Washington, D.C. September 14, 1979.

Welling, Conrad G. "The Economics of Marine Mineral
Production: A Private Sector Profitability
Analysis." Paper delivered at the Marine Sciences
and Ocean Policy Symposium. University of
California, Santa Barbara. June 17-20, 1979.

Kennecott Cooper Company. Sunken Treasure. Corporate
pamphlet. September, 1977.

Interviews:

Agarwal, Jay. Charles River Associates. Boston, June
1970.

Wright, Rebecca. Dicksteen, Shapiro and Moran.
Washington, D.C. March 1979.

Drucker, Milt, Arthur Kobler, and Ray Meyers.
Department of State. Law of the Sea Advisory
Group. March and October 1979. Additional
interview with Meyers, June 1980. Washington, D.C.

Pardo, Arvid. Senior Fellow at the Institute of Marine
and Coastal Studies, University of Southern
California. February, June and September 1979;
June, August and November 1980.

Kitsos, Thomas. Legislative Analyst. House Merchant
Marine and Fisheries Committee. March 1979;
April, October 1980; March 1981.

Ryan, Alan. Office of International Fisheries. National
Marine Fisheries Service, National Oceanic and
Atmospheric Administration, Department of

Commerce. U.S. negotiating team on Antarctic matters. October 1979 and June 1980.

Kimball, Lee. United Methodist Law of the Sea Project. March 1979; April, October 1980; November, December 1981. Washington, D.C.

Kildow, Judith. Department of Ocean Engineering, Massachusetts Institute of Technology, Boston, March 1979; April, October 1980; March 1981; September, October, November, December, 1981.

Welling, Conrad G., Vice President, Lockheed Ocean Systems. June 1979. Telephone interview March 1981.

Dangler, Ed. Lockheed Ocean Systems. Telephone interviews June 1980; May, September, October, November, and December 1981.

Richardson, Elliot. Former U.S. Ambassador to Third United Nations Conference on the Law of the Sea. June 1979, Santa Barbara, California.

Lawless, James. Office of Ocean Mining and Energy. National Oceanic and Atmospheric Administration. Department of Commerce. Telephone interview March 1981; consultation November, December 1981.

Letters:

Amsbaugh, J.K., President, Ocean Mining Associates, to James L. Malone, U.S. Ambassador to UNCLOS III, date June 2, 1981.

Statham, A.P., Vice-President, INCO Limited. September 3, 1980.

Halkyard, John E., Manager, Ocean Nodule Project. Kennecott Exploration, Inc., Ocean Mining Office. October 8, 1980, February 15, 1980.

Dangler, Ed. Assistant to Senior Vice-President, Ocean Minerals Company (Lockheed). November 19, 1979, September 3, 1980, June 6, 1981.

Atwood, Brian J., (Assistant Secretary for Congressional Relations, Department of State) to Senator Alan Cranston on the Moon Treaty. October 15, 1979.

Ratiner, Leigh S., to Ms. Carolyn Henson (L-5 Society) on the Moon Treaty. August 15, 1979.

U.S. Senator Jacab Javits and U.S. Senator Frank Church,
to the Honorable Cyrus R. Vance (Secretary of
State) on the Law of the Sea Conference and Moon
Treaty. October 30, 1979.

Breaux, John (U.S. House of Representatives) to the
Honorable Jimmy Carter, on the Moon Treaty.
November 7, 1979.

Forsythe, Edwin, and John B. Breaux (U.S. House of
Representatives), to President-Elect Ronald Reagan
on deep seabed mining. December 3, 1980.

Overton, J. Allen, Jr., President, American Mining
Congress, to President-Elect Ronald Reagan on deep
seabed mining. December 15, 1980.

Newspapers:

Washington Post. Sea Law Treaty Being Blocked at White
House. March 4, 1981.

Washington Post. Editorial. Deep-Sixing the Law of the
Sea? March 7, 1981.

Washington Post. Reagan Orders Strategic Stockpile
Purchases. March 14, 1981.

Wall Street Journal. Reagan Seeks Total Review of Ocean
Treaty. March 10, 1981.

Los Angeles Times. U.S. to Insist on Mining Rights in
Ocean Treaty. March 6, 1981.

New York Times. Mineral Takeovers Critized. March 16,
1981.

Christian Science Monitor. U.S. Blocks Law of the Sea
Treaty. March 9, 1981.

The Economist. London. The sea-horse-traders. March
7-13, 1981.

Ocean Science News and Strategic Materials Management,
are both excellent sources of weekly ocean and
resources development news. Published by Nautilus
Press Inc., Washington, D.C.

Index

329

334

340